The Trial of Ca

Edgar Pangborn

Alpha Editions

This edition published in 2024

ISBN : 9789362096739

Design and Setting By
Alpha Editions
www.alphaedis.com
Email - info@alphaedis.com

Contents

1 .... - 1 -

I .... - 1 -

II .... - 9 -

III .... - 14 -

IV .... - 25 -

2 .... - 27 -

I .... - 27 -

II .... - 35 -

III .... - 46 -

IV .... - 52 -

3 .... - 54 -

I .... - 54 -

II .... - 63 -

III .... - 69 -

IV .... - 78 -

4 .... - 81 -

I .... - 81 -

II .... - 89 -

III .... - 99 -

IV .... - 109 -

5 .... - 112 -

I .... - 112 -

II .... - 123 -

III .... - 135 -

IV .... - 146 -

6 .... - 149 -

I .... - 149 -

II .... - 157 -

7 .... - 171 -

I .... - 171 -

II .... - 185 -

III .... - 191 -

8 .... - 206 -

I .... - 206 -

II .... - 218 -

III .... - 227 -

THE TRIAL OF CALLISTA BLAKE .... - 236 -

1

Now laws maintain their credit not because they are just, but because they are laws. That is the mystic foundation of their authority: they have no other.

MONTAIGNE, *Of Experience*

I

Doves wheeled above the city's winter morning, vanishing by a turn of wings, reappearing in a silent explosion of light. Judge Terence Mann saw smoke rising through windless cold from a thousand chimneys, and saw, beyond a bleak acreage of city roofs, the apartment house that contained his bachelor burrow; further on, the Veterans Hospital shone not as a temple of sickness but a shaft of splendor in the sun. His eyes smarted as he turned away from the brightness. That was partly from a lack of sleep. The Judge remembered that, like this robing-room, the detention cells also looked up across the long rise of land where, for something like three hundred years, the city had been haphazardly expanding, fattening on river commerce, and becoming—in the American sense—old.

Some day, should the small gods in the state capital approve, the city of Winchester would own a Civic Center near that hospital, with a new county courthouse. Judge Mann had seen an architect's dream picture in the Egypto-lavatory style, a kind of streamlined cake of soap—optimistic in a time when Winchester's population of 80,000 was remaining constant while suburbs oozed in heedless growth over the once magnificent countryside. In any case this late-Victorian-Gothic firetrap downtown would have to serve for the ordeal of *The People vs. Blake*.

He shoved the black sleeve clear of his wrist watch: 10:10. Short, slight, his temples silvering at forty-seven; few wrinkles yet; a thin flexible mouth suggesting kindness; in his square forehead the pucker of certain chronic doubts. He checked his pockets for reading glasses and aspirin while his attendant Joe Bass brushed at imaginary lint.

"Mr. Delehanty says there's quite a crowd, Judge."

"Do they need more bailiffs out there?"

"I wouldn't think so—just noisy. They all want in." Pink-faced, lightly wrinkled, Joe could shift at will from a glorified valet to a literate old man. "Maybe the rumors about the girl's deformity make them curious, same as if she were a Hollywood dish."

"Oh, I understand her deformity's pretty slight. It's just the radio and papers—sensationalism—public wants a circus. Well, I'm late."

"Technically, sir, you are. But after three years on the bench, you know it isn't ten o'clock till you pass through that door."

"Uh-huh—Joshua never had it so good. Well, here we go ..."

"All rise!" Mr. Delehanty's tenor burbled the lusciousness of a clarinet. "The Honorable Judge of the Court of General Sessions in and for the County of Winchester!" Judge Mann saw them rise, for what the tradition said he must be and therefore was. "All persons having business before this honorable court draw near, give your attention, and you shall be heard!" Seating himself with a twinge of annoyance at pomp and circumstance, Mann observed a virgin scratch-pad beside his minute-book. He suspected Mr. Delehanty of rescuing judicial doodles from the wastebasket: to Mr. Delehanty any new judge was a potential Great Man till the bloom wore off. "This court is now in session."

Three years a judge, less than a year in General Sessions—it had been sure to come, the first case overshadowed by the death penalty. He had faced the certainty and argued it out with himself, well before those scrambled days of the election campaign two years ago which had settled him securely in office after the uncertainty of an interim appointment. He had supposed the answers he arrived at then were still valid: *The law is man-made, therefore imperfect: as its servant, my function is simply to interpret, trusting that time and natural process will permit the law to continue growing, not petrifying, as men gradually become a little wiser (if they do).* And so on—respectable answers, unoriginal but having the sanction of history, of just and generous minds. Yet last night, after a final reading of the grand jury minutes in the Blake case, he could not sleep. And this morning, so far, he was merely insisting to himself that those answers had better stay valid, since the sovereign state of New Essex was stuck with him for another twelve years.

Perhaps, he thought, his uneasiness was not so much at the ethical position as at the Blake case itself—too one-sided. He saw at present no good prospects for defense counsel Cecil Warner except in delaying actions, skirmishes, the unpredictable chances of courtroom drama, and the doctrine of reasonable doubt—which is, to be sure, a doctrine broad enough to take in the whole expanse of human affairs, philosophically and not legally speaking.

He surveyed the arena, wiping his reading glasses, hoping his eyes didn't look too bloodshot. The prospective talesmen spilled into the rows beyond the press tables. Then the anonymous; and from outside, a beehive snarl of the disappointed, who might dwindle away presently, unless the papers had succeeded at blowing the case up into a sexual circus. Portraits of the dead woman showed a pretty face, but Ann Doherty had after all been a respectable suburban housewife, not a glamor girl. Catering to the perennial hunger for a scapegoat, most of the papers were writing of Callista Blake on a note of hate just inside libel—Crippled Teen-Age Intellectual, Prodigy Girl in the Monkshood Case. But that carried a phony note, for Callista Blake had managed to remain so essentially unknown that so far there was really no one to but a paper image. Some voices dissented, too. One sob sister had declared Callista was a woman, with human needs, feelings, a tragic childhood. That writer might have read an article on psychiatry—even two articles.

There were certain letters, from Callista Blake to her lover James Doherty, the last one written about a week before Doherty's wife was found dead— poisoned and drowned. If those letters arrived in evidence over the protests of Cecil Warner, they would demonstrate Callista Blake's humanity more intensely than any journalistic gulping.

Judge Mann had read them, Cecil Warner and District Attorney Lamson present. James Doherty, Lamson said, had handed over the first three voluntarily. The fourth, found in Callista Blake's possession, had not been mailed to Doherty. For Mann, to read them had been like blundering into a private room where lovers clung together with locked loins and tortured faces; like being compelled to watch, afterward, when the woman was alone and wounded with loss. He had skimmed, his mind wincing aside, knowing it was not possible to understand the letters under those conditions. They had not been read to the grand jury. Some passages in them might be construed as admissions of guilt—or not, as you pleased. Warner evidently felt that this notion could be demolished.

As for beauty and glamor, the prosecution would introduce other photographs of Ann Doherty that were no pretty portraits. Old Warner would object routinely and be overruled; the jury would then meet the unmitigated spectacle of a death by drowning. When Ophelia perishes offstage you don't think of post-mortem lividity or foam on the mouth.

"Mr. District Attorney?"

Assistant District Attorney Talbot J. Hunter nodded briskly but solemnly: he was being the man who profoundly regrets what he must do. That had not been altogether predictable. Dealing with professional crooks, T. J. could act downright jolly in a ferocious give-nothing way, often sweeping a jury along. With a tiger's grace, handsome in spite of too much chin and early frontal baldness, Hunter could have been athlete, actor, singer. He was a near-professional with the Winchester Choral Society, having once gone splendidly through the baritone solo in the Brahms *German Requiem* when the guest artist turned up with laryngitis. Mann, himself a serious pianist, had heard that achievement, and remembered it at times when Hunter's courtroom personality annoyed him: the man could hardly have sung that well unless there was in him, somewhere, the element of compassion. In the law, Mann supposed, Hunter could use and enjoy his musical and histrionic abilities and at the same time make a living. "Call the Blake case!" The voice, Mann observed, was in top form, rich, melodious, and acceptably stern.

"Mr. Warner?"

"The defense is ready." Cecil Warner was standing also, heavy and old, a man listening to other voices though capable of employing his own heavy thunder. The other voices were conscience, tradition, books; overtones of what witnesses and lawyers don't say. The seamed ancient face was fat, the kindness obvious but not the strength. Mann wondered occasionally whether Warner had ever, like Darrow, faced all the implications of a certain pessimism that colored most of his opinions. A fracture imperfectly set had crippled Cecil Warner's left arm in childhood; he could not bend the elbow beyond a ninety-degree angle. And Warner's mind, the Judge speculated, might suffer a similar limitation, never hitting with quite all its power. He would need it all in the next few days.

"The People of the State of New Essex against Callista Blake."

Reasonable words; but as Mr. Delehanty intoned them, the Judge's mind perversely visualized an army of five or six million, uniformed, with rifles, tanks, flame-throwers, advancing in ponderous wrath against one cornered chipmunk with tinfoil helmet and paper sword. Foolish, he knew: the individual was not alone, and faced not the People roaring and multitudinous but merely their representative, who might be no more powerful a champion than his own counsel. Yet the image had pestered Judge Mann before now, and faded in the style of the Cheshire Cat.

At other times he could not avoid the impression that the adversary system was too distressingly close in nature as well as origin to the absurdities of medieval justice, in which truth could be determined by the beef of a hired champion. Were prosecutor and defender today any more concerned with truth than those bumbling muscle-men? Were juries?

And judges?

"Counsel to the bench, please." They approached, Hunter light on his feet, Warner slow and carrying too much weight in the middle. "When we get started, gentlemen, I intend to bear down on the formalities, some. I think it's that kind of case. Anything more we should discuss now?"

Warner's hand rested on the bench. Mann noticed the pale freckles, the frailty of deep-crinkled flesh, blurred rims of the irises of Warner's melancholy brown eyes. Cecil Warner was sixty-eight. "Don't think so, Judge, unless T. J.'s got some load on his mind."

Hunter murmured: "Can't imagine a plea—poison and drowning."

"My God, do you imagine us taking one?" Mann frowned; Warner's anger was rumbling too loudly. "We're here for acquittal. My girl didn't do it. It's that simple, and that's where we stand."

Hunter nodded gravely, courteously, unmoved.

In the night, Terence Mann had felt he was not asking himself the right questions. If as prosecutor he could frame them, allowing rational objections from himself as defender, perhaps as witness (or accused?) he might find answers acceptable to himself as judge, jury, and appellate court. But under torment of insomnia the many selves of the mind may abandon the congress of reason and start a rat-race. And now—well, this was full tide; he could not let counsel stand there wondering what ailed him. "That's it, then. Let the defendant be brought in."

As they returned to their places he sketched on the doodle-pad two egg-shaped boxers: tangled eyebrows for Cecil Warner, for Hunter too much forehead and shovel chin.

A police matron appeared, and a court officer. A hush, then a murmur, each voice swelling but slightly, the crescendo joining others in one uproar that expresses no more than the human need to make a noise under stress. Heads turned, weeds under water. Mann heard the s-whispers, water over sand: *Callista Blake—Callissssta ...*

She walked with a barely noticeable limp—polio in childhood, Mann recalled from the record. She was also very slightly hunchbacked, her thin pale arms seeming too long. As Warner escorted her to the defense section, Judge Mann saw she wore no make-up, though powder might have hidden the narrow scar that ran from her left ear to her jaw. Dark blue suit and white blouse were neat, unobtrusive, severe. A natural curl held her black hair in lines of grace above a skin of porcelain white.

She was ignoring Warner's arm, and walked alone.

She was nineteen.

Her eyes were the blue of undersea. Mann searched for other compensating beauty—hard to find. High cheekbones, large nose, small abrupt chin, high forehead modified by the curls but still too high. The extreme whiteness of skin made one think of marble, or heart disease. The medical report declared that apart from the unimportant deformity she was quite healthy. And the State's psychiatrist was prepared to testify, following the quaint barbarism of the once useful McNaughton Rule, that Callista Blake was legally sane. As the jargon had it, she knew the difference between right and wrong, the nature and consequences of her acts.

With no word yet, Callista Blake rejected sympathy, dared the world to pity her, indicated a readiness to spit in its eye.

Warner said: "Give the clerk your name for the record."

Mann heard a strong contralto drawl; it might have sounded warm and pleasant at other times: "Which is the clerk?"

Some idiot woman in the back row giggled.

Warner spoke quickly: "Up there, my dear, that's Mr. Delehanty."

The girl glanced casually at the clerk's dapper dignity, and resumed her level examination of Judge Mann. "I am Callista Blake."

Judge Mann opened the record book and wrote: *State vs. Blake, Dec. 7, 1959.* Eighteen days to Christmas and he still hadn't bought that Diesel train for David, his brother Jack's youngest.... The Blake girl sat down, Warner on her other side where his bulk might partly shield her from the assault of eyes. She moved with grace, the deformity a nothing; the disturbing grace of a wild thing—a cat, a snake, a soaring bird, who makes never one waste motion but appears to flow with no instant of transition known. On the scratch-pad Mann's pencil labored through the fussiness of Old English script:

𝔚hich is the Clerk?

He said: "If you're ready, Mr. Hunter, we can choose a jury."

The squirrel-cage squeaked. Mr. Delehanty called: "Peter Anson."

The bald stubby man waddling forward looked neither calloused nor hypersensitive. Thirtyish; young enough not to be too congealed in acquired prejudices, old enough to have rubbed off some of the certainties the young must use in place of experience. Mann imagined for him a cute pink-and-white wife, two kids, mortgage, Chevvy. Anson might do.

As Mr. Delehanty called more names, Mann ripped off the top sheet of the doodle-pad, to bury it in the minute-book instead of the wastebasket. Never mind Mr. Delehanty's feelings. Some later page might show only cats, mermaids, stripteasers—he could have that one.

Relaxed and genial, T. J. Hunter spoke to the potential jurors as well as to those first called: "I'm Talbot Hunter, assistant district attorney who will try this case. Judge Terence Mann is presiding. At the other table is Mr. Cecil Warner, defense counsel, and beside him is the defendant Callista Blake. She's not a resident of Shanesville, by the way, though she lived there till about a year ago. I don't think any of you come from Shanesville—very nice town, about three miles beyond the city line." Mann drew a lightning sketch of the Governor's mansion, and wrote: *Nice town, but alas, T. J., wrong county!* "Callista Blake is the daughter, by an earlier marriage, of Mrs. Herbert Chalmers of Shanesville. Callista's father, Kramer Blake, died in 1947. In 1951 her mother married Dr. Herbert Chalmers, Associate Professor of English at our own Winchester College. Miss Blake lived in Shanesville until July of last year, when she took an apartment by herself here in Winchester— 21 Covent Street. Then, and up to the time of her arrest, she was employed by a portrait photographer, Miss Edith Nolan—"

"Still is," said a thin red-haired woman among the spectators.

Mann's rap with the gavel was reflex action. "That can't be permitted." The redhead sat frozen in evident astonishment at herself. It would be Edith Nolan, Mann guessed; he could feel no genuine annoyance. "The Court assumes the impulsive remark just made by a spectator was inadvertent, an accident. Disciplinary action will be necessary if anything like that happens again. All relevant statements will be made properly, at the proper time. Go ahead, Mr. Hunter." A blush flooded the woman's keen homely face; she nodded, no doubt a promise to behave. In the early thirties, tense, intelligent, explosive, but without the look of a crackpot; Mann expected no further trouble there.

Hunter said: "Please search your memories. Are any of those names familiar? Blake? Chalmers? Nolan?... Don't worry if you've read or heard of Mr. Warner. He's a very distinguished attorney. It'd be more surprising if you hadn't heard of him. That's not the sort of familiarity I mean—wouldn't disqualify you."

Mann noted the purloined Warner special. Now if the Old Man tossed his opponent verbal violets he would appear imitative and absurd.

"Other names—Nathaniel Judd, senior partner in the real estate and insurance firm of Judd and Doherty. Ann Doherty—that is, Mrs. James Doherty.... Welsh? Jason? No familiarity? Good." Hunter swept on his reading glasses, which were perhaps clear glass. "This paper I'm holding charges that on the evening of Sunday, the 16th of last August, Callista Blake, at her apartment at 21 Covent Street, Winchester, gave to Ann Doherty, who was about to leave that apartment after a short visit and return to her home in Shanesville, a drink of brandy containing the poison aconite. It charges that within the half-hour thereafter Callista Blake followed Ann Doherty to Shanesville, and found her near a small pond which lies at the edge of the Dohertys' property. It charges that Callista Blake, willfully, with malice aforethought, drowned Ann Doherty in this pond. The State will ask for the verdict of murder in the first degree."

Under spreading silence, words moved sluggishly in Judge Mann's mind—words remembered from the hours when he could not sleep. He had lurched sandy-eyed out of bed, prowled at the bookshelves, settled by the chilling fireplace with a volume of the *Britannica* and a shot glass of brandy. "*The cerebrum is totally unaffected by aconite, consciousness and the intelligence remaining normal to the last.*"

His diaphragm twisted in a spasmodic yawn. He covered it swiftly, but the reporters would have seen it. He thought: *Let them!* But he must not start woolgathering. Plump Mr. Anson had folded his arms and declared that he was a plumber by trade. T. J. Hunter was asking: "Have newspaper or radio accounts caused you to give any advance opinion?"

"No, sir, I b'lieve I can honestly say they haven't."

"Have you read the editorials in the Winchester *Courier* or the morning *Sentinel* on this case?"

"Well, no, I kind of let the wife do the heavy reading."

Crowd laughter mildly rumbled; Anson evidently didn't mind it.

"Have you ever been the victim of a robbery or burglary?"

"No, sir, never was."

Routine questions continued a while, Hunter relaxed and casual yet really wasting no time.... "Mr. Anson, my next question has been under a good deal of discussion in recent years. Like any good citizen, you must have given it thought. Have you, sir, any conscientious objection to the death penalty?"

"Well ..." The man was unhappy. "I been asking myself that, ever since I got called. All's I can say, if I was certain-sure about the guilt, I mean the first-degree thing, I wouldn't hesitate to vote for the ch—for the death penalty—if I was certain-sure, that's what I'd have to do."

"And you would do it?"

"I would," said Mr. Anson. "Seems—seems only right."

Another yawn assailed the Judge. He groped for causes of his weariness other than lack of sleep. "*The world is too much with us*—" if too much for

Wordsworth long ago, what about now? A tractor-trailer answered the thought, groaning through the street three stories below, a Cyclops in anguish, rattling windows, sending elderly foundations into a sympathetic shudder. Judge Mann wondered if he might be coming down with a cold.

II

Edith Nolan studied eleven faces, and the twelfth now giving the prosecutor stiffly reasonable answers. She wondered if Cecil Warner would dislike, as she did, Mr. Francis Fielding's buttoned-in upper lip. A statistician in the records office of Winchester's biggest department store, forty, consciously literate, rather too good to be true. Edith sensed the fanatic, the acrid mind that must be always right. But such a disposition might harden in favor of acquittal instead of conviction.

Since her tasteless sandwich luncheon, the afternoon had been for Edith a desert of echoes, all voices unfamiliar except Cecil Warner's. Fast work, she supposed, to have a jury almost complete, and the hour not quite four. The heat had been turned higher after the noon recess, the courtroom growing sickly with a mustiness of flesh, disinfectant, dust. Edith's head ached, a dull frontal throb. The hard seat nagged at thin buttocks, unpadded backbone. When Callista looked her way, Edith wriggled and grimaced, trying to add a mild humor to her silent message: *Head up, Cal! We're going to win.* Briefly, Callista smiled.

Imaginary pressure of eyes at the back of her neck was a misery. Callista's mother and stepfather were two or three rows behind. At the noon recess they had been unwillingly jammed against her in the corridor outside. Mrs. Chalmers would have liked to cut her then, Edith thought, but washed together so in the loud human tide, that hadn't been quite possible even for Victoria Chalmers. The Pale Professor might even have rebelled at it—he was bravely friendly, pleased to stoop in his weedy tallness and shake hands, keeping haunted uncourageous eyes obstinately turned away from the great stone face. And so the Face had talked, pronouncing deadly commonplaces in Victoria's public manner, which always suggested the need of an organ obligato—a spate of commonplaces, all of them somehow conveying the implication that Edith Nolan was at the very least a Bad Influence.

Edith had never discovered much resemblance between Victoria and her daughter, except for prominent cheekbones and uncommonly white skin. Victoria's nose was classically straight, without the irregularity that gave

Callista's features an almost Indian cast. Victoria's smoky-pale hyperthyroid eyes somehow lacked alertness, as though she could not be bothered with anything so simple as direct observation. Her hands were stodgy, unalive—nothing there of Callista, and nothing of Callista in her mother's rugged frame and Madam-Chairman chestiness. Edith could picture that bust inflating for voice projection when Victoria was about to read a paper before the Thursday Society of Shanesville—they "did" book reviews and current events. She had met Victoria on her home grounds twice, when Callista had invited her out to Shanesville with wry warnings. At home, Victoria was invincible, a conversational Juggernaut riding over a crumpled evening with every adverb in place.

And yet now, Edith thought, Victoria was probably suffering, in her fashion. She would be regarding Callista's trouble as an unwarranted attack of the universe against Mrs. Victoria Johnson Blake Chalmers; but with whatever strength of emotion remained, with whatever capability of love may exist in a person who must be always right, Victoria would be feeling a genuine distress for her maverick daughter, perhaps also for dead Ann Doherty, even for Jim Doherty. Maybe. Or maybe Callista had been right in the quick, casual, bitter remark that Edith remembered from many months ago: "Something was left out when Mother's chromosomes got slung together—I believe it was humanity."

Or the truth could lie as usual somewhere in the middle. In the noon recess, it had seemed to Edith that she glimpsed flickerings of real pain in Victoria—some kind of pain; under such conditions it might be hard to tell the difference between grief and the pinch of a tight girdle. Then the crowd had thinned enough to let them escape, and Victoria, still resonantly talking nothings, had marched Professor Herbert Chalmers away, a trainer jerking the leash on a shambling mournful Great Dane.

The electric clock behind Mr. Delehanty clicked and twitched, another scrap of eternity chipped off as Mr. Fielding declared: "I have no objection to the death penalty, and would make no exception for a woman."

The bald athlete Talbot J. Hunter stepped aside, and Cecil Warner, wilted and ancient, took over. The Old Man was tired, his questions a mere mopping up of areas Hunter had ignored: Fielding's newspaper reading, length of residence in Winchester; perhaps he just wanted to hear a few more overtones. In this case Cecil Warner—(Edith understood it fully today for the first time)—was not interested in the fee, the publicity, or the abstraction of justice. He was there because, with the curious devotion of an old man, he loved Callista. To use one of his own worn phrases, it was that simple. Since a woman of thirty-one does not live in the world of a battle-worn man of sixty-eight, Edith knew she could grasp the quality of that love from the outside only, with the mind only: enough, to accept the fact. But didn't a defense counsel need some inner coldness to sustain him?

She studied the twelve faces, their names already carved into her memory. She would retain the look of them as vividly as though each juror had sat in her studio under the clever lights while she examined the faults, planes, good points, chatted with them to let self-consciousness and vanity subside, searched for the portrait they wouldn't see, and at last finished her shots—one to please the customer if possible; one, if lucky, to please herself as a frozen instant of relative truth.

Peter Anson—oh, if he were furry instead of bald you could use color film and get a pink panda. That notion was not quite her own, but like something Callista might have said in one of her fantastic moods, more impudent than funny, more funny than spiteful. Anson's chubbiness would be deceptive, his good nature not the kind that he would maintain under serious pressure. His kindness would be limited to what he understood. Beyond that limit, Anson could be cruel.

Dora Lagovski, twenty-four, mammal, housewife. Dora would want to be photographed with a big mouthful of teeth, and you better do it.

Emerson Lake, newsdealer, sixty-five. If not born in a cool pocket of the White Mountains, he should have been. Humanity gleamed in him like an ember under the crust of a clotted briar pipe.

Emma Beales, forty, housewife. Smooth round conscientious face, all hell on civic duty. Never plagued with an original idea, capable of talking both arms off at the deltoids, but not a bad old girl. Edith estimated that she must have made about twenty portraits of Emma every year; it was only in the bad moods that they all looked alike.

Stella Wainwright, thirty-seven, grade school teacher. Her brown hair curved in what Edith decided was a natural wave, not helped by her dowdy muddy-brown dress. The kids probably liked her; she would not be expected to teach them much about the passion and confusion of the world: not for Stella the sweat and garbage, the sunrises and the music of moon-drenched nights, the labors of love, the fields of cornflowers, the screaming in the disturbed ward. They had people to take care of all that stuff while Stella taught social studies. But on this jury Stella would do her best, and it might be good enough.

Elizabeth Grant, twenty-six, housewife. How could life write on a face of dough? Unfair, maybe; nevertheless Edith distrusted Mrs. Grant, reflecting what atrocious cruelty can be accomplished by well-meaning souls devoid of humor and imagination. The woman was opaque, her simplest answers under voir dire examination sounding like quotations from a wholesome family magazine.

Ralph LaSalle, thirty-one, shoe-store clerk. Cecil Warner and Hunter, Edith supposed, would both have recognized the minority he represented. His mask was good, the too-long blond hair and somewhat mannered accent betraying it. Cecil Warner might be counting on LaSalle to show fairness toward a white crow of another sort; Hunter possibly expected him to be hostile toward all women. Both lawyers could be wrong; Edith expected LaSalle to act and think simply as a human being with a good intelligence and rational sympathies.

Rachel Kleinman, housewife, forty-eight. They would be needing Mother Rachel at home; Edith hoped there was a daughter old enough to cook. But Rachel would stay with it; warmth and gentleness were in her; she would not knowingly burn another woman for a witch. And when Edith took the stand, she might look for this woman Rachel to understand why Callista Blake had smashed the heater and poured ice-water into her tank of tropical fish when she knew she was to be arrested.

Emmet Hoag, hardware salesman, twenty-nine. A little bit handsome, Edith noted—like a healthy pig. He would consider himself hell on the women until snared and housebroken by some broad-beamed breeder who knew what she wanted. A born No. 12 sure to go along with the majority: what else could he do? Well, Edith thought in a gust of weariness, he could drop dead.

Dolores Acevedo, secretary, twenty-nine—and actually not over thirty-five. Hair midnight black and skin of honey brown, born to be beautiful and surely knowing it with a simplicity too placid for vanity. By rights Dolores should be a rich man's mistress, maybe was. Edith also guessed that anywhere outside the region of sexual competition Dolores might be generous and kind, even very kind—and admitted that it was no more than a guess. For that matter, would a woman as outrageously lovely as Dolores ever get far enough from the sex arena for other elements of her nature to dominate? Nothing cold or contrived about *that* kind of beauty—warm as tropic night, Dolores. Yet she might also think, and reason, and be kind—she just might.

Helen Butler, fifty-two, gift-shop proprietor. And a Sunday painter, Edith doubtfully remembered. She had met Miss Butler a few months ago, when prowling the gift shop for book ends. Callista had not gone along, and Edith recalled she had not given Miss Butler her name, though they enjoyed a quarter-hour of small talk. Books mostly; some deprecating mention by Miss Butler of her landscape painting, or was it still life? Nothing in that to make the lady disqualify herself from the jury, if she remembered. A salty spirit with independent opinions, laughter wrinkles at the eyes, unmalicious wit. A bit old-maidish, maybe no great force of character. But intelligent, moderate, good.

They were the Twelve.

Edith looked again at the slight and silver-templed man in black. No schoolmastery fuss from him at that bad moment of the morning when impulse had betrayed her into speaking out of turn. Even a kind of friendliness behind the rebuke he had been forced to make. He would be harder to photograph than any of the jury, or ambitious Hunter. Harder than anyone present except Callista herself, and Cecil Warner who had posed for Edith in actuality a year ago.

And Cal had drawn one of her three-minute cartoons of Warner, which delighted the Old Man—their first meeting. Had he adored her then? Why, then, a year ago, Cal's ordeal of love with Jim Doherty had not even begun. It occurred to Edith that for the human race a magic power of foresight would be a burden unendurable. Fair enough to guess, and plan within limits, but no one should ever know to a certainty what will happen in the next hour, or day, or year.

The time might arrive when Callista would be forced to know that—or perhaps almost know it, and be tortured by a series of meaningless reprieves. In Salem, less than three hundred years ago, they had crushed Giles Corey to death by gradually adding rocks to the pile on his breast. Edith warned herself sharply: *Stop that!*

Cecil Warner was moving away from the jury box, straightening his round shoulders with a tired twist. "Thank you, Mr. Fielding. May it please the Court, the defense is satisfied with this jury."

Mr. Delehanty announced: "The jury will rise." In Mr. Delehanty's pocket a gleaming triangle of handkerchief shone, still perfect, spotless at the weary end of the day. And the jury was standing.

Graceless in the group and clumsy, they mutely apologized to each other for their elbows, raised their hands for the burbling of Mr. Delehanty of the perfect handkerchief. They swore. Too much finality. A true verdict render?—but what is truth? No, too much. Behind the half-comic front, too vast a thing for the Hoags, Lagovskis, Kleinmans.

But, Edith thought, that's how it's done. And we persuade ourselves that what we wish to call truth may emerge from it. We accept the ludicrous fancy that you multiply wisdom when you multiply one by twelve.

Mr. Delehanty laid down the Bible. Flushed, important, the jury took their seats. The prosecutor stood. Edith's stomach twisted. She bent forward, covering her face. Too much.

She thought: But I *know* Callista!

Frail, damaged, miraculous body; wild, difficult, exasperating, wholly irreplaceable brain that understood, needed, desired so much—everything that was Callista could be and might be charred to rubbish, to satisfy the mythology of a still vengeful and superstitious race. Surely not even guilty; but if she were—

Edith knew then that the same emotional storm would have struck her if she had believed Callista Blake guilty of this and a thousand other crimes. A storm including personal shame and horror at taking part, if only by silent presence, in an act of barbarism.

What are we doing here?

III

Cecil Warner turned toward the cold gleam of the courtroom window; an eastern window, the winter sunshine long gone. In the morning he had watched a glint of the sun on Callista's black hair, and on the polished bleakness of the table where her arm rested. The daily journey and decline of the sun affected him more deeply now than in past years, left him irrationally disappointed on the gray days, less willing to accept the approach and arrival of night. On such days, or at the tired conclusions of winter afternoons, the age of his body oppressed him—as now, when he turned his heavy head and felt a wobbling sag of cheeks, unwilling droop of eyelids, slight but irritating deafness, uncertainty of his powers. And in all activities between foggy waking and not quite desired sleep, a fading, a knowledge of relinquishment. If his eyes sought and cherished (as now) the delicate swell of Callista's breast, his mind said: *My hand will not follow that curve, not ever.* Or it said: *Even the inner and almost hidden love that keeps the spirit alive and sometimes strong and sometimes angry—even that is only for a little while.*

T. J. Hunter was up on his feet being stately and important. Warner advised himself: he must not, would not fall into the dangerous error of hating or even disliking T. J. Enact hostility, yes, whenever it might have a useful effect on the jury—enact anything at all, from sputtering rage to glacial contempt—*but don't feel it!* He could not afford to feel it, without a far more flexible control of his private emotions than he now possessed: much too easy for an angry man to look like a fool. And yet not hating T. J. was going to be intolerably difficult at times; for Callista could die, and T. J. was after all a good deal of a bloody bastard.

Hunter said: "Your Honor, I see it's getting on to four. My opening will be brief. If agreeable to the Court and Mr. Warner, may I make it now?"

Behind his mask Warner felt flustered and unready. He could protest; Terence Mann would obligingly call an early adjournment; Callista would have some rest, if you could give that name to her unknowable hours in the detention cell. The advantage T. J. probably hoped for, in having the jury sleep on his opening masterpiece, might be no advantage at all—a jury can forget impressions as well as facts.... Startled, he realized that Terence with his curious courtesy was deferring, looking down from the bench with harmless reminders of a ten-year friendship in his face, waiting for the defense to speak first. He said: "My client is very tired. However, I assume from what Mr. Hunter says that his opening will not run much past five o'clock—is that correct?"

"I'm sure it won't, sir. I only intend to summarize, to outline what the State expects to prove."

Sir from you?—gah! "In that case, the defense has no objection."

"Members of the jury, Callista Blake is the daughter of an artist, by all accounts a loving father, who died when she was seven, and a lady who is known to a wide circle of acquaintance as a devoted wife and mother. This lady, and Callista's father and stepfather, gave the girl a careful, decent upbringing. Callista's stepfather Dr. Herbert Chalmers of Winchester College is a distinguished man, author of a textbook in English widely used in the secondary schools. Her mother is active in the Presbyterian Church, past president of the Shanesville P.T.A.—in short I know of nothing in this girl's history or family surroundings to account for her present situation unless you attach more importance than I do to certain childhood accidents. As a baby she got a nitric acid burn, later repaired by plastic surgery. She had polio, which left her slightly lame, very slightly—as you can see, Miss Blake is not disfigured, and not at all unattractive. And don't we all know of cases where ugly accidents have happened to children without turning them against the human race?

"What are the origins of crime? Does anyone know? Psychiatrists? Well, the State is prepared to offer psychiatric testimony, if the defense elects to do so. I can't see the necessity myself. I can't imagine an insanity defense being made here. I think it's a case where the individual must be held clearly responsible for a wanton and cruel act, the one act that strikes most dangerously against the welfare and security of human society: namely murder. It was, and the State will prove it, a murder motivated by sex jealousy, but obviously not in any gust of passion. No, it was coldly premeditated, planned, and heartless."

Warner fought down the perilous anger. This was simply Hunter's opening barrage. *I can roar, too.* Yet he wished that without disturbing her by a touch he could will Callista to look toward him for comfort. He checked an impulsive motion of his hand. Still-faced, she was watching a spot on the wall above the gaunt grim skull of the juror Emerson Lake. She would turn to him and listen if he whispered, maybe even smile. But it might be that she needed those withdrawals, a kind of rest.

"In 1950, Mrs. Blake and her daughter Callista moved from New York City where Callista was born, to Winchester. Mrs. Blake was employed in the Registrar's office of Winchester College, and there met Dr. Herbert Chalmers; they were married in 1951. Dr. Chalmers had bought a Shanesville property a few years before—1946, I think. Callista lived there till she graduated from the Shanesville High School, Class of 1958—with high honors by the way. Dr. Chalmers wished to send her to college. She is a girl of exceptional intelligence, and don't forget it." (*So, T. J.? She's on trial for unauthorized possession of a brain?*) "But immediately after graduation, Callista Blake preferred to seek employment, and found it as an assistant in a photographic studio—Nolan's, on Hallam Street here in Winchester. Well, Dr. and Mrs. Chalmers have always wanted to satisfy any reasonable wish of Callista's." (*Have they?*) "They offered no objection to her taking this job. In fact for her eighteenth birthday, July of last year, Dr. Chalmers bought her a car of her own, a Volkswagen—it will be important in the evidence."

Important enough, Warner admitted. If there were any way to deny or even cast doubt on Callista's presence out there in Shanesville that night—but there was not. Callista herself would not have it so. On the stand, he knew, she would tell the truth so far as she knew it—the whole impossible clouded story that left her no defense except a reasonable doubt as to criminal intent. And if she did not take the stand, there was no defense at all.

"In that same month last year, July, Callista took an apartment in Winchester, at 21 Covent Street. Again her family indulged her and made the best of it." *Indulged, you fool?* It had been Callista's own money from her father's estate, plus her salary from Edith. Warner felt some wry pleasure, although it meant nothing, really, except an opportunity to rub Hunter's nose in a minor blunder. "There was no break in the family relation, members of the jury—so far as we know. We assume that like many parents, they simply wanted the child to have what *she* wanted." (*And now, T. J., do you think you can transform her from a child into a woman fit for burning?*)

"Another family is involved, a family now broken up by murder. When James Doherty, originally from Massachusetts, met and married Ann Pierce in Philadelphia, he was twenty-seven. He had served in Korea, finishing college on his return. They were married in 1955, and moved to this neighborhood. Mr. Nathaniel Judd of Winchester is the father of a friend of James Doherty's killed in Korea. Mr. Judd grew acquainted with Doherty through correspondence, and in '55 offered him a partnership in his real estate and insurance firm, now Judd and Doherty. In the spring of '55 the Dohertys purchased a house and land in Shanesville township adjoining the Chalmers place. I think Ann Doherty was a happy young wife that year. She started a flower garden."

Callista had a garden too; she poured ice-water in it. Warner glanced up to the spectators' benches, looking for Edith Nolan, feeling a warmth for her that puzzled him by its sudden increase. He supposed one got the habit of taking Edith too much for granted, of turning to her in trouble or weariness (Callista had done it too) without remembering that Edith also was vulnerable, quite as likely to be in the grip of fatigue or sorrow. Edith would be remembering that magical water garden, the emerald illusion of infinity, the darting, shifting arrows of living light that could not move without grace. His first sight of it had been about a year ago, an invitation to the little apartment at Covent Street soon after Edith had done his portrait and Callista's rapid pen had drawn that strangely affectionate cartoon of him, comedy without spite; as if at eighteen the girl could incredibly glimpse the quality of sixty-seven and find something there for the unhurtful entertainment of both of them—and of Edith, who had remarked laconically: "What the hell good is a camera?" Well, he thought, many thanks to the human species for Red Nolan, and he would send her flowers tonight and take her out to dinner like a boy with a date and why not? Never mind the boy—he was dead long ago: take her out like an old man still capable of friendship with a lively, tender, witty woman who understood friendship herself.... Edith met and acknowledged his look across the anonymous crowd—yes, she would be remembering that water garden, and its end, untouchable beauty transformed to a pathetic mess for the janitor to remove.

Two rows behind Edith he saw without pleasure the angular haunted features of James Doherty, and the opaque calm of the black-clad man on Doherty's left. It would be Father Bland's habit, Warner supposed, to show at all times that careful benignity smooth as quartz. Without pleasure, without much interest, he wondered in passing how it felt to be certain of one's own serene rightness.

Hunter's noise—oh, geography. Giving them the lie of the land.

"Those properties are on the outskirts of Shanesville proper. You go out Walton Road about three miles beyond the city line. There's a fork, and the right branch, Summer Avenue, reaches the village limits of Shanesville in a mile; Walton Road runs on south to Emmetville, Pritchett, other towns at the south end of the county. The Doherty place is near that right-angle fork of Summer and Walton, back from the road, its drive opening north on Summer Avenue. The house itself stands about a hundred yards west of the fork. The Chalmers house is south of Dohertys'—entrance on Walton Road about the same distance from the fork. Except for not very heavy traffic, the region's isolated. Peaceful. Closest neighbor is about a quarter-mile down Summer Avenue from Dohertys', a Mrs. Phelps Jason, who manages her twenty-acre place as a wild-life sanctuary. The back land behind it is unused pasture and woods belonging to the Chalmers property, which used to be operated as a farm.

"The Chalmers and Doherty houses are separated by a grove of trees that reaches all the way to Walton Road. On the west side of Dohertys' the woods are continuous, except for Mrs. Jason's place, to Shanesville. You can think of the Doherty place as a pocket cut out of woodland. The two families used a winding footpath through the grove for visiting back and forth. And you must imagine the region as it is in summer, leafed out so that the two houses are quite hidden from each other. Maple, pine, hemlock, oak—some very big pines at the edge of Walton Road.... In the grove near the property line there's a natural pond, fed by a brook from the Chalmers back land. Its outlet runs through the grove, into a culvert near the fork of the highway. The pond is small, oval, fifteen feet across at the widest, less than five feet deep last August because of several weeks of drouth.

"From the spur path or the pond, you can't see either house in summer. On the night Ann Doherty died there, it might have been possible to catch a glint of light from the Chalmers house, through the leaves. A hazy night, hot, a nearly full moon shining through the overcast. A still and oppressive night."

And that night, Warner remembered, the night of Ann Doherty's death and of Callista's longer and stranger ordeal, he had been at Mrs. Willoughby's discreet establishment on River Street, sharing a well-perfumed sheet with one of her young professionals. The memory remained clear because there had been no more such nights since August; the many other nights of hired love stretching back across thirty-odd years tended to blur and run together—here and there a face remembered, a word, a special instant of intensity, annoyance, amusement. The night in August had been delightful; relaxed, no attempt to achieve a counterfeit of youth, and no wish for it. Leisure of a sort was possible—it ought to be, at Mrs. Willoughby's rates!—and the girl, small, brown-eyed, pert, had been convincingly friendly; more so, once she understood that the Old Man, in spite of being sixty-eight and too fat, didn't care for elaborate variations but wanted only the bread-and-butter-steak-and-potatoes of natural intercourse. They had talked a while, he recalled, she comfortably smoking, braced up prettily naked on a thin elbow and chattering—perceptive enough, by the way, not to call him Daddy.... There might be no more such nights: a final recession of the need, or perhaps a suddenly yielding blood-vessel, a cancer taking over, a tumble in a slippery bathtub—*never mind*.... He could almost remember walking home from River Street (thinking very likely of Callista), but it must have been after the moon was down. A hazy night—"*Out of the cradle endlessly rocking—*"

T. J. Hunter was still pausing over a drink of water. Warner remembered— old things mainly, their intensity dissolved by distance in time; remembered, under the illusion of detachment that can make existence appear truly like a river, yourself able to look back upstream at nearly forgotten vistas: trees, meadow and town, eddies, dubious shoreline, floating trash. Warner shielded his face with his hand, closing away even Callista, as he had found he must sometimes do.

Boyhood was the sound of ocean, medicinal reek of kelp washed in on the night tide to wait for bare feet and a poking stick. It was the breakers, green ridges advancing out of the ever-distressed Atlantic and growing a snowy froth, never pausing yet seeming to pause when the froth spilled over the crest. Then a toppling, crash, inward flow. A receding; a mysterious acceptance of an end, soft hiss and sigh and aftermath, swirl of light water become thin and harmless on the sand.

Boyhood was fishing boats and Montauk Light, gravely busy clam-diggers, Manuelo whom Cecil wasn't supposed to play with. It was the unseen journey of hollow-voiced titans in the fog; pressure and majestic riot of storm. It was an afternoon of watching the disappearance of an unknown sail over the southern curve of the earth. School, too. Helpless rage at long division; Papa's dry-goods store that was always going to do a little better next year; Manuelo in the empty boathouse showing off how many times he could do it in half an hour; Great-aunt Harriet who turned up every Thanksgiving, who liked to announce abruptly out of her world of deafness that she'd been in Ford's Theatre when Lincoln was shot—then she would read lips a minute while the company hollered how wonderful that was, and then, eating loudly and cheerfully, she would slip back contented into the mist of ancient times. Boyhood was windy nights, and surf hammering the muffled drums of sand a quarter-mile away; stillness also in the dark, and moonlight pouring into another midnight of black water. Tide inexorably rising to clean away the dead jellyfish and driftwood, blotting out barefoot stories written on the low-tide beach; clear sunshine over the whitecaps; and long gray days.

Out of the cradle endlessly rocking,
Out of the mocking-bird's throat, the musical shuttle,
Out of the Ninth-month midnight,
Over the sterile sands, and the fields beyond, where the child, leaving his
bed, wander'd alone, bareheaded, barefoot ...

He had been twelve—anyway it was soon after Mother died—when he discovered Whitman. One of the volumes chastely silent behind glass, in the parlor over the store, undoubtedly a book of Mother's. Carried off to his room and secretly saved from disaster when his stepmother dismissed all the books in the parlor that didn't have pretty red or brown bindings. The fury of that ancient wound stirred. At sixty-eight, Cecil Warner smiled slightly, unknowingly, and shifted in the disagreeable courtroom chair to ease a discomfort in his defective left arm.

So much, so many million other images, reflections, happenings, accidents, in the forty-nine years of the river's journey before Callista Blake was born, the nineteen years since then! None of it (said the doctors) totally forgotten. *"I, Cecil, take thee, Ellen...."*

He remembered making the necessary uproar about his bad arm's disqualifying him for military service; most of it sincere enough too, in spite of a deep private happiness with his young wife. He remembered damning the Kaiser. The murky spooks of Stalin and Hitler bulked so much larger in the years between, in front of them the mushroom cloud—hard to reconstruct true images of 1917. Then 1918, and influenza, and Ellen dead. She couldn't be—not abruptly, incomprehensibly *gone* like that; but she was. He returned half willingly to a winter day of 1959.

At sixty-eight it is possible to look ahead—some; to form a purpose, with caution, remembering that if you don't make it, they'll say charitably: "Think of that! Sort of getting on, wasn't he?"

He would not drink tonight. Well—dinner with Edith, maybe (and flowers), so maybe a glass or two of wine, nothing more—

Never more shall I escape, never more the reverberations,
Never more the cries of unsatisfied love be absent from me,
Never again leave me to be the peaceful child I was before what there, in
the night,
By the sea, under the yellow and sagging moon,
The messenger there aroused—the fire, the sweet hell within,
The unknown want, the destiny of me....

T. J. Hunter dropped the folder of notes he had been studying, possibly for effect, and turned back to the jury.

"In May of this year—the State will prove it—an illicit relation developed between Callista Blake and James Doherty, the husband of that Ann Doherty whose death, as you know, is the reason for this trial. Not to mince matters, the word is adultery, and I must remind you now, members of the jury, that Callista Blake is not here on trial for adultery. She is on trial for murder, nothing else. The State will prove the fact of adultery to establish motive—

which, as you may also know, is not legally required, yet I think a rational mind is bound to demand it. How can we reasonably condemn anyone without at least some understanding of what made him act as the factual evidence says he did?

"I want to make one thing clear. In a case of this sort the husband is automatically suspect, the chance of conspiracy so obvious that the police would be derelict in duty if they didn't examine it to the last scrap of a clue. That's been done. If anything at all had been uncovered involving James Doherty in this crime, you know he would not be at liberty. Nothing of the sort has been found; everything points the other way. He decisively broke off the affair more than a month before the murder. He tried to make amends for his folly. The State is convinced that in the death of Ann Doherty, Callista Blake, consumed by hatred and jealousy—and by a certain fear for herself, since she was pregnant—acted entirely alone.

"I am sorry for her—who wouldn't be? You will be. Her difficulty was great, her position tragic. But as the State's representative, I remind you that instead of the many fair and decent solutions for her trouble that she might have chosen, the one she did choose was premeditated murder.

"On the evening of Sunday, August 16th, Ann Doherty called at Callista Blake's apartment, 21 Covent Street, leaving at 8:30. No third person was present, no one knew she was going there except Callista Blake who, by her own admission, had telephoned and asked her to come. James Doherty had gone to New York City by train the morning of that Sunday and did not return until Monday evening.... Before leaving Callista's apartment, Ann had a little drink of brandy for the road. It was poisoned, with aconite.

"On her way home, Ann was stopped by a state trooper because her driving was a bit erratic. The trooper dismissed her with a warning, and then followed her home because he thought she might be ill, felt uneasy about her welfare till he saw her drive in safely at her house on Summer Avenue—8:43 by his notebook. This trooper, Carlo San Giorgio, is the last person known to have spoken with Ann Doherty before her death. He will testify.

"At 9:10, less than half an hour after Ann reached home, Callista Blake's Volkswagen was parked on Walton Road, between the fork and the Chalmers house, hidden by the trees. At 9:40, another half-hour later, Callista Blake drove that car part way into the Chalmers drive, backed out and drove off in the direction of Winchester—no stop, no visit to her mother's house, just in and out and away.

"Ann Doherty died, by drowning in that pond in the woods, between quarter to nine and quarter to ten; this we know from medical evidence. We have excellent circumstantial evidence for most of Ann's actions after San Giorgio saw her reach home. She stopped her car in the driveway, off the gravel, almost colliding with the front porch. She turned off headlights and motor but left the car door open. Her key ring, with house and car keys, fell by the porch steps. She dropped her handbag on the path leading through the woods to the Chalmers house. Aconite causes numbness of the extremities, nausea, thirst, general muscular collapse, but usually no impairment of the intelligence. Evidently Ann's mind was at least clear enough to remember her husband was away, and the nearest help in her sudden sickness would be at the Chalmers house. She probably couldn't recover the key ring after her numb fingers dropped it, and that's why she couldn't get into the house and reach the telephone. She had locked up when she left, her custom whenever Jim was away.

"Coming down that path, Ann fell several times, she vomited, she lost one of her shoes. She fell again, half-way down the spur path leading to the pond. Why did she go that way, and not straight on to the Chalmers house? We don't know, for certain. Took the wrong turn in the moonlight, being sick and confused?—possible. She was found in the water, drowned. Stumbled and fell in, couldn't get out?—that also is possible, remotely possible. Admittedly the circumstantial evidence is imperfect at this point, and it's one of the questions of fact that you, members of the jury, will be called on to decide."

Grim, slow, brooding, Hunter returned to the prosecution's table for another sip of water, and Warner's gaze wandered to the face of Judge Terence Mann. *What are you going to do to us, Terence?*

In a sense, the Judge would do nothing. Warner assumed without reservations that the quiet introspective man up there would try his best to preserve an ideal impartiality. It seemed to Warner that Mann was almost devoid of vanity, incredible as that might seem in a judge. No fanaticism in Terence Mann, no insistence on the rightness of a view because it was his own, no false identification of self with idea. Incredible until you remembered that Terence was a judge more or less by accident, an interim appointment later confirmed by an election in which he had peacefully refused to do any serious campaigning.

Warner recalled their first meeting ten years ago, soon after Mann had been appointed special prosecutor for an investigation into county road construction frauds. The rats were running, and Terence, a youngish thirty-seven, appeared to be enjoying it. In the book-leather and walnut surroundings of Mann and Wheatley, Terence had looked at first like a revised version of his uncle Norden Mann who had died the year before. A superficial resemblance. Old Norden had been a born pettifogger, loving legal labyrinths for their own sake. Terence, skeptical, a bit sharp, would look for the simplest way to pass through a labyrinth and come out on the other side. Terence had served his apprenticeship in Norden's firm, re-entering it after his discharge from the Army. Until that graft-hunting appointment no one had heard much of him. Warner had gone to the office on Wilson Place off Main Street—"Lawyers' Hollow"—for a luncheon engagement with Joe Wheatley. Terence had been halted for a handshake, and Warner had fallen into a pose he could not always avoid: the aging lion. Terence wasn't scared. "Do you intend to be a famous prosecutor? Scourge of the unrighteous, huh?"

The loaded questions—they came out too, Grandfather roaring. Terence hadn't minded. "No, sir, I don't exactly see that ahead of me." No word of what he did see. Later they met at the University Club and began a more relaxed acquaintance over a few drinks. Then an invitation to Terence's apartment that became an evening of Chopin and Bach. Music was an aspect of Mann's life unsuspected, discovered by Warner with the abruptness of an opened door. The lawyer vanished; the hands were "beyond technique"; the keyboard voice spoke with the authority of intense feeling governed by insight.

And Warner recalled another meeting with someone else, in an almost empty bar, a few days after the election that confirmed Terence Mann in office. Idle for the afternoon and in a cool beery mood, he had glanced down the damp mahogany and noticed a sagging red-veined blob, the face of Boss Timmy Flack of the Third Ward—who, in a way, *was* the politics of Winchester, the half-submerged and partly useful human force, neither honest nor demonstrably a crook, The Man You Went To See. Himself honored and ancient, professionally secure, in any case seldom giving a damn what others said of him or of the company he kept, Warner had moved down the bar and bought Timmy another drink before The Man could buy him one. "Hear tell we got a new judge."

"Uh-huh."

"Happy, Timmy? Civic virtue and so on?"

"Shit."

"If not happy, what are you going to do about it?"

"You needling me, Counselor?"

"Little bit."

"What the hell's anybody going to do, now he's in? The son of a bitch doesn't *want* anything!"

Which was certainly not true, but just as certainly true in Timmy's sense. And Cecil Warner understood that he now feared Terence Mann only because Terence's mind demanded demonstration, when a demonstration of relative truth may be more arduous than any labors of the gods.

"Yes, she might have stumbled and fallen in. The State contends this is not probable. You will of course hear all the evidence that has led us to this conclusion. The State contends that Callista Blake followed Ann Doherty, searched her out, found her there helpless on the path, dragged her the rest of the way into the water. Perhaps even held her under, the way you might drown an unwanted kitten."

Chilled by the voice in spite of forty courtroom years, Warner saw Callista gazing down at her fingertips, frowning slightly as if bothered in the midst of concentration by an irrelevant uproar in another room.

"On Monday, August 17th, Detective Sergeant Lloyd Rankin of the Winchester Police was sent to Callista Blake's apartment, acting on information received from the State Police at Shanesville. The poison aconitine was found there, in two forms—in an opened bottle of brandy, and in a canister that held chopped-up monkshood roots, the source of aconitine, steeping in brandy. The State will prove Callista's opportunity to secure monkshood roots ten days earlier, from her mother's flower garden in Shanesville.

"The State contends that Ann Doherty could not have received that poison by accident. The State contends that Callista Blake gave it to her with malice aforethought, with full intent to cause her death. The State contends that the final act, the drowning, was done by Callista Blake, and that she is guilty of murder in the first degree."

Hunter was sitting down and mopping his face. Warner discovered that he himself had risen, for now his body was wavering in vertigo and he must grab the back of his chair and wait. The clock hands stood at three minutes past five. The Judge was gazing distantly down the slant of an unmoving pencil. "Your Honor, a word before adjournment if I may?"

Terence's voice was soft and friendly. "Certainly, Mr. Warner."

"The defense will waive the opening. At this time, before evidence, before the jury has had opportunity to learn the truth, I have nothing to say except that my client is innocent."

Whereto answering, the sea,
Delaying not, hurrying not,
Whispered me through the night, and very plainly before daybreak,
Lisp'd to me the low and delicious word DEATH ...

IV

Judge Mann followed Joe Bass to the elevator that clanked them gravely to the relative holiness of the sixth floor, where Mann's chambers occupied a corner with a north view. The windows were dark, under a windy spatter of unexpected rain. Mann glimpsed gold blurs of downtown windows, white hurry of headlights, a flow of them two blocks away at the corner of Main and Court, Winchester going home to suburban bedrooms. "Nasty night," said Joe Bass. The red eye closed, the green eye opened; a file of wet bugs poured up the Court Street hill. "Going home directly, sir?"

"I think so. You were in court, weren't you, Joe?"

"Yes. I ducked out before the end of Mr. Hunter's speech. Did Mr. Warner waive the opening?"

"More or less...." Joe Bass never hovered, or clucked. A sure instinct had told him Judge Mann preferred to light his own cigarettes. But he did not like to be dismissed before the Judge went home, preferring to read or meditate in the anteroom until any hour of the night. He had not much to go home to— a boarding-house bedroom uptown, his wife dead, children married and gone. "I wish Mr. Warner would cut down that belly. Too much work for the heart at sixty-eight."

"Sixty-eight, Judge?—I hadn't realized." Joe chuckled faintly in the shadows. "I'm sixty-seven. Apropos of old age, I took the liberty of browsing through your Thucydides a while ago—have the same paperback edition at home, and very good, I'd say—may I?" He was already drifting to the bookshelves. For Joe, there was always a quotation. It seemed to Judge Mann that this was at least the magpie instinct at its noblest, for Joe did not gather them as random bright beads, but for personal use and to be shared. "It's from a speech of Pericles at the funeral of those who first died in the war—and I wonder sometimes if the Peloponnesian War wasn't as great a disaster as the latest? If the Greece of Pericles could have survived—well.... Here it is: 'As for those of you who are too old to have children, I would ask you to count as gain the greater part of your life, in which you have been happy, and remember that what remains is not long, and let your hearts be lifted up at the thought of the fair fame of the dead. One's sense of honor is the only thing that does not grow old.'"

Judge Mann thought: What of one who dies young?—a child hit by a car? Ann Doherty? What of one who dies young by act of the State, with no fair fame? "I think, Joe, we've become a more complex people."

"Aren't the essentials much the same?"

"Not quite. I think there's even a new humanitarianism, new in the last hundred and fifty years. In the time of, say, Edmund Burke, there was still officially approved slavery even in England, where they got rid of it before we did. Hangings as public entertainments. Cats burnt alive for fun on Guy Fawkes Day. The modern stomach pukes up that sort of thing. Alongside the mushroom cloud, the decade of insanity that was Hitler's bloom, the damned impersonal devices for butchering unseen millions by throwing a switch, you try setting up the way people actually live, or try to live, from day to day: there's a difference. If the difference means as much as I think it does, if we get through another hundred years without blowing up the planet, modern medicine should have a great share of the credit." Joe looked puzzled. "In a time when any bad sickness or injury was probably a death sentence, a general fatalism would be almost unavoidable, don't you think?"

"Mm, yes."

"Cruelty and beastliness got taken for granted. If we value life more now, it's because we know more about maintaining it and reducing its miseries. It doesn't have to be 'nasty, brutish and short.'"

"'One's sense of honor'—I liked that part."

"Other things don't grow old. Knowledge. What you learned as a child is with you at sixty-seven. Some kinds of love remain young, so long as the body can support our curious brains where love is born."

2

It is extraordinary that a system hoary with age, extravagant and wasteful to the highest degree, should not be supplanted by some method of getting at facts directly, and having them passed on by men who understand the controversies that they seek to solve.

CLARENCE DARROW, *The Story of My Life*

I

The wolves sat on their haunches, or stood, or crouched belly to earth with snouts on forepaws, while others maneuvered in the shadow beyond the tree-border of the clearing. On the other side of that border spread such a blackness as the mind imagines for the sea a mile down, yet here and there it was relieved by the gray of stone; everywhere, also, a coldness. Grayness in the clearing too; no flowers, nothing of the sun, but phallic-bodied toadstools and a ground-vine twisting a serpentine life among scattered rocks. Callista remembered being told that someone had died in there, in the blackness where no one could see it happen. The wolves would have eaten the body.

The wolves were old, possibly several thousand years old. "A geeolawgical malformation," said the child in her lap, speaking with precocious insight.

Callista moved her hand with its dangling bracelet over the fine black hair, tiny ear, bony shoulder, indistinct body. Her intention was a caress; likely the child knew it. She grew interested, not urgently, in learning the child's sex. What was the difficulty?—not a diaper. Apparently the little thing possessed only a negative pink blank between skinny thighs, like the crotch of a plastic doll. "The Merican Ideal," said the brat, rolling china-white eyes. "See?"

"Well, shut up, darlin'," Callista said. The wolves had crept closer during her preoccupation. Such was their habit (she had been told) if you neglected to look them straight in the eye. She watched them in contemplative pain resembling fear, and they continued moving, slowly, a stirring and gliding that seemed aimless until Callista understood one of them was being pursued, a thin bitch wolf, scar-faced, nearly black, with a crooked leg, devil-eyed but in her demoniac way pathetic. Callista was moved to remark: "Hasn't a chance."

And yet, poor beast, her own wickedness was plain. You could see the drip of poisonous saliva from her mouth, and the fetuslike thing impaled on a lower tooth—it couldn't be her own, so she must have stolen it somewhere. No wonder they were after her. Serve her right! (Or if the fetus was her own she ought to have taken better care of it)—therefore one could understand the primitive justice of it as the gray jaw of a pursuer hooked over her narrow rump. His hind legs massively firmed themselves. Callista could observe the sudden scarlet erection, sense the weight of the one lifted gray indifferent paw; but he did not swing about to rear up and clamp her loins, he merely held her in the angle of his jawbone and under that paw while others closed in to slit her throat—she womanly now lying on her back as a clean white fang thrust out of a surgical mask to run deftly down from the throat along the mid-line of the body, opening up the internal apparatus not for eating but for a better clinical view.

"Like a theater Oh-doctor," said the child's intelligent profile in Callista's arms. Someone said: "Gentlemen, this is the pancreas—a remarkably pancreative bitch to be sure, aware of nature and consequences. Notice the inadequate uterus, a primipara yes yes, but evidence of miscarriage early in term—and by the way, Potter's Field is bungfull of that type."

"I resent that," Callista said. Able now to pick up the child and walk away with her through the woods where all light was granite-gray, she did so, seeking her father to show him a long overdue report card on progress in pancreation. The little girl—naturally, a little girl, with that lyre waist and tumbling hair and dainty genital groove—said to her: "I am so sorry, Callista Johnson Blake, I have to stop here and paint a picture. Can I look at that thing?"

"I got my paw stuck in it."

"Irrelevant," said the little girl. "Incompetent Callista."

"All right," Callista said, and walked away from her through the grayness, uncertain whether she could find her father. He sat (she thought) behind a gray screen, by a lighted window. "*Daddy, please!*—"

Now the bracelet on her wrist had caught, snarled itself in a tangle of black vines, and Callista called: "Daddy, I can't seem to fix it. Can I go now?"

She could not go, because in front of her beyond the vines were the two doors, so very nearly alike, and someone—NOT Daddy, because Daddy NEVER said anything so unkind—someone said: "It's one or the other."

Callista tried then to scream with all her power: "*Daddy! My back hurts*—" nothing in her throat but a mumble, hardly even that, a scream in silence without breath: "Daddy! *Please* come—my back hurts—"

Callista sat up drenched in sweat that soaked her pajamas, and shivering. No relief at first, rather a frustrated anger, since in another moment her father might have been able to hear and answer. Comprehension then; reorientation; qualified relief—*Is waking any better?*

It was, of course. Steadier, anyway. The familiar exchange of selves: What I was in the dream, I am not; what I am, I was and was not in the dream.

The grayness before her eyes yielded the image of a cross, and a second horizontal bar grew visible—there all the time. A window, the same one through which yesterday, by straining on tiptoe to the limit of pain, she had succeeded in watching the wheeling of doves. The same effort now would give her the field of winter sky before dawn. If the rain had stopped, a few stars incorruptible, indifferent.

She did not rise, but pulled her feet under her for warmth and drew closer the scratchy antiseptic-smelling blanket. At this hour the cells were quiet. Another prisoner snored, probably the old woman who had been brought in drunk last night, her high defiant monotone of obscenities temporarily hushed.

A few months ago Callista would have reached for the notebook by her bed to write down what she could recapture of the dream. Edith had wondered if all that intensive reading in psychology wasn't too one-sided, introspective-making. "Maybe, Cal, you ought to be meeting people more and thinking less about their insides." But to meet one person is to meet a thousand selves; and it seemed to Callista that she had remained critical, as Edith probably feared she wouldn't. "Cal, I wish you had more counterbalance, too, for those psychologists in print. I've read them. They don't look out of the windows enough. Why not contrast them with the exact scientists?—who often have the same fault but in a different style?" Something in that.... "There isn't one of those boys, going back to Papa Freud himself, who wouldn't be improved by a refresher course in first-year biology."

And Edith had gone on to urge her, once more, to go to college next year— Callista, inwardly, very nearly ready to agree. She recalled the crystal April afternoon, and Edith standing, her back turned, looking out the studio's north window, the light a clear perfection on her red hair—why must Edith imagine herself homely? "Here—may I say it?—you're not quite far enough away from your Mom."

"A million light years."

"Of course, darling, but not in the flesh. And I keep thinking that right now maybe you ought to be farther from me." Edith shrugged and sighed. "For your sake, that is, certainly not for mine. Right now I could be a little too rich for your blood."

"No. If not for your sake, then not for mine."

Edith had come back to her then, standing with the great cool light at her back, looking down in one of her sudden moods of softness and gravity. "All right, Cal. But think about college for next fall?"

In agreement more than half sincere, Callista said: "I will—I'll think about it. You ought to marry, Edith."

"Narrow pelvis, distaste for an overpopulated world. I don't think it's my dish. I like men. The few that I've thought I'd like for keeps turned out to be guys who didn't want me, or at least not that way...."

But as for the reading in psychology, Edith's opinion remembered was still not quite acceptable. Freud and his successors still seemed to Callista like the best available guides into the nearest and most tormenting section of the jungle. One could rule out those who had fallen into worship of the sofa-pillow god Adjustment, and in doing so lost sight of the individual self or never noticed it. One could also remain critical of any guide, since the self must learn the sound of its own voice and discover its own country.

Yes—but all that was before Ann Doherty drank poison.

Once more laboriously, appearing to herself rather like a high school child hungry for a good mark, Callista attempted to review her knowledge of that night last August. Not only as it would be presented when she took the stand (as she must do whether Cecil thought best or not) but as it would be declared to the court of her own intelligence before that court could grant any acquittal. The face of Judge Mann intruded, however, again and once again, when her toiling revery reached the Blank, the lost moment, the miserable blur of amnesia where the crucial thing, the one answer Callista must have, was surely lying hidden. A quiet face, probably wise and certainly not vain, with the small chronic frown, the sense of cleanness and good health, the gentleness that Callista believed no face could wear if it were functioning as a mask—very well then: admit the face of Judge Terence Mann to this lonely privacy and make use of it.

Let the empty wall beside the barred door dissolve a little. Blur the flat plaster, doubtless reinforced within; it looks like stone and by daylight shows a few sad scribblings of the last tenant, not quite scrubbed away: *Why can't they let me read what the wench wrote and criticize her bit of a drawing that might now be either a baby or a phallus?*—blur that, and let the high walnut bench stand there. Give him the gown—*black, please!*—and the pencil, and the look, startled but not unkind, that he wore when the spiteful child said: "*Which is the Clerk?*" He would be less ghostly if now and then, there in the foggy opening of the wall, he could move his thin hand in the writing—could it possibly be drawing?—up there in the dignified isolation where even Mr. Delehanty, the Clerk-which-is-the-Clerk, couldn't watch it. *All right now? Go ahead!*

Begin with the talk, the flustered moment when Ann came into the apartment a little fogged up with wondering what it was all about. If she was wondering—hard to be sure, since dewy-eyed confusion was one of Ann's best faces: look-how-cute-I-am-when-I'm-thinking-about-something. Not that a talk with Nancy could ever decide anything except that she would continue certain of her own placid rightness. *Your Honor, it had a bearing on my state of mind—and by the way, my cantankerous cattiness and unfairness are duly noted and admitted. I couldn't stand her. I never could stand her, even before—before Jim. I can't stand people who cuddle continually inside one ready-made idea like babies growing old in the crib. Yes—granted—they can't help it.*

YOU ARE ADMITTING YOU HATED YOUR LOVER'S WIFE?

No, I'm not. I said I couldn't stand her. It's not the same thing. Wasn't that correct? A difficult point, but not too difficult for Judge Mann—he with his calm face, his busy pencil: without the black robe, in ordinary clothes, what would you take him for? Doctor? Scientist? Teacher? *Besides, your Honor, on that night he was no longer my lover. That was the night of the 16th of August, with a hazy moon. He had been my lover from the first of May to the sixth day of July.*

DO YOU WISH TO TESTIFY ABOUT THAT?

I think I should like to have the hazy moon admitted in evidence.

CALLISTA, WILL YOU NEVER UNDERSTAND THAT MOST HUMAN CREATURES ARE AFRAID OF LAUGHTER? GET TO THE POINT.

All right.

She could skim over the first half-hour of that talk. It had been mere sparring, Ann vaguely friendly on the surface, chattery, perhaps sensing just enough of trouble to want to hold it away. Then Callista had made a stumbling approach of blurted hints, Ann gradually comprehending because she had to, gradually perching nearer the edge of her chair, hands not in their usual flutter but folded and tightening in her lap, her lovely face abnormally attentive; listening—she had to, that once!—watchful and still. Not openly resentful or hating, never entirely distorted out of beauty. Incredible, but it must be that Ann had never guessed, and Jim had been a better actor than Callista dreamed. Ann had not even been hurt, really; not inside. Too secure. And then—"Poor Callie!"

Your Honor, I then said: "Oh, for Christ's sake!" and was sick to my stomach.

She lived again (nearly forgetting the ghostly, not unkindly seated figure in the blurred wall) her blundering rush for the bathroom with a handkerchief at her mouth. Ann had followed, of course. Callista had not quite slammed the door. Ann was out there, bleating, and then inside. "Callie, you mustn't feel so bad! Don't you see? God will forgive you. If you'll only take the right attitude!"

Yes, your Honor, I retract the word "bleating." "Her voice was ever soft, gentle, and low, an excellent thing in woman"—Lear, Act Five, last scene, I forget the number of the scene, do you mind? She also put her arm around me while I was heaving, and—

"Let me alone!"

"Poor Callie! It's all right. Let me get you something."

"God damn it, Ann, go away!"

Ann had not gone away, not then. Callista remembered running from her again, into the bedroom, slamming that door and locking it, dropping on the bed unable for a while to move or cry out. The beginning of the blank, probably. A mental door slammed, but surely not locked. But mind is continuing action: it doesn't have doors, levels, thresholds. *I know, your Honor, I know; I'm tired out, therefore thinking in stupid terms, because I wish I could go back to sleep. The blanket stinks, but I do wish—*

WHY DID YOU ASK HER TO COME AT ALL, MISS BLAKE?

I believe I thought we might be able to talk of it like adults, but I never even got as far as telling her I was pregnant. When half the truth was out I saw it was no good. I'd forgotten her God had a blueprint for all these little difficulties. I goofed.... This business about doors: admittedly Freudian slanguage is treacherously pictorial, deceptively so, as Edith pointed out once, only, damn it, it FEELS like a slammed door. Not quite locked. Now may I—please—

Once upon a time there was an orange-gold-brindle kitten named Bonnie who lived (happily ever afterward) at Aunt Cora Winwood's flat in Greenwich Village, and she was sentimentally tame, small enough to curl up in two human palms. Which Aunt Cora liked to demonstrate, transferring the sleepy morsel to Callista's hands. They had called it "pouring the kitten." After Papa died, reason after reason why she mustn't go visit the Winwoods. Only three subway stops away, and Papa's own sister. "Tom Winwood drinks, dear, and is not reliable. I do not intend to have My Little Girl exposed to Anything Like That. Nor do I wish to be reminded, Callista, that your father approved of your going there. His judgment was not *always— entirely—sound.* Mr. Winwood was in fact largely responsible for certain aspects of your father's Condition. Now I think I need say no more." *Yes, Mother, and No, Mother. Yes, Mother, now and forever you need say no more.*

Eyes closed, cheek wincing at the blanket—but twitching over to the left side would be no better—Callista resolved not to remember nor count the days since she had last drawn down her lover's face to her, seen gaunt cheekbones grown large beyond vision above her, accepted the pressure of his desire and her own. And therefore, inevitably, remembered and counted the days. Sometimes his hands sweated and were cold.

Not the first time, that May-Day afternoon in the woods—why, then (at first) Jim had been almost pagan, natural, free, coming on her suddenly in the damp green hollow where spring growth was riotous. Startled and—yes, temporarily set free. He must have been, or he could not have acted with such quick certainty, tenderness and aggression blended for once in a most invincible rightness. In the very first moment, when he pushed aside the hemlock branch and saw her, his face had been comically legible as his mind abruptly discovered a woman in place of Homely-Blake-Girl-Who-Used-to-Live-Next-Door. To the best of her memory, Callista had not smiled; only sat waiting where spring sunlight lay scattered, random gold; waiting and looking up, needing words no more than a grown-up Bonnie would have needed them at the first cruel-kind approach of a yellow-eyed lover across a back fence. Still she had used words, a few, standing up, leaning back against the rough gray body of an oak, something foolish: "Oh—I'm afraid you've started up a dryad." He might not even have heard that, his hands pressing the tree on either side of her face, his growing need as obvious as the sunlight. *I think he never so desired Ann. Such hungers (I know he thought this) are not for good women.*

His first kiss had fallen in the thin hollow of her shoulder. He had carried her to a softness of hemlock needles. *I think I helped him a little with my shorts.* Pain of course, the wrench of the torn hymen a required crash of dissonance in the symphonic flow. *I suppose I screamed—had my teeth in his shoulder for a minute—he understood that. Drowsy exhaustion afterward deeper than his—*

Soles occidere et redire possunt:
Nobis cum semel occidit brevis lux,
Nox est perpetua una dormienda....

"What, Cal? What did you say? Was that Italian?"

"Latin. Thing—happened to remember."

"Oh."

She had come wide awake then: no Kotex of course, tiresome clinical necessity of a handkerchief for the unimportant bleeding—and had presently given him some sort of English translation that stumbled along on two left feet: "Suns may set and rise, but when our brief light is gone, the night is an eternal sleep." Jim hadn't liked any of that, much. The Latin, or the bleeding. That must have been the first time that the worry-wart crinkle appeared between his thick black eyebrows, the first time the poor guy had said: "Cal, darling, what the devil are we going to do?" *I think I laughed at him, a bit. Not inside me of course.*

SHOULDN'T WE (MY DEAR) GET BACK TO THE PEOPLE VS. BLAKE?

Very well, Your Honor, but I don't admit that the episode of adultery (terminology by T. J. Hunter) is irrelevant.

NOT IRRELEVANT (MY DEAR)—BUT WEREN'T WE DISCUSSING THE DEATH BY VIOLENCE OF ANN PIERCE DOHERTY?

All right. I lay frozen in my bedroom wishing the good little bitch would go away, and I DO NOT KNOW whether or not I heard what she was up to in the kitchenette. You're not helping, Judge. You're not helping me remember.

Eyes wide, she saw the dull wall had grown a little brighter with dawn, and wished that the man on the bench might appear as a genuine visual hallucination: it would be interesting. But he lived in the brain only; her outer eyes would not create him. *I did hear her knock on my bedroom door, call my name, say something else stupid, go away with a tap of little high heels. Get it, Judge? This is the Blank, this is the thing you're not helping me remember:*

If I did hear her take that brandy bottle out, if I wasn't too hysterical to remember what was in it and why, then—

(Spot of soup on Cecil's coat sleeve. Old, half-sick, drinking too much, his wife dead long ago and nobody to look after him—when he's dead who'll even remember what he was, the courage and the kindness? Cesspool known as the world—people are already forgetting Darrow, aren't they? and every other who's tried to clean it out, dig channels to drain away the filth of human stupidity?)

If I heard her and remembered what was in the bottle, then I murdered her. If I didn't, then as a potential but incompetent suicide I was merely maintaining a public nuisance. As a good man well known to you would say, it's that simple. But that is the Blank, Judge, and you're not helping me.

I therefore address my closing remarks to other gentlemen of Winchester County, specifically District Attorney Lamson and his subordinate Talbot Jesus-wept Hunter. I wish to apologize to them for laughing, being convinced that the noise just heard in my apartment was laughter and not rats. I have no wish to laugh and hurt your feelings, but it IS funny. Honest, isn't it funny how the judge and jury inside me (with some inconsequential imaginary help from that rather nice joe Judge Mann) can make me squirm and whimper like a gut-shot rabbit, while YOU CAN'T?

II

Edith Nolan watched the cherries wobbling on Maud Welsh's hat as the woman perched in the witness chair, a sparrow ready for flight. T. J. Hunter purred and soothed. "Your occupation, Miss Welsh?"

"Guess you could say housekeeper." The voice was dry, brittle as the woman's skin. Merciless morning light played on Maud's wrinkles; bad judgment had tricked her into using dabs of make-up.

On her two visits to the Shanesville house, Edith had been aware of Maud as not much more than a background flutter and squeak; Callista had filled Edith in on the family history that explained her. Long ago, long before Herb Chalmers and Callista's mother were married and while Herb's father Malachi Chalmers was still alive, Cousin Maud had been asked to come and keep house. She stayed. Father Malachi had been a Full Professor, also a sort of *fin de siècle* Great Man who wrote a book (or something) and whose memory, Edith gathered, served as a squashy but invincible paperweight holding down the remainder of Herb's polite life. Maud Welsh had evidently done much to keep that memory functional. By the power of the meek, and because she *was* useful *and* a cousin, she just stayed, a small household tyrant given to vigorous church attendance and good works, enlarging on the time when the Professor was alive as a golden age to keep his degenerate son in line, dusting and sweeping intensely at unseasonable hours, putting up interminable preserves, and carrying on a picayune war with Victoria Chalmers, a war of sniffles and grievances which (Callista said) both of them enjoyed so much that there was never any serious question of sending Maud on her way. In the cellar, said Callista, there were five six-foot shelves of plum jam alone— Maud's atomic reserve. Anyhow, she raised quiet Presbyterian hell if any of it was used. And Callista in the studio had drawn a pen-and-ink of Maud lurking all alone underground in a desolated world, grown obese (in garments meant for a thin woman) on a thick diet of plum jam. Edith had said: "Oh, damn it, Cal, after all!" and kept the sketch.

"Where are you employed at present, Miss Welsh?"

"Well, see, I'm kin to—"

T. J. Hunter showed half-amused worry wrinkles. "Just my question, please. You know, limit your answers to the question."

"Oh, you did tell me that, didn't you? Well, I live in with the Chalmerses, I mean Dr. and Mrs. Herbert Chalmers of Shanesville."

"Doctor—that's an academic degree, isn't it?"

"Uh—oh yes. A Ph. D." Her voice made it an ailment.

Hunter's morning sleekness annoyed Edith, who felt dowdy and unkempt after a bad night. Aspirin, insomnia, a dripping faucet in the bathroom, meaningless noises in the studio—probably mice.

"Is there a street number on the Chalmers house?"

"No, just Walton Road. Same's when The Professor was alive and we lived in Winchester, all you had to say—"

"Yes, I understand. Just limit your answers, please."

"I'm sorry. I'll try."

Judge Mann also was dark under the eyes, as if his sleep had been poor. He was not busy with his pencil. His ignoring of Hunter's wry glance was perhaps a way of saying: She's your chicken. Callista, drooping and still-faced, was again partly hidden by Cecil Warner, who looked a little better this morning with a fresh shave. The flowers last night, the rather elaborate too-expensive dining out, the antique gallantry—very sweet of him, Edith thought, and in his idiom not at all strange. He had wanted of course to talk about Callista, but at dinner and later, after toiling upstairs to the studio for drinks and quiet, he had hardly been able to, seeming happier when Edith carried the conversation away to more impersonal regions.

Edith twisted in her seat, winning a timid nod from Herb Chalmers, a calm glare from Victoria. Back of them was Jim Doherty, again with Father Bland. Jim did not acknowledge her glance either, but probably because he didn't see it, a man alone on an island and hurt, trying to interpret contradictory voices in the wind. Edith twitched her skirt back into place and settled herself to endure the first day of testimony.

"Are your duties as housekeeper fairly general, Miss Welsh?"

"Might say so. I do everything but heavy cleaning, we have a woman on Tuesdays for that. I cook, see to things."

"You go away on vacations?"

"Visit my sister in Maine two weeks every summer, two in the fall."

"You did so this year?"

"In June, not the fall. Because of the trouble, I thought I should stay, couldn't do less."

"Were you in Shanesville on Friday, August 7th of this year?"

"The 7th—oh, the picnic. Yes, I was."

"No, limit your answers, *please*. I just want to verify your presence on certain dates. Were you at Shanesville all day Sunday and Monday, August 16th and 17th?"

Arthritic claws clenched on her handbag. "Yes, I was."

"At about 10:30 Monday morning, August 17th, who beside yourself was present, to your knowledge, at the Chalmers house or on the grounds?"

"Just Herb, I mean Dr. Chalmers. I think Mrs. Chalmers'd gone to the supermarket in Shanesville, anyhow she wasn't home at 10:30."

"Where exactly were you at that time?"

"On the back porch fixing snap beans for lunch."

"What part of the grounds could you see from that spot?"

"Well, part of the lawn runs around the north side of the house, between it and the grove, and there's the vegetable garden in back."

"Is there a path through the grove?"

"Yes, from our house to Dohertys' place."

"Will you describe that path, please?"

"Just a footpath, tramped ground, pine needles." Maud Welsh swallowed. "Goes near a pond that's right about on the Dohertys' line."

"From the back porch could you see the opening of that path?"

"Yes."

"Did you see Dr. Chalmers at 10:30 or thereabouts?"

"Yes, he came out on the porch and we talked some. Weather mostly I guess. It was a scorcher, and real humid."

"What did he do after your conversation?"

"Went to look at the vegetable garden, then into the grove—not by that path though: he went into it at a place beyond the garden, where our brook goes under the trees. We were watching that brook on account of the drouth."

"When did you next see him?"

"A few minutes later. He came out of the woods, by the path that time, stumbled, shouted to me. I dropped the beans and went to him. I saw his clothes were wringin' wet, and he looked awful white. I helped him into the shade on the back porch. He talked kind of—"

"Just the substance of the conversation, please. That is, if he explained what had happened to upset him—did he?"

"Not—not to say explain, exactly. He said—"

"I think we'll just omit the conversation and go on to what you did next. Just what you did, you understand. After helping him into the shade, what did you yourself do?"

Clearly the biddy was already giving T. J. Hunter a case of jitters. Cecil Warner's crooked half-smile underlined the fact for Edith. Would he now be able to bring out poor Herb's first addled words, whatever they were, in cross examination? Would they help, if he did? And if he testified for the defense, what would Herb himself do about them? Last night Cecil had said, into the bright depth of his second Martini: "First law of the courtroom: never count on a jury's respecting logic."

"Well, sir, I went to the pond. His clothes wet, I knew it—"

"Just what you did, not what you thought. You went to the pond—wait a minute. We'll go back a little at this point, Miss Welsh. You were well acquainted with Ann Doherty—Mrs. James Doherty?"

"Well, I sh'd hope—I'm sorry, sir. Yes, I was."

"When did you first meet her?"

"In 1956. They moved in that year. Good neighbors, her anyway."

Edith saw the Old Man rising, and steady too, monumental. "May it please the Court, the defense is not concerned with the character of James Doherty, but I object in principle to that kind of innuendo."

"Sustained." The Judge's voice was cool. "The witness's last remark beginning with the words 'good neighbors' will be stricken."

Edith relaxed, aware of the primitive quality of her gratification: one for our side. Not that Jim belonged to the defense—Jim was lost, or trapped. All the same, the defense had spoken. She also recalled unhappily other words Cecil had spoken to that Martini: "Why did I order that thing? I was going to make it wine. Will you slap my fat wrist if I do it again?" He had made it wine, at the studio, and gone home sober. After, of all things, kissing her hand.

"Miss Welsh, was your relation to Mrs. Doherty one of close acquaintance? Casual? Just what was it?"

"Kind of close. We'd—oh, visit back and forth."

"When was the last time you saw Mrs. Doherty alive?"

"Two days before—I mean Saturday, August 15th. She came over for some bacon. She'd forgot it in shopping."

"Did you, for instance, call each other by your first names?"

"Ayah, did, matter of fact. I'm a mite old-fashioned, but we did."

"All right. Now back to the Monday morning. You went to the pond. What if anything did you find there?"

"She—in the water—I couldn't reach—"

"Miss Welsh, try to be impersonal, won't you? Remember the jury never knew these people. Now: when you came to the pond, just describing things impersonally, what did you see?"

"I saw—the body of a woman in the water."

"How was she dressed?"

"White blouse. Powder-blue skirt, blue jacket to match."

"Any head covering?"

"No. I saw her hair, that real pretty reddy-gold—auburn—"

"Could you reach the body from the bank?"

"No. I went in a few steps. A mud bottom—I—"

"Do you feel all right?"

"I'm all right. I touched her, the whole body turned—"

"We can spare you those details, I think. You turned the body until you could see the face, right? And knew positively that it was—?"

"It was Ann—Mrs. Doherty. I couldn't lift her out, anyway she was—cold. I went and called the state police, thought I should—"

"Did you talk again with Dr. Chalmers?"

"Yes, he was still on the back porch. I just said I'd called the police, said I'd go back to the pond, way they told me. So I did."

Maud Welsh, Edith thought, might have loved Ann in whatever flustered way she was capable of loving. For Edith the memory of Ann, met only three or four times, hung suspended in the past like an antique picture: something by Fragonard, say, in a frame of fussy gilt. Dainty, a bit undernourished— Ann pestered herself with diets now and then—and insipid. You couldn't quite imagine the angelic face distorted or transfigured by extremes of passion, or wrinkled by thought. With no overtone of spite, Callista had said once: "Ann isn't vain. I think she likes to share her prettiness in a nice way, the way you'd share a box of candy. She feels it was very pleasant of God to make her so pretty, and so going to Mass and keeping confession up to date like a good bank account, that's a matter of genuine gratitude as well as a sort of spiritual hygiene."

"While you waited for the police you didn't move or change anything?"

"No, sir, I just sat there and prayed for her."

Most of the jurors looked vaguely gratified. The faces of Terence Mann and Cecil Warner were politely blank as a church door on Monday morning. Edith could not see Callista, for Warner leaning forward at that moment shut her away. And T. J. Hunter at the prosecution's table was fumbling at a plastic bag.

"Miss Welsh, do you identify these garments as those that Ann Doherty was wearing when you found her body in the pond at Shanesville?"

"Yes, I—let me see the blouse again—yes, sir, I do."

"These stockings: can you identify them as the ones Mrs. Doherty was wearing?"

"Well, I suppose—I mean, that type, they look so alike."

"I'm putting my hand in this one, the right. Here's the heel. Now as near as I can manage it, my wrist is about where an anklebone would come—does that help you?"

"Oh, the hole! Yes, it's the same."

"When you lifted the body part-way from the water, you saw a hole like this one in the right stocking, correct?"

"Yes, I did."

"As a housekeeper, you know dressmaking and such things?"

"You could say so."

"Does anything about this hole strike you as unusual, peculiar?"

"It's not where you'd get a run. I can't see how you'd get it unless you bumped or scraped your ankle across something."

"When you found the body, was this hole visible above the line of a shoe, do you recall?"

"Oh—the right shoe was missing."

"Only the right one, you're sure?"

"Yes, she was wearing the left."

"This blue left slipper I'm now holding. Do you identify it?"

"Yes," said Maud Welsh, and fumbled at her face with a sodden handkerchief, while Edith's gaze swung in futile desperation to study the jury. Mrs. Kleinman was crying and, rather surprisingly, the cool black-haired beauty Dolores Acevedo. *So could I.* Instead, Edith looked down. She held away the irrelevant pathos of those garments on the State's table, the mud-spotted frilly blouse, crumpled blue skirt and jacket, the single water-streaked shoe, by contemplating the dark green tweed suit that she herself was wearing. Less than perfect. Needed pressing. A small spot, maybe watercolor paint, near the bottom of the skirt (*well, hell!*)—but having thought of it this morning, she could wear no other costume, for once last winter at the studio, in March or February, Callista had glanced up and remarked apropos of nothing: "Fact, I love that thing on you. Makes your thatch a sort of bonfire off in the green woods." And seeing it when she entered the courtroom, Callista had smiled.

"Miss Welsh, we'll go back to the evening of Sunday, August 16th, about nine o'clock. Where were you then and what were you doing?"

"Setting out on the front porch. It was dark enough so I'd put my sewing things aside some time before. I'd gone out there about eight, I guess, when the light was still good. Usually do."

"Did you see or hear anything you particularly remember?"

"Didn't see anything special. Heard a car stop, on Walton Road, out of sight of me behind the pines."

"Did you notice any glow from its headlights?"

"I don't think I did."

"Anything distinctive about the sound of that car?"

"Well, a buzzy thing, and of course I—"

"Was the motor shut off?"

"Not right away—oh, I remember something. A rattle, while the motor was running, loose metal, like a license-plate or something."

Edith saw Callista lean to Warner for a quick whispered conference; Cal seemed unexcited, but the Old Man was pleased. His back turned, Hunter would have missed it.

"Motor not shut off right away—how long did it run?"

"A minute, maybe, before the car door opened and shut."

"Can you establish the time you heard that car stop?"

"Yes; ten minutes past nine. Looked at my watch. You see, I wondered if the Chalmerses were expecting anyone, didn't think they were. Anyhow, all the talk you hear about juvenile delinquents in parked cars, naturally I—" her voice dwindled and came alive again briskly: "My watch runs good."

"Did you hear any other sounds beyond the pines, or maybe in the grove, after you heard that car door close?"

"No, not for half an hour."

"Is there an outside light on the Chalmers' front porch?"

"Yes, shines right down the driveway."

"Was it turned on that evening, and if so, when?"

"It was, about 9:40."

"Half an hour after the car stopped. Did you turn it on?"

"No. Herb, I mean Dr. Chalmers, came out on the porch about half past nine. He was the one turned it on—not right away though."

"Well—the car door closed at 9:10, then no sounds from that direction for half an hour. You did hear something then? If so, what?"

"Car door again, motor started, same buzzy noise, and then the car came into the driveway—it had just the dimmer lights on, I remember—and that's when Herb turned on the porch light. It was that little German car of hers, and she—"

"A moment. You're positive of the car? You read the license plate, or something like that?"

"No, sir, I never memorized her license number, but I knew the car, the shape, and the maroon color. Anyhow C'lista herself was driving it, I could see her face in the porch light, just as plain. Alone, she was."

"Did she call to you, or wave?"

"No, sir, just backed for the turn and scooted off again, direction of Winchester."

"Was Dr. Chalmers standing in the porch light?"

"We were both in plain sight, Mr. Hunter. That porch light, it's real bright, lights up everything."

"When had you last seen Callista Blake before that appearance in the driveway Sunday evening?"

"Evening before. Saturday. She came out to the house, about 8:30."

"An ordinary visit?"

"You never knew what was ordinary for Callista."

"Your Honor, I must object—the patience of the defense is not everlasting." Warner had risen; Edith could see the heavy tremor of his thick hand on the back of his chair. "This kind of spiteful side-remark—inexcusable."

"The witness's entire last remark will be stricken. Mr. Hunter?"

"Miss Welsh, just state briefly the circumstances of Callista Blake's visit to Shanesville Saturday evening."

"Well, I was on the porch same as the other time. Mrs. Doherty'd come over for some bacon—guess I said that. I wrapped some for her, then I remembered I wanted to show her an embroidery piece I was doing. I'd already taken my things out to the porch before she came. We went out there, were setting there when C'lista drove up to the house alone, walked right by us, not a word except to ask kind of sharp where her mother was. Ann had spoken—you know, 'Hello, Callie!' or something like that, but I don't believe C'lista answered her. Anyhow I told her, I said I thought her mother was upstairs somewhere, and she went on in. Slamming the door."

The defense can't object, Edith thought, because those are facts. That was Callista, no use denying it: the often needlessly cruel abruptness, indifference to social necessities, inability to suffer a fool with patience. On that black evening Maud Welsh and Ann had not even been fools, just harmless little people acting as usual at a time when Callista was burning, a tigress with an arrow festering in her side. And today, in smouldering cherished resentment, Maud Welsh was not harmless.

"Did you see Callista Blake again that evening?"

"No, went to my room before she left. I did hear her, talking to her mother upstairs in a wild sort of way."

"Wild? Do you mean quarreling? Loud?"

"No, sir, I give C'lista credit, she was never one to raise her voice, anyhow I wasn't eavesdropping, only Mrs. Chalmers' bedroom happens to be right over the porch where I was. Ann had gone home then and I couldn't help but hear her crying, Mrs. Chalmers I mean, and the stuff C'lista was saying about forgive me this my virtue."

"Miss Welsh—"

"Which didn't make any sense, besides being no sort of way to talk to her mother, only I wasn't eavesdropping."

Edith winced at the courtroom laughter. At any rate the nervous uproar, quickly subdued by Judge Mann's gavel, was probably directed more at Maud Welsh than Callista.

"Miss Welsh, we established that you were at the Chalmers house on August 7th, ten days before Mrs. Doherty's death. Does any particular event fix that date in your memory?"

"Picnic. The Chalmerses gave a picnic that afternoon."

"Informal?"

"Ayah. We do it three-four times every summer. Mostly friends of Herb's from the college, but that one was more for Shanesville folks. Hot dogs, hamburgers and like that. Croquet, pitching horse-shoes, badminton. Real informal."

"Do you recall who was present, August 7th?"

"Yes. Mrs. Phelps Jason—she's our nearest neighbor except the Dohertys. Mr. and Mrs. Wayne of Shanesville and their two kids Billy and Doris. Billy's nine, Doris going-on-twelve. Mr. and Mrs. Doherty of course. Mr. Judd drove out from Winchester. And C'lista did too."

"What time was the picnic?"

"From two in the afternoon to about five, five-thirty."

"Do you know when Callista Blake arrived?"

"Early, near two I think."

"When did she leave?"

"Didn't see her go. Noticed her car was gone at four-thirty."

"How was she dressed, if you recall?"

"Green blouse, brown skirt I think. Anyway I'm sure of the green blouse, she was partial to it for some reason."

"Any special accessories that you recall?"

"Big shoulder-strap bag. I remember thinking how those things are sort of out of style, but C'lista liked that one because it was roomy, she could carry her field glasses in it. Partial to Nature and stuff like that—bird watching."

"Did she have her field glasses that day?"

"Didn't see them, Mr. Hunter. Just the bag."

"Are there bushes, scrubs, likely places for birds or nests, near the part of the grounds where you had that picnic?"

"Yes. Back of the lawn there's a flower garden, and beyond that a sort of half-wild area. Things planted there that more or less take care of themselves—ground-cover, perennials. Pair of catbirds nested there last summer, likely others."

"Are you familiar with the perennials in that wild spot?"

"With some of them." Maud Welsh cleared her throat and swallowed. "Day-lilies, myrtle—monkshood."

"You have seen monkshood growing there, with your own eyes?"

"Yes. Mrs. Chalmers pointed it out to me once, wondering if she ought to keep it, spite of the pretty flower it has. Yes, it grows there—I mean it did last August. Of course the police—"

"Yes, never mind that. On the afternoon of August 7th, did you see Callista go into that wild garden?"

"I did."

"Was she then wearing that shoulder-strap bag?"

"She was."

"Was she alone?"

"Yes."

"How long did she remain there?"

"I don't know for certain. Half an hour later Mrs. Chalmers wanted her to lend a hand with the grill. I called her. When she came—which she didn't right away—it was from there."

"Was she still alone?"

Edith thought: *She is always alone, Mr. Hunter. Clinging to that fool Jim Doherty, she was alone. The one time when she cried in my arms, she was alone.*

"She was alone."

"Your witness, Mr. Warner."

III

Judge Mann watched Cecil Warner approach the witness chair like an old bull: heavy step, flaring nostrils, lowered head, eyes communicating nothing but a brooding truculence. He halted ponderously, an old bull arriving at the dubious barrier of a fence, and—just stood there. Judge Mann's pencil drifted across the scratch pad in a rapid script not much like his normal writing:

Forgive me this my virtue;
For in the fatness of these pursy times
Virtue itself of vice must pardon beg,
Yea, curb and woo for leave to do him good.

He grew fully aware of the writing with a partly pleased astonishment: almost a true dissociation. His brother Jack might be interested; he would save the page. It must have been three years since he had last read *Hamlet*.

He understood also, waiting out the darkness of Warner's silence, how his own self might become a battleground. Why fool himself? It had already become one. The deeper occasions of the battle, the relative wrong and right, his true position within it, not clear. *More light!* He had been assuming two nights ago, and less certainly last night, a mental clarity he had not yet won. Then look at it this way: the assumption had been a folly and a vanity and a failure in self-appraisal; therefore dismiss it. Accept for the moment simply the fact of inner conflict; and then what? His pencil hand stirred and advanced:

Sit you down,
And let me wring your heart: for so I shall,
If it be made of penetrable stuff....

The conflict itself was no illusion. He could oblige his mind to draw somewhat apart and provide illusive imagery for what was no illusion; an imagery, sharp enough, from happenings fourteen years ago that had been (in their time) no illusion. Northern Luzon, 1945: all they'd done that night was drop a few daisy-cutters. Why should he remember that night and not some of the livelier ones? Perhaps because his mind had been rather detached then too, his body not much scared, not much concerned. A darkened earth, flares, smoky glimpses more deceiving than dark, thunder of .75's and mad red flight of tracers; long drone overhead of the angry bug evading crossed searchlight swords, or trying to—too high for flak; we hadn't got the poor bastard. And a sudden sense in Sergeant Terence Mann of the medics, who shortly before had been annoyed mostly at the interruption of a poker game with himself three bucks ahead, of the humanly vast forces involved, the courage and hate and fear and death and love with which the stars are not concerned at all. Trying for the supply dump near Dagupan, all Joe had got was the backside of a church and two buffalos. Above, behind, including all, a sense of the flow of time that renders every victory and every defeat a part of eternity. And every moment of compromise ...

"Miss Welsh, were you with the Chalmers family in 1951 when Dr. Herbert Chalmers married Victoria Johnson Blake?"

"Yes."

"Did you attend the wedding?"

"I did." She was biting her words now, not chattering.

"In what month were they married?"

"July."

"When did you first meet the defendant, Callista Blake?"

"Guess it was August that year, 1951." Warner studied his shoes. "Well, I *know* it was, because C'lista was away in girls' camp while they went on a honeymoon, me with the house on my hands—" she clamped her mouth shut, glaring. Mann found it possible to be sorry for the woman. Warner's massive pauses were tough on any witness.

Warner said at last, mildly: "Thank you." The back row idiot briefly giggled. "Callista was not present at her mother's wedding?"

"Certainly wasn't."

"Why 'certainly,' Miss Welsh? She was eleven that year."

"Because you never knew when she'd throw a tantrum."

"You consider that unhappy children should not have tantrums?"

Hunter declared: "Improper question, if I ever heard one."

Mann thought: *Sorry, Bud!* "The Court will rule it admissible in cross-examination. Answer the question, Miss Welsh."

"Well, I don't know what she had to be unhappy about, with—"

"Miss Welsh, may I have a responsive answer to my question?"

"Haven't a notion what the question was all about."

"It may be too difficult. I withdraw it. You have known Miss Blake, by sight that is, for eight years. During that time, has your relation with her ever been cordial?"

"Naturally I tried to put up with—"

"I will repeat the question. During the eight years since 1951, has your relation with Callista Blake ever been cordial?"

On the doodle-pad a freshly drawn bull contemplated a tiny spinster—angular long skirt, hat with cherries, defensive umbrella. No fence between her and the beast. Mann drew one, post-and-rail, the top rail fallen. He felt rather proud of the bull: a fine solidity in the foreshortened barrel body; grandeur and melancholy. He sketched in grass and bending daisies to answer the curves of huge elongated scrotum and ponderous sheath. In the right foreground he added a miniature rabbit bundled up in a black gown. Cecil might enjoy the damned thing, on some relaxed evening far in time from the present hour.

"I don't—I don't understand the question."

"Very well—I withdraw it. Is that wrist watch the one you were wearing on the evening of last August 16th?"

"Yes."

"Does it have a luminous dial?"

"No, I don't want radium and things in my system."

"But last August 16th, in the deep twilight after nine o'clock, you could easily read it?"

She smirked, recovering. "Lights were on in the living-room."

Judge Mann watched Hunter's faint smile appear and fade.

"Thank you for remembering that now, Miss Welsh. Is it your custom to look at your watch when anything captures your interest?"

"I explained why I did that when I heard the car."

"Yes, you were concerned about juvenile delinquency."

"I didn't say that!"

"Why, I thought I heard a reference to the menace of juvenile delinquents in parked cars."

"Oh, that—dare say I was thinking out loud."

"I see. Thank you. Had you other reasons to check the time?"

"Well, I wondered if the family was expecting C'lista, so I—"

"Miss Welsh, in direct testimony you said you wondered if the family was expecting *anyone*, no names mentioned. Then you admitted this deep concern about juvenile delinquents in parked cars. Now we learn the family might have been expecting Callista. All three statements true?"

"Oh, what's all the fuss? I knew it was her car."

"But preferred not to say so in direct testimony. All right—how did you know it was her car?"

"I *explained* that. Loose license plate, and that buzzy noise."

"You did testify to hearing something like a loose license plate. You didn't say Miss Blake's car had one."

"Well, it did, and I heard it."

"Miss Welsh, a hypothetical question. If, when the defense opens, you learn that Miss Blake's Volkswagen had a garage check-up on Friday, August 14th, and that the license-plate holder was repaired at that time, would you, if recalled under oath, still claim you heard that plate rattling on Sunday evening, August 16th?"

The passion of resentment simmering behind the woman's blinking eyes was a kind of sickness. Once or twice she opened her lips without sound; then: "All I got to say, it wasn't natural how men went crazy for her—not even pretty—any man, garage man, anything in pants—"

Mann thought sharply: *Okay, that's torn it.* He saw Warner turn slowly, facing the bench. "Your Honor, I respectfully request that this witness be held in contempt of court."

Mann flipped the doodle-pad face down. He said: "There will be a ten-minute recess. Counsel in chambers, please. The jury will remain." Entering the dingy retreat off the courtroom, he was aware of T. J. Hunter standing aside to let Warner precede him. "You don't want to toil up to the sixth floor, do you? I suppose I could locate a nip of something."

Warner said: "No, Judge, I'm too fat to ride that thing you call an elevator. It busts, I'm liable for have-his-carcass."

"All right—shouldn't anyway. We'll settle for a smoke."

Warner sat down, an old man and weary, impersonally accepting the impersonal courtesy when Hunter snapped a lighter for his cigarette. His fat hand waved aside the curling fantasy of smoke between him and his enemy. "Okay, T. J., I think you asked for it. Why couldn't you establish *corpus delecti* with Herb Chalmers? Could've, no sweat."

"Grab off a natural defense witness when I don't have to?"

"What makes you think I want Herb?"

Hunter chuckled and strolled to the window. "Just fishing."

Mann asked: "What's your view, T. J.?"

The back of Hunter's neck was calm. "Just among us girls, Welsh certainly goofed. Honest, I sweated blood trying to give her the rudiments of courtroom behavior. Seems it was mostly hooting down a rain-barrel."

Warner said: "They goofed the same way over Joan of Arc."

Hunter swung around and exclaimed: "After all, Cecil!"

"No comparison between the principals," Warner said, "except age and sex. You admire Joan? I don't, much. But there's an obvious parallel between twentieth- and fifteenth-century attitudes toward the accused maverick. Takes more than five hundred years for the human race to learn anything important." His slow voice was acquiring a snarl. "You know, T. J.—you know what the newspapers have been doing. Far as Welsh is concerned, I don't care a fractionated brass-bound tinker's fart whether she's held in contempt or not. I do care about keeping this thing from turning into a witchcraft trial. I'm not sitting peaceful on my fat ass, understand, while they turn my girl into a succubus."

Hunter said stiffly: "I think you could trust me to prevent any nonsense of that kind." Warner studied him, dark eyes searching and sad in their slightly yellowed and bloodshot fields of white. Hunter went on: "Your hypothetical was a dilly, by the way. The defense introduces testimony at this point? You want the State to pack up and go home?"

"Why wouldn't I?"

"Fine! You going to claim the Volkswagen wasn't there?"

Warner shook his head indifferently.

Mann said: "T. J., I still want your view, on Welsh. I'd be half minded to throw the book, only I'm not sure Welsh is that important."

"Well, I don't think she is, Judge. But I'm sort of indifferent. The facts of her testimony will remain with the jury, and that's all that concerns me. The contempt thing—important to the Court, and to me as a lawyer, but not so important to *People vs. Blake.*"

"For a prosecutor," said Warner, "you're curiously frank, T. J. Now that she's squeezed in her 'anything-in-pants' remark, you're content, you can go fishing—that's what you're saying."

"Look here—"

Judge Mann struck the desk lightly with the flat of his hand. "Cecil, do you have many more questions for her?"

"Not many, Judge. Ought to be done in a few minutes, before one o'clock anyhow."

"Hope so—I'm unjudicially hungry and I'll be glad to see the last of her. I'm not holding her in contempt, Cecil, unless she pulls another one. It's not quite justified, I'm not even too sure of the ground, and—" he rubbed out his cigarette, glancing at the somewhat frozen face of T. J. Hunter—"I particularly don't want to make a martyr out of her. Let's get back on the job."

Maud Welsh's rigid face told him the ten minutes of anticipation might have been punishment enough. He had not intended that: merely a courtroom happen-so. "Miss Welsh, contempt of court is a serious thing. It must be, to preserve respect for law. For willfully disregarding the instructions given you about limiting your answers and avoiding prejudicial comments, you could, if this court so ordered, be severely punished." *There she goes sniffling, and to some of the jury she'll have the face of Mom.* "It is not the present intention of the Court to hold you in contempt. You are being let off with a warning, for the last time. Consider yourself fortunate. Mr. Warner?"

"Miss Welsh, I quote to you certain words: 'Assume a virtue if you have it not.' Are those words familiar to you?"

Her streaked face glowing, perhaps with relief, Maud Welsh also looked bewildered. "No—no, sir, I don't think so."

"Have you ever read Shakespeare's play *Hamlet?*"

"I'm sure we had it in school, but—" she smiled placatingly—"that's quite a while. I never get the time to read much."

"Here are some other famous lines from the same source: 'Forgive me this my virtue; for in the fatness of these pursy times virtue itself of vice must pardon beg'—familiar?"

"That's what I heard C'lista say to her mother."

"Did you overhear anything else?"

"I wasn't eavesdropping, sir."

"You're not accused of it." Warner was speaking gently. "We're only concerned with what you heard. Was there anything else?"

"Well, like I said, I heard Mrs. Chalmers crying."

"Can you be certain it wasn't her daughter you heard?"

"Yes. Their voices are mighty different."

"You had heard Mrs. Chalmers cry before?"

"Yes, sir, now and then."

"And Callista?"

"She never cried."

"Not even as a child, having tantrums?"

"No, she'd just go white and—walk away, or—is it all right to say this?"

"Go ahead."

"Walk away, or sort of run away sometimes, I mean off into the woods or like that, and practically have to be dragged home. I thought it was—can I say this?—I don't want to say anything wrong, I—"

"Go ahead, Miss Welsh."

"Well, just—I thought it was real unnatural, that I never heard Callista cry."

"No further questions."

IV

Callista sampled and pushed aside the inoffensive meal. The state of New Essex was feeding her well. Treating her well too—a star prisoner. A room of her own and, now that the trial had begun, meals in private, on a tray no less. No utensils of course except a spoon. She rose and performed the infinite journey of three steps from the barred door to the barred window a few times: shorten stride and you could make it come out to four steps. *Best room in the hotel, southwest exposure 'n' everything—gee!* She adjusted the blanket on her cot to sharp military precision: it would make Matron Flannery happy. A pity to sit down now and spoil all that wonderful work. Anyway Biddy Flannery would be along in a minute for the tray, with her usual not unfriendly clash of keys; then back to the courtroom for the afternoon.

Callista gazed at the flat-faced wall where smears of old writing had been not quite obliterated—for everything in this building was more than a little tired, peevish, ineffectual. Indifferent mop or washrag took a swipe at the graffiti, to keep busy; the law took a swipe, the best it could manage, at the perennial smears of human confusion, dishonesty, violence. High up—the woman must have been tall—enough remained of a lipstick inscription to indicate a heart symbol enclosing a pair of names: DAVY & ——: the other name had defied Callista's months-long effort to decipher it. She tried again now, bemused, and once more gave it up, although somehow this time she did feel a bit nearer success. It was exasperating as a sore tooth.

She gave up also another effort to interpret the almost destroyed black-pencil picture below the heart, probably someone else's contribution. A thick phallus not quite erect, a baby with the facial features gone, perhaps just a round-petaled flower or geometric design? No use. Call it a Rorschach blot— but even for that, the months of seeing it had made it impossible to see it at all. Callista turned away, glancing with an amusement that held the warmth of gratitude at the third and last writing—off in the corner, tiny and squeezed, it had almost escaped the washrag's faint assault, and still transmitted a cocky, not too cryptic message: WE DID IT IN A SNOBANK ON LINCAN'S BIRTHDAY 1957.

In the death house too they would feed her well and treat her very kindly, within the meaning of the statute. Callista examined this, perplexed, trying to recall what form of the auxiliary verb her thought had used. *Did the gray cells say WILL or WOULD?*

She journeyed again, to the window that for all its cramped ugliness was a friend, because of its messages of night and day, cloud, sunlight, and the wheeling of doves. And returning, she made a discovery, with the suddenness of sunshine. She could read the red writing up there on the wall, the other name. Amazing that it could have eluded her so long:

DAVY & ME.

Bewildering too the quick starting of tears to her eyes. *Why, I never cry. Well— once, when Edith helped me talk.*

DAVY & ME.

"This helps too, dear." She must have said that aloud, for the cell was alive with the memory of a private sound. *They couldn't take away the Me, could they? Shoplifter, whore, drunk, another murderer maybe? Doesn't matter. Went out of here to die, get drunk, go back to work in a cathouse or pushing dope—I don't care. They couldn't quite do it to you.* Down the corridor, keys rattled. *They couldn't take away the Me. Ever.*

3

Once a trial judge or jury has determined, on conflicting evidence, a question of fact, that determination is final. It is binding upon the appellate courts. If there has been an error of law the defendant has a remedy by appeal. If there has been an erroneous finding of fact the defendant has no remedy. He is forever bound by the finding of the trial judge or of the jury.

Now it should be obvious that trial judges and juries aren't that good.

ERLE STANLEY GARDNER, *The Court of Last Resort*

I

Cecil Warner remembered the night, a corridor of hours, a windy darkness of winter streets, a homecoming to solitude and too much thought and the uncertain consolation of sleep.

After leaving Edith's studio a whim had urged him to walk home instead of calling a taxi. By that time the rain had stopped, the winter pavements were damp and harmless. It would have been pleasant to drive alone out of the city on quiet side roads, perhaps winding up in a suburban bar for an hour's casual amusement. Not so long ago he would have done it, but last year, after a few near-disasters, he had ruled out driving as too great a hazard for aging faculties, and sold his car: from there on the world could wait on him a little, a good enough arrangement so long as you can pay for it.

Walking was good for you, they said—in moderation, of course. Ten blocks, say half a mile and none of it uphill, from Edith's studio to the small old house on Midland Avenue that for the last twenty-five years had grown wrinkled and out of date along with him, dignity and seediness of antiquity together; maybe you couldn't have one without the other. Yes, a nice walk, colored by a grudging admission that there was no great harm in doing what they said was good for you, so long as you did it in moderation. A winter wind has many voices, not all of them edged by grief.

The best part of that walk was the long block past Trinity Church and its tiny cemetery where time had pushed many headstones aslant and long since worn down all grief to a stillness. No large extent of time really: Trinity was built in 1761, said its cornerstone: a mere two centuries, enough to give the more respectable ghosts the privilege of wearing three-cornered hats. In Trinity churchyard they were bound to be respectable and, through no fault of their own, quaint, like George Washington's wooden false teeth. Leaving there, crossing Quire Street, you passed too suddenly into a splash of gaudy twentieth-century glare, the uptown movie house. Cecil had gone by it last night when the theater was about to close, a late crowd spilling away presumably cheered by a long gulp of Bardot bosom and eye and flank. Then two decent residential blocks, other detached houses like his own yet virtually unknown to him, keeping their own counsel in the quiet street. And the three front steps that needed paint, the key, the cantankerous welcome from the squeak of the front door which could have been fixed in a minute by the drop of oil it wasn't going to get.

There was the not quite musty flavor of the little front hall: Cecil didn't like it but would have disliked its absence. At every homecoming there was the confidence, as he stumped into the shabby living-room, that Mrs. Wilks would have left everything just so before retiring to her world upstairs, except that of course she'd never learn not to put match-cards in ash trays. Some time the long sorrow that Mrs. Wilks lived with upstairs—a husband paralyzed for twenty years, unable to walk or feed himself, not quite able to die—would arrive at an end. Like all sorrow. Cecil had not gone up last night for his usual visit and chess game with Tom Wilks. Too late; too tired.

Now in the bleak courtroom remembering the night, relaxing in his chair beside Callista, still feeling thirty cents' worth of virtue for having resisted the siren voice of mince pie for lunch, Cecil Warner remembered—suddenly, like a reward of effort—one of the answers his mind had given him during the hours before he could sleep. Perhaps it was the only answer worth remembering out of many. There had been many, some no better than mumblings of fatigue. That one had come to him by the mind's magic when the night beyond his window was in a moment of supreme clarity and peace, and Trinity's delicate chimes had struck the morning hour of two o'clock, and the wind died: *The defense never rests.*

The air was still today, pure and sharp, the sky a clean splendor above the smear of the city. Something of it could be felt through the high eastern window behind them. Callista would have looked upward into that strong blue of infinity through the detention cell bars. She liked the brilliant days. They would enrich her artist's vision, he supposed, revealing depth and detail that duller eyes saw without seeing. A pleasant day, a good (light) lunch, and T. J. Hunter at the moment engaged in nothing more harmful than getting a police technician's map of the Shanesville properties admitted in evidence. A fine map, laboriously honest. Nothing required right now except an outward appearance of grumpy indifference suitable to the Old Man.

His gaze passed over the Twelve, the ordinary, respectable, appalling faces, and turned aside. He studied his blunt, unskillful hands, examining the blur of an old scar. A small racing unthinking motion of Terence Mann's fingers up yonder reminded him of the last occasion when he had spent an evening at Terence's apartment. Quite a while ago—July, he thought, anyway some time before Callista's trouble. A hot evening, Terence reviewing some of his Army habits of speech when the old building's air-conditioning unit goofed.

Terence that night had been in a Chopin mood; temporarily fed up with Mozart, he said, the weather too hot for Brahms. In passing Cecil wondered what the little guy would be working on these days. Something certainly; Terence liked to keep two or three compositions currently at concert pitch— no reason, he claimed, except that it satisfied a whim. The reason could lie deeper than that. With only a listener's knowledge, Cecil felt that music might have lost something important when Terence Mann went into the law. Something held back, possibly some old unhappiness or inhibition, when Terence said his keyboard ability—and he would have to call it that, instead of talent or spark or musicianship!—fell far enough short of the top so that it wasn't worth exploiting for more than private enjoyment.

Get with it, Old Man!

Spotless law and order was taking the oath. Sergeant Shields of the State Police would never allow any dust on the sparkle of his shoes; undoubtedly he could dissect his .32 and reassemble it in the dark. Yet he was also young, and human. A sidelong glance gave Warner Callista's face, composed, neutral. As usual, too remote. During the police testimony, the jury might not resent that too much, might vaguely understand her need for self-control. Later on he must make another attempt to persuade her that you can't just brush off the human race—not when it's after you.

"Your full name and occupation, please?"

"Samuel Arthur Shields, Sergeant, New Essex State Police. I have been stationed at Emmetville Barracks for general duty since January of last year."

"How were you employed on Monday morning, August 17th last?"

The Sergeant's notebook rested in his hand; Warner guessed he was not likely to need it. "I was operating State Police Car No. 48 on highway patrol between Shanesville and East Walton."

"Is Car 48 equipped with two-way radio?"

"Yes, sir."

"In your own words—I believe you don't need any coaching in the requirements of legal testimony—in your own words, Sergeant, please state what you did and what you observed, in line of duty, at or about 10:30 and subsequently, that Monday morning, August 17th."

"At 10:36 I received a radio call directing me to proceed to the house of Dr. Herbert Chalmers on Walton Road south of the junction with Summer

Avenue, in Shanesville township. I was informed that the body of a woman, apparently drowned, had been discovered in a pond near that house. No further particulars were given me by radio. I drove to the site immediately, arriving at the Chalmers house at 10:40. I knocked, received no answer, saw no one until I walked around to the back. There I found Dr. Herbert Chalmers, who is and was then known to me by sight as a member of the Shanesville Presbyterian Church, to which I belong. He was sitting on the top step of the back porch, and appeared to be ill or in shock: white, breathing with difficulty, leaning against the porch rail with his eyes shut. When I spoke to him he roused, recognized me. I learned from him that he had found the body of a woman, whom he named as his neighbor Mrs. James Doherty, in a pond in the woods bordering his land. He pointed out a path into the woods."

"Will you indicate it on this map for the jury, Sergeant?"

"Yes, sir. Here it is." Warner watched him from under the famous lowered brows. A good boy, decently ambitious, standing by the map's tall frame, a brisk young schoolteacher interested in facts. He stayed there erect and impressive as he went on talking: "Dr. Chalmers mentioned a heart condition, saying he didn't feel able to go with me to the pond; afraid of blacking out, or words to that effect. He told me his housekeeper, Miss Maud Welsh, had also seen the body and had gone back to the pond after telephoning my headquarters. I followed the path to this spot here, where you see a short spur path leading to the water. There Miss Welsh saw me, from the pond-side, and called to me. I asked her to stay where she was, since I had noticed footprints and other marks that ought not to be disturbed until examined. These marks were all in this area here, along the spur path; none on the main footpath where the ground was quite hard and dry." He stepped back to the witness chair. And nothing, Warner thought, would ever influence or shake the boy except more facts, the sharp and tangible truths that you can weigh or photograph or look up in a textbook. And yet the continuing actions of the mind, the swift and dark events gone in a moment, misunderstood or "forgotten" or never glimpsed at all: *Those are facts too, Sergeant: did you know?*

"Go on, please."

"I went to the pond along the undisturbed ground at the side of the spur path. In the pond, submerged, I saw the body of a woman dressed in a light blue skirt and jacket and white blouse. Later in the day I measured the pond and found the maximum depth to be forty-two inches; a high-water line on the banks indicated that when full the greatest depth would be about five feet. On August 17th, however, the inlet was a mere trickle, the outlet practically dry—there's probably some underground drainage. Before stepping into the water I saw that the woman's arms were somewhat extended, and the hands were not clenched as I have seen them in other drowning cases."

"You have seen a number of them, Sergeant?"

"I have, sir. Boating, swimming accidents, a few suicides."

"You stepped into the pond?"

"I did. On lifting the body I found that rigor was complete, and post-mortem lividity noticeable in the face and hands."

"Please explain those terms for the jury, will you?"

"Rigor mortis is the stiffening that takes place, usually from two to six hours after death, and may continue from twelve to forty-eight hours. Post-mortem lividity is a discoloration caused by the settling of the blood to whatever parts of the body are lowest when the heart action ceases."

"Did that trickle into the pond create any current?"

"No, sir, hardly a ripple. Too small."

"Later on did you check the temperature of the water?"

"Yes—evening after dark. The weather that Monday evening was about like the evening before. The pond water at 9 P.M. Monday was at 68 degrees Fahrenheit."

"Was the water clear?"

"Some roiling, before I stepped in. The bottom has a layer of dead leaves and silt. Miss Welsh told me she had gone into the pond—her skirt was wet. I'd also noticed (I forgot to say) that Dr. Chalmers' slacks were quite wet, consistent with what he told me. The body was that of a woman in the early twenties, of slight build, about five feet two. Since there was no question of life remaining, I let it back into the water, to disturb the situation as little as possible before examination by my superiors. The foam on the lips was noticeable, but less than one expects to see in a drowning."

"What is the significance of foam on the lips, in a drowning?"

"Well, sir, a medical expert—"

"Just drawing on your own experience and police training."

"Well, it means a struggle for air. Air and water mix with the secretions of nose and throat."

"So, if a body not breathing enters the water, you won't see foam?"

"That's correct, sir."

"And in this case there was some, but less than normal?"

"Sir, I don't think I'm qualified to say what would be normal."

"Well, again, Sergeant, I just want to draw on your police experience. You said, I think, 'less than one expects to see'—correct?"

"Yes, sir, I can go that far, but it's only a—a layman's opinion. I've been with the state police only three years altogether. In that time I haven't seen any *large* number of drowning cases."

Warner suppressed a smile. T.J. should have known better than to push this man. His retreat was quick and graceful. "Quite right, Sergeant, and maybe I was a bit out of line. Would you now please describe the elevations of the ground in that area? I notice our map omits that."

The Sergeant looked pleased to be on his feet again; he might have been happier still with a pointer and a blackboard. "Here, where the spur path begins, the main footpath is going over a rise of ground. The spur itself runs level for about half its distance, then there's a ten-foot slope to the pond, rather steep." Hunter seemed bothered, perhaps getting more than he wanted. "That slope is the only one in the area you could call steep. Elsewhere the ground slopes toward the pond more gradually."

Yes, it was steep. Falling there, in the hazy night, sick with a cruel poison, Ann Doherty could easily have rolled down that short slope into the water. In cross-examination, this level-minded fact-lover would willingly say so. *Sick*—Warner's body involuntarily shuddered. He felt suffocated, and as though he too were falling in a darkness, nothing upholding him but a single thread of belief: *Callista had no criminal intent.* A belief that could never be demonstrated as a truth; never at least by the sort of demonstration that would be rightly, intelligently demanded by such a man as Sergeant Shields. *No criminal intent: how do I know?* No answer except the legally unacceptable and meaningless answer of trust, friendship, insight, love: *I know because I know.*

Sergeant Shields cheerfully continued: "The Chalmers house is on another moderate rise of ground, and going toward Dohertys' on the main footpath from the beginning of the spur, there's a gradual slope as far as the place where the pond's outlet crosses the path—just a little ditch you step over; then another slight rise to the Doherty house. The outlet runs fairly straight through the grove—just barely enough drop of the ground level to carry it into the culvert near the fork."

"Thank you." Much pleasanter for T.J., Warner guessed, to have the blocky sandy-haired athlete sitting down. "After letting the body back in the water, what did you do next, Sergeant?"

"I made a superficial examination of the ground. Then with Miss Welsh I went back to the main path, and requested her to stay there in sight of the pond while I went to report. After doing so, I returned to the edge of the woods and remained with Miss Welsh, in sight of the pond, until others arrived: Lieutenant Kovacs, the photographer Sergeant Peterson, Trooper Walter Curtis who brought equipment for making plaster casts, and Trooper Morris. The coroner's physician Dr. Devens arrived soon, and the undertaker's vehicle from Shanesville. However, Dr. Devens directed that the body be taken to the Winchester City morgue, where I understand there are better facilities. Trooper Morris and I lifted the body from the water, and Dr. Devens made a brief examination at the scene. We then placed the body in the vehicle, Dr. Devens gave his car keys to Trooper Morris, and went himself in the undertaker's vehicle. Trooper Morris followed with the doctor's car."

Smart and careful boy. It might still be necessary for T.J. to soothe down little Dr. Devens if he got snippy about testifying to the same technicality. Common sense says: Who's going to switch bodies on the doctor? The law says: All right, but let's just make sure nobody does. Not for the first time, Warner thought: *Granted, the law is an ass; but better listen when it brays. Sometimes it's right.*

"Go on, Sergeant."

"Under Lieutenant Kovacs' orders, I examined the pond's banks and the immediate area, with Peterson and Curtis. Eliminating the marks made by Dr. Chalmers, Miss Welsh and myself, only two sets of footprints were found near the pond. Mrs. Doherty's were identifiable by the high-heeled print of one shoe, and the stocking print of the other foot. The second set was size six, low-heeled, blunt-toed, the right shoe showing a slightly different sole-pattern from the left. I assisted Trooper Curtis in making casts of the prints, and initialed them as he did. Mrs. Doherty's footprints ended on the spur path, at the top of that slope I mentioned. Where they ended, a blurred mark on the fairly soft ground suggested that someone had fallen. It was not a very clear mark; all it really indicated was some recent disturbance of the earth. And from my experience of woodcraft and trail-reading—I think I can honestly claim a bit of expert knowledge there, by the way—I would say that all the marks from the beginning of the slope to the edge of the water were quite indefinite; that is, I think they could be interpreted in several different ways, all except one."

"And that one?"

"A heel-print belonging to the second set, the low-heeled set, superimposed on the blurred mark where someone had apparently fallen. And this mark told nothing except that whoever made it set her heel—that is, the heel of a low shoe, size six—on top of the other mark."

"Only one heel-mark?"

"Only one. The sole, and the other foot, must have rested on the hemlock needles and other loose stuff. The ground was only partly bare."

"Could you tell whether the person was standing or squatting?"

"Not for certain. I'd say standing, but I could be wrong."

"Where else were the footprints of that second set?"

"On the left bank of the pond—that is, left as you approached by the spur path. Two fairly clear imprints, left and right, pointed toward the water. The ground was somewhat moist there. We found a few other, partial prints of the size six shoes in that area, all partly obliterated by other footsteps. That left bank is the place where access to the water is easiest. That's where Miss Welsh had stepped in and out, and Dr. Chalmers had stumbled out on the left bank, slipping once by the way, although he had approached the pond from the other side."

"You say the marks on the slope of the spur path were indefinite. But would you describe them a little more, Sergeant?"

"They just weren't readable, Mr. Hunter. Mere disturbances of the earth. Let me put it this way, sir: simply on the basis of the trailmarks, Mrs. Doherty might have fallen and rolled into the water—it's just about steep enough for that; or she might have been pushed after she had fallen; or she might even have crawled or dragged herself into the pond. At the bottom of that slope, by the water's edge, the top of a wide flat boulder is exposed. Most of it's under water, but the top is bare, a shelf of rock that would show no marks if a person slipped over the edge into the water. And the water there is almost as deep as in the middle of the pond."

"Did you extend your search beyond the pond area?"

"Yes, sir, with Sergeant Peterson. We went to the Doherty house, examining the footpath. In the brush by the path, we found two marks of falling; at one of these places, evidence of vomiting. At the ditch where the pond's outlet intersects the path, I found a blue shoe, a right, matching the left one on the body. The footpath ends at a gravel turning circle in front of the Doherty house. There we found a blue and white four-door Pontiac sedan, later identified as belonging to Mr. James Doherty. The front bumper was almost in contact with a pillar of the porch. Tire gouges on the gravel indicated the brakes had been slammed on at the last minute. The front door on the driver's side was open. The ignition had been turned off and the key removed; because of the open door, the inside light was still burning."

"Does the gravel drive extend to Summer Avenue?"

"Yes, sir. We examined it for signs of another car, but found none. That drive would take no mark when dry except the kind the Pontiac made."

"Did you find anything else by the house?"

"A key ring, on the porch by the door. After the leather case of the key-holder had been checked for fingerprints, I tried the keys. They fitted the Pontiac and the outside doors of the Doherty house—those doors were all locked at that time, when Sergeant Peterson and I arrived there. On the driveway, near the opening of the path into the woods, I found a woman's blue handbag, monogrammed A.P.D. Its catch was open, and a lipstick pencil and compact had tumbled out."

"Did you check the other contents of the handbag?"

"Yes, sir." Sergeant Shields at last opened his notebook. "Lipstick pencil of a light shade, gold compact monogrammed A.P.D., one handkerchief unused, three Kleenex folded, engagement book of red imitation leather, mechanical pencil with chromium finish, single stub from motion picture theater, fifteen dollars in bills, one dollar and fourteen cents in coin in change purse, page torn from a memorandum pad with date August 15, 1959 and with writing evidently a grocery list, four bobby pins, a scrap of green rayon possibly a dressgoods sample, identification card belonging with handbag but not filled out, a—a paper clip."

Warner watched the histrionic tenderness of T. J. Hunter's hands. They moved over the already identified garments, not quite touching but with the sense of a caress. Corn, of course, but how marvelously served up! Gently the hands lifted a plastic bag.

"Sergeant, this bag has a tag with your initials—is this your identifying mark?"

"Yes, sir."

"And do you identify what I show you here, a woman's blue slipper, size five?"

"That is the slipper I found on the path in the woods, between the pond and the Doherty house, the morning of last August 17th."

Sit still, Old Man! No protest possible that the jury would not resent. How can you make legal protest against the gentleness of a pair of hands? Against a voice that by its very restraint compels the subject to cry aloud? Ann's garments, her poor fallen possessions, needed no advocate: four bobby pins, a paper clip. Best to sit still, the face a little hidden, as Callista was still, and hidden.

And to wait, because the defense never rests.

"Your witness, Mr. Warner."

He wondered whether it was worth the trouble of rising. Maybe. As a fact-lover, the Sergeant understood the existence of grays between black and white. One dim blur of gray across the clarity of Shields' testimony might stir a slight wonder in a few jurors. "Sergeant, when you found Dr. Chalmers on the back porch, did you speak first?"

"Yes, sir." Quite as polite as he had been to the prosecution.

"He roused at once and answered you?"

"He did, sir." Yes, polite, and well aware of what was coming.

Mildness and indifference were needed here: "What did he say?"

Then the expected noise: "Objection! This conversation wasn't introduced in direct examination."

Mildness, indifference? "Your Honor, I submit that the substance of the conversation was introduced."

"Yes—admissible in cross examination. Objection overruled."

T. J. Hunter shrugged and let it go. A masterly shrug.

"Well, Sergeant, what did Dr. Chalmers say?"

Sergeant Shields also was mild. Not indifferent; on the contrary, the level fact-loving eyes were kind. A contemplative kindness that could do the defense no service even if the jury were able to glimpse it and grope at the meaning of it.

"Dr. Chalmers said to me: 'Sam? My God, Sam, I can't believe it.' I said: 'I just got here. What's happened?' And he said: 'Ann—Ann Doherty—she's killed herself.'"

II

Weariness had grown like an external pressure, the encroachment of a rising tide, the waters of darkness. Callista had supposed that when Cecil walked over there to cross-examine the tide might recede, even release her entirely. It had not, not entirely, but it might be no longer rising; maybe this was the turn. She had heard Cecil speak, and had listened. Listening, she had felt within the weariness that hint of inarticulate continuing surprise which is an element in any manifestation of love. It did not seem to her that she had actually understood what he said, or what the Sergeant said. "Ann Doherty— killed herself." *What?* Oh—he was repeating what poor Herb had said to him. Herb could always be trusted to say something idiotic.

Important as testimony?—nobody thinks she killed herself. But the tide might very well be turning. Her eyes were no longer blurred. She could discover the thousand crow's-foot wrinkles in Cecil's face over yonder. Callista understood that she would not faint, nor collapse, nor die for some little time to come.

Threescore and ten is also a short time. Long enough to wear down a rugged boy's splendor to a burden of exhausted flesh—Cecil must have been a magnificent youth. Hardly long enough (Edith suggested once) to comprehend the pattern of a May-fly's wing, since for that you'd have to comprehend the protein molecule. When we can do that, Edith said, we shall still be ignorant, learning all new things with reluctance, initial rejection, stubborn retention of obsolete notions, superstitions, cruelties. Maybe, Edith said, the sickly bromide "at the last analysis" is the most arrogant verbalism human beings ever slung together.

What? Cecil's voice had spoken something more. With effort and a little panic, Callista recaptured it out of the counterpoint of thought. It was very simple. He said: "No further questions."

Edith had gone on to wonder how the coming centuries would handle their heretics. Burn and hang them like the seventeenth and earlier centuries? Listen to them a little, unwillingly, like the nineteenth, until revolution stiffened into respectability, congealed in half-truths? Wall them off, like the twentieth, with the soft barrier of democratic smugness or a steel barrier such as Marxian demonology? Maybe, Edith grumbled, the twenty-first century would return to punishing dissenters with open savagery: they'd be locked in delightful rooms with plastic food dispensers, ingenious mechanical attention to all the body's other needs (sure, all of 'em) and not a God-damned thing to do except watch television.

Cecil was coming back to her.

Cecil would agree with Edith; and in agreeing would not remind her how much farther his own life had ranged within the threescore and ten, how much of wonder and experience, speculation, pleasure, suffering had burgeoned in him during the half-century that spread between his age and her own: for he was kind.

Surely if now she cautiously turned her eyes toward the wall clock, the hands would have struggled a little nearer to five. The Old Man was sitting down by her, covering her hand briefly, his own heavy and hot. The clock hands had pushed a small weary way beyond two. "Are you all right, Cal? You don't look good."

"I'm all right. What's happening now?"

"Looks as if T.J. was going to try a bit of redirect. Sore too. Nothing makes a prosecutor madder than an impartial policeman."

To Callista the suave gentleman in the gray suit didn't look mad. "Sergeant, when you first saw Dr. Chalmers he was in a state of shock?"

"He appeared so. Color and breathing bad. Spoke brokenly, with difficulty. And as I said, later he mentioned a heart condition."

"In other words he was in a state where you'd hardly expect him to make a clear interpretation of anything he'd seen?"

"I can't answer that, sir, because I've noticed some people can think pretty straight in spite of a bad shock. I don't know Dr. Chalmers well enough to say whether he could or not."

She heard the Old Man exclaim under his breath: "Brother! good thing I didn't bother to object." But after Hunter's leading question Callista had seen the smooth jowls of juror Emma Beales bobbing with gratification at the way nice Mr. Hunter had gone straight to the point.

"Has Dr. Chalmers, in any later conversation with you, again brought up the theory that Mrs. Doherty might have committed suicide?"

"No, sir, he has not."

Hunter dropped it there. Callista was aware of the Sergeant rising, meeting her glance for an instant with something in his own not at all unkind. It was not understanding, perhaps not really compassion. He had never spoken to her. She thought she remembered his face among others at District Attorney Lamson's office during her worst time of questioning. He had said nothing then; would have given Mr. Lamson his information at some other time; maybe he had turned up there (if he really did) just to have a look at her. What she read in him now might be a simple adult refusal to condemn, by a busy man, not involved, not personally much excited or concerned, his thought and daily life filled with a thousand other matters. And now he was marching away. With nothing of the sarcasm that would have distorted the words if she had spoken aloud, Callista thought: *Good-bye—nice to have known you.*

The next witness, Sergeant Peterson the photographer, unwound his scrawniness from some part of the outer blur and strode into the arena to take the oath. Dark hair, a pallor as if bleached in his own hypo. Unexpectedly Callista's fingers itched for a pencil, to draw Peterson's lank face as an expanded kodak. She could ask Cecil for a pencil—no, he was getting up. Hunter had rather lovingly produced a big Manila folder, and now came Cecil's sonorous: "May it please the Court—"

Those would be the photographs of Ann Doherty dead, and Cecil would try to keep out the most lurid ones.

Over Callista swept a weight of memory. Even the smell of the District Attorney's office—tobacco, book leather, a peculiarly penetrating shaving-lotion stink. She saw again the half-star shape of a spot on the wall behind Mr. Lamson's shoulder, an imperfection in the paint like a chip flaked off the man's pinkish face; and the face itself in all detail, slightly ascetic in spite of that healthy glow, under carefully theatrical gray hair. She saw his manicured hand, womanish except for a scattering of black hairs, reaching across the desk to her, in a reek of too much hygiene and primping, presenting a Manila folder like the one Hunter now cherished, possibly the same one. "By the way, Miss Blake—" tone polite, fruity, luscious with some kind of enjoyment that perhaps the man himself did not recognize—"you might glance at this folder, if you will."

So I held her in my hand. Ann's arms reached upward in rigor out of the shadow of earth, for in that first photograph they had let the drowned girl lie on her back while the camera peered impersonally at wet skirt tumbled down from flexed thigh (the knee discolored), and soaked white underpants, the position pointlessly (accidentally?) erotic: *Death, my lover.* Accidental surely, for the camera had given a sharper focus to the bedabbled mouth, darkened cheeks, empty eyes. Why must the small breasts push up so urgently? Why, a happen-so: she was drifting face down, arms and bent knee probably holding her up a little from the pond's bottom, when rigor began—*all right, I understand.* The lifted hands were a blur, foreshortened, ghostly; innocently acquisitive hands transformed to shadows incapable of holding fast to anything, even pity.

The second picture was an enlargement of the face to life size, no detail spared. Drops of pond water blurred the eyes; a black twig was caught in water-soaked hair. Discoloration, and foam.

The third picture was one taken at the morgue, after rigor had passed off, and though the face was still a comment on the brevity, the insecurity of beauty and warmth, Ann's no longer vulnerable nakedness conveyed no great sorrow. It was just a portrait of death; apart from the drowned face, not unlovely. Callista remembered that in Mr. Lamson's office she had very nearly remarked aloud: "Never knew she'd had an appendectomy." The lividity, yes; but one could think of that as simply the shadow of death. This photograph, Callista supposed, would hardly go to the jury, for in the morgue nobody had bothered to toss a prudish towel over the innocent little triangle. Maybe they had fixed up another one for the purpose, that wouldn't distress the sensibilities of Mr. Emmet Hoag. Yes, granted, certainly, that Ann had been very pretty and desirable, a long time ago.

Callista recalled what it was she actually said aloud in Mr. Lamson's office: "I'd like to be sure I understand. If these pictures shock me, that's evidence of remorse, in other words guilt. If I don't display any shock, that means unnatural coldness; in other words, guilt. Is that correct?"

Someone behind the chair in Lamson's office where she sat facing the desk light had made a noise. Not T. J. Hunter; Sergeant Rankin maybe; or could it have been that young Sergeant, Samuel Arthur Shields? An indistinct word or suppressed grumble; not significant, but Mr. Lamson's cool gaze had flicked upward at the sound, not liking it. "No, Miss Blake, I don't think you have it quite correct. A girl of your intelligence and background ought not to be taking that world-is-all-against-me attitude. One expects it from common criminals—we look for it—but surely not from you."

"I've never thought the world was all against me. I used to think it was a place where you could get by fairly well by telling the truth, minding your own business, trying not to hurt anyone."

"You don't think so now?"

She herself had heard the wiry unpleasant note of pain in her voice: "No comment." And Mr. Lamson had heard it, and could not quite hide a brief flare of gratification, a thin spear of flame shooting up from an ember behind his eyes. Oh, he was doubtless a decent and respectable man, father of a family, pillar of the church. It would be only her sickened imagination that made him something with a whip out of Krafft-Ebing.

"Miss Blake, you ought to understand that what we are trying to do here is to discover the truth."

"What is truth?"

"No comment."

"Mr. Lamson, since she must have got the poison in my apartment, and since I shouldn't have had it there, I do feel remorse. But I am not breaking down and screaming at sight of these pictures, because that is not my way."

"Oh, now, the pictures aren't all that important, Miss Blake. No occasion to make such an issue of the pictures. I thought it might be to your interest to look at them, since a jury will. The whole point, my dear girl—the whole point is we just don't believe your story."

Cecil Warner came back from the side-bar discussion, looking rather blind. He murmured: "Couldn't do much, Cal. They're all going in. An open protest would just antagonize the jury."

"Does it really matter? She'd look the same whether she fell in or was pushed."

"Dear—I'll be saying that of course. But it assumes that twelve minds can respect logic."

Hunter and Sergeant Peterson were being immensely fair. Finished now with the portraits of death, they were showing a photograph of a blunt-toed shoe superimposed on another mark. Peterson was even wordy and boring, explaining unnecessarily how you could tell that the footprint was made later. Then came photographs of the disturbed areas at other parts of the bank, and of the flat rock by the water's edge that would take no sign.

The rock. Cecil ought not to be looking so distressed for her. Behind her hand she whispered: "Peterson must have held his camera right where I stood. If the moon hadn't come out of a cloud—I wonder, Cecil—would I have refused to understand she was there? It was a small cloud but deep, suddenly come, suddenly gone. The rock—I used to sit there for hours when I was a little girl, and dabble my feet. It was the first thing I saw, and suddenly, you understand?—because of the moon."

"The moon—"

"Yes, 'the moon, the inconstant moon'—don't you remember I told you? The way the light strengthened in that gap of the hemlocks, and there was my rock, and then the whiteness in the water. Her arm, or that blouse—no, her jacket hid the blouse, she was face down. It must have been her arm, that whiteness, don't you think?"

"I suppose. Cal, this isn't the time—"

"I know. Hunter will ask: 'Why didn't you go into the pond, if your story is true? Why, Callista? She might have been alive.'"

"We'll deal with that in direct examination."

"He'll come back to it, though. 'How could you know, Callista? How could you *know* she was dead?' And then I say: 'Sir, dead or not, she was so quiet I couldn't disturb her rest.'"

"Cal, please!"

"Are you going to cross-examine Sergeant Peterson?"

"I don't think so—nothing to gain."

"Ah, I was hoping you'd ask him why his damned silly face looks like a camera bellows."

"Hush! Shall I come to see you this evening?"

"Oh—no—no, I am unwell. I mean—that is, I would so like to have two candles, one for you and one for—I'm sorry ... I'm all right now. I'll be quiet. But don't come tonight—I did mean that. It's something—I can't explain it."

"All right, my dear. Maybe tomorrow evening."

"Yes, without fail. Let me tell you one thing more?"

"What?"

"I think I'm discovering that I want to live."

III

Sergeant Peterson had droned his last and had been succeeded on the stand by Trooper Curtis, brisk and dry, with his plaster casts and fingerprints. Both men, Edith Nolan understood, were competent, honest, not deliberately wasting time. Hunter himself was not really unduly slow at this business of hammering home what was already clear and established: Callista had been there. The fingerprint evidence at Shanesville was quite negative: no prints except Ann's on handbag or key case, none but hers and Jim's on the Pontiac or the Dohertys' front porch. All right and so what? It was half past three before Hunter and Curtis were solemnly finished with that apparent futility. It had never occurred to Edith that any part of this ordeal could be a bore. But it was.

Then in a brief cross examination Warner brought out the fact that a police search of the grove between the pond and Walton Road had produced nothing at all. It could not matter. Curtis and Peterson had both acted rather pleased with their casts and photographs of the Volkswagen's tire marks on the shoulder of Walton Road. They liked things complete, well wrapped. But it couldn't matter, for in her statement to District Attorney Lamson Callista had admitted taking the Volkswagen first into the Dohertys' driveway, following the footpath, seeing Ann's body in the pond. She had admitted leaving then, driving around to Walton Road, parking there out of sight of her mother's house.

And the prosecution would surely not trouble to deny or even question Callista's story of what happened then, in that half hour. She had stumbled off into the thick second-growth woods on the other side of Walton Road, a tangle of saplings, briers, poison ivy, wiry bushes, and young locust trees thorny in the dark, to get through a miscarriage in secret like a wounded animal and have done with it. To Edith, on the first occasion when with Warner's help Edith had broken through the barriers and won a visit with Callista in the detention cell, Callista had said tersely, in haste to change the subject: "The brambles were the worst of it." And that visit was not a time when she would accept any word of consolation. Something held back, Edith knew, some private tormenting reason why, even to her, Callista could not speak freely about that agony in the woods. Later, maybe. Everything now must be qualified with such words: "later"—"some time"—"after all this is over, Cal, and you are free."

Curtis was gone. Something smart and bright-eyed was down there swearing to tell the whole truth and nothing but the truth.

"Your full name and occupation, sir?"

"Sutherland R. Clipp. I own and manage Clipp's Garage on Duke Street, uptown—you know, repairs, gas, body work, matter of fact we do everything, you'd be surprised."

In startled disgust Edith thought: *Everything? How lovely for you, Mr. Clipp!* With the utmost geniality, Mr. Clipp went on to testify that on the evening of Sunday, August 16th, he had been driving home to Winchester by Walton Road, after delivering a 1956 Buick in the nicest condition you could imagine to a customer in Emmetville. He wanted to emphasize that the Buick was a dish, in spite of—well, low mileage. He had practically robbed himself, but that was his way, the customer came first, and it paid off—oh—yes, he'd been watching the time that evening because he had to pick up his wife after a church supper; got talking with that (completely satisfied) Emmetville client, and besides, the car he'd taken in exchange was kind of a sad heap that wouldn't safely do anything over forty, and you know how women are if you keep them waiting, not that she—yes, he had passed the junction of Summer Avenue and Walton Road between 9:10 and 9:15, no later. He had seen a maroon Volkswagen parked under the pines, not too well off the road either, careless parking, one reason why he'd noticed it, although he always did notice them cheap foreign cars, which weren't too bad if all you wanted was economical transportation, like, however—what?—no, there wasn't anybody in the Volks or near it, unless somebody was scrouched down back of the dashboard when his headlights got there, but you couldn't hardly do anything like that in them foreign cheapies—"Your witness, Mr. Warner."

Mr. Clipp's hurt, astonished look inquired: *Is that all?*

Without rising, Warner asked: "You do front end alignment?"

"Well, no, sir, that calls for pretty tricky machinery. Still, the way we're growing all the time—"

"Interior finish?"

"No, sir, that's mostly factory. Of course, in a pinch—"

Edith heard Hunter begin snarling: "What possible bearing—"

"None, sir. I just wanted to make sure Mr. Clipp hadn't left out anything. No further questions."

During the short courtroom roar, checked by the gavel, Edith thought she could read exasperated forgiveness in the face of Judge Terence Mann. But foreman Peter Anson, she saw, was not amused, nor Hoag, nor Francis Fielding. Business is serious: to make fun of a man when he's advertising is something like interrupting him in the men's room.

State Trooper Carlo San Giorgio, solemn, deceptively fresh-faced and young, followed Mr. Clipp. He had stopped a blue and white Pontiac, license JD1081, on Walton Road two miles beyond the city line, at 8:34 P.M., Sunday, August 16th. The driver was a young woman who gave her name as Mrs. James Doherty, which agreed with her driver's license. Her driving had been unsteady, with some wavering over the white line.

"Was she driving fast, exceeding the limit?"

"No, sir, rather slow. Just unsteady."

"Did she seem in good command of herself when you spoke to her?"

"Yes, but I did ask if she'd been drinking a little."

"Was her response satisfactory to you as a police officer?"

"Well—yes, sir, it was."

"Did you notice any smell of alcohol on her breath?"

"A trifle." San Giorgio fidgeted. "Just barely noticeable."

"But according to your observation, she wasn't what you'd call drunk, is that right?"

"No, sir, she certainly wasn't. Spoke coherently, understood what I said—real polite and—and nice."

"Did anything in her appearance suggest she might be ill?"

"She was slightly hoarse. I'd stopped her car where there was a pretty good light from a house across the road, and I thought her eyes looked very slightly inflamed. Enough to suggest she might be—oh, perhaps coming down with a cold. You understand, sir, these were very slight things, otherwise I couldn't have let her drive on."

Back of all that, Edith knew—back of the hedging, the slowly chosen words, back of Hunter's questions blunted by the hearsay rule—was the thing that San Giorgio knew and keenly remembered and could not say. Warner's dark eyes had narrowed to cold watchfulness, and Judge Mann's pencil was still. There wasn't any hearsay rule in Mr. Lamson's office. But here in the arena, Carlo San Giorgio couldn't say: "*She said she'd had one little shot of brandy. And I said: 'Oh well, Miss, I guess we won't throw the book at you for that.'*"

Last night at dinner, Cecil Warner had done some thinking out loud about Trooper San Giorgio, who would have in his own young mind no reasonable doubt. San Giorgio could not repeat Ann's words on the stand. And yet if he could, the Old Man said, it ought (if juries were logical) to make no essential difference. For there was no defense, he said, except a reasonable doubt as to criminal intent. "Reasonable doubt!" he said, and set down his glass because his fat hand was shaking. "You see it, Red? T.J. can say that criminal intent and premeditation are proved up to the hilt by the mere presence of the poison in Cal's apartment. He will. He'll rub their noses in it. Against that and a flock of other circumstantial facts, we've got just one fact, the fact of something that happened in Cal's mind. Is it a fact?"

"You and I both know it, don't we? She had no intent to kill."

But instead of answering directly, the Old Man had said: "Red, do you understand she's not certain of it herself?"

Edith had not quite understood it, until then.

"Did you give her a ticket, Trooper?"

"No, sir. From the address on her driving license I knew she had only about a mile to go. I told her she'd better head straight for home, and I told her I'd follow along behind till she got there, which I did."

The youth was reliving it, Edith saw, and perhaps painfully. A pretty girl, hot night and hazy moon—had he hoped to be invited into the house for a quick check on burglars and a little drink? Oh, probably not. Ann had carried an obvious flag of conventional virtue. San Giorgio would have recognized and respected it, and done no more than a bit of summer's-night dreaming.

"You drove behind her car, as far as the house on Summer Avenue?"

"I did, sir. I saw her turn in at the driveway, and since she made it all right, I drove on."

"Did you note the time?"

"Yes, sir: 8:43."

"Mr. Warner?"

"No questions."

Later last night, up at her studio, watching the fire in the grate through the prism of his wineglass, the Old Man said: "Who started the legend that the law court is a place devoted to search for truth? Answer, lawyers of course. But not counsel for the defense, Red. We know our function is to persuade. The prosecution may fool itself now and then, and kick the word 'truth' around; we can't afford to."

Edith had said flatly: "The system stinks."

He wasn't startled; he only grumbled: "I agree. The adversary system stinks. But working inside of it, my own position has logic enough to satisfy me. I get it out of a hypothesis, Red—not abstract truth, but working hypothesis. I say a human being once born has a right to live, if the word 'right' is going to mean anything—or let's say, a right not to be murdered, judicially or any other way. In other words, I'd defend Cal if I thought she was guilty as hell."

Crew-cut gray hair and dignity marched to the stand, the face under the gray brush unknown to Edith but carrying a nearly unmistakable professional stamp. This would be bad. *Look towards me, Cal! I'll wear this old green suit tomorrow, too.* "Arthur J. Devens, M.D." *Look toward me!* But telepathy is like other kinds of magic, she knew: fun to play with as a notion; if it worked, we'd run screaming. "A.B. Columbia, 1930, M.D. from College of Physicians and Surgeons." And maybe soon, another century or so, there'll be no such thing as privacy on earth except in the dark center of a few minds not quite overwhelmed. The desert shall blossom like the rose: distilled sea water, atomic-power pumps, sure, nothing to it, but no room for roses, and no hiding place—"active as Coroner's physician for Winchester County, New Essex, since 1952." *But friend, if something happens inside the mind I don't know, to make you remember me, to turn your head toward me, I will smile. I'll say with my lips: "We're going to win."*

"—preliminary examination made on the scene. The body was that of a young white woman in the middle twenties, of slight build, height five feet two. Rigor was complete, a light reddish post-mortem lividity noticeable, the face not markedly cyanotic. A moderate quantity of white cohesive foam adhered to nose and mouth. The hands, though stiffened in rigor, were not clenched as one often finds them in drowning cases. The conjunctivae were congested. Cutis anserina—gooseflesh—was pronounced on the thighs and upper arms. Gooseflesh," said Dr. Devens politely and patiently to the jury, "is frequently evident after death by drowning, if the water is far enough below body temperature, as it ordinarily is even in the tropics. To sum up that preliminary, superficial examination: it suggested, but did not prove, that death had occurred with less struggle than is usual in a drowning. It did prove that life was not extinct when the body entered the water. There was at least some breathing, possibly the shallow breathing of unconsciousness, but enough inhaling and exhaling and choking reflex to cause that foam."

"Doctor, a hypothetical question: if a person were stunned, I mean knocked entirely unconscious, before falling or being thrown into the water, and then perished by drowning, would you expect to find the body, after twelve to thirteen hours of submersion, more or less in the condition of Mrs. Doherty's at the time you made that first examination?"

Edith saw Callista start as if struck in the face. Her dark brows gathered in that quick frown of hers, and she was leaning to Cecil Warner, whispering. She looked, Edith thought, more disgusted than angry. Cecil's poker face remained in control. He only listened, shook his head, patted her hand.

"Oh, hypothetical—well.... I dare say the findings wouldn't be inconsistent. Of course, Mr. Hunter, I looked for any sign of head injury, a matter of routine, and found nothing of the kind."

"Isn't it possible, Doctor, to receive a head injury, perhaps from a padded thing like a sandbag, that won't leave any marks?"

"No superficial marks, maybe. I think you'd find post-mortem evidence, likely subdural hemorrhage."

"Even from a blow that merely stunned?"

With some acid and faraway amusement Dr. Devens remarked: "Even as Coroner's physician, I'm not too versed in the lore of sandbags. But I think that a blow heavy enough to stun, followed very soon by death from another cause, would leave some internal evidence."

"Did you look for such evidence?"

"I did."

"Is that standard procedure, by the way, when there's convincing evidence of drowning?"

"I can't say that I lean very much on standard procedure. So far as I'm concerned, any case that reaches the Coroner's office is unique. When there's any possibility of homicide, I try to think of everything, including the apparently far-fetched. Yes, I examined the head: cranial section—well, I don't suppose you want those details. Head, neck vertebrae, all perfectly normal, uninjured. In fact the one and only injury on the entire body surface was a trifling abrasion on the right anklebone, which could have been caused in any number of ways—a fall, or the anklebone scraping against something: impossible to say. I also examined the palms for earth marks, such as she might have got if she'd fallen forward and tried to break the fall with her hands. There weren't any, but I dare say several hours' immersion would have removed them if they were ever there. The skin of the palms was perfectly clear."

"I see. Go on, please."

"The body was placed in the mortuary wagon from Shanesville, and at my suggestion was taken to the Winchester morgue. I accompanied it there; it was at no time out of my sight. I began the post-mortem at about 1:30 P.M., assisted by Dr. Miles Dennison and with the authorization of Mr. District Attorney Lamson. I think I should say at this point that shortly before I began the post-mortem, I was notified by Winchester Chief of Police Morgan Collins that there was a possibility Mrs. Doherty had drunk poison, thought to be aconitine. I therefore had this in mind before beginning the examination, and I consulted by telephone with the toxicologist Dr. Walter Ginsberg, and prepared the organs, blood samples and so on, that he told me he would need for his study. The body weight was one hundred and ten pounds, slightly undernourished. There was an appendectomy scar, old; no other scars, no evidence of chronic illness or disorder, no marks of violence; the subject had never given birth. The nasal cavities and bronchi contained some stiff foam and a few dark brown and black specks identified by microscopic examination as fragments of dead leaves. No algae were found. Some water was in the lungs, but very little. The heart, not markedly distended, contained fluid blood, but that is not diagnostic: clotted blood may appear in a drowning case. The viscera were quite noticeably congested."

"That is diagnostic?—congestion of the viscera?"

"No, sir—may appear in many other conditions."

"Including some kinds of poisoning?"

"Yes, Mr. Hunter."

"For example poisoning by aconitine?"

"Yes."

"Did you employ the Gettler test?"

"Yes—inconclusive. The blood in the left side of the heart had a slightly lower concentration of sodium chloride than the blood on the right. If that difference had been pronounced, you could call it fair evidence of inhalation of fresh water, but it was too slight. I don't attach any significance to it."

"Could the *lack* of a positive finding be significant?"

"I don't think so. It's a good test, but plenty of things may confuse it. For instance, a drowning may occur from pharyngeal shock—a spasmodic throat contraction that causes asphyxia before much water is inhaled. Logically still a drowning death, but no water to speak of, so there goes your Gettler test."

"You looked of course for evidence of aconitine poisoning?"

"Only in a limited sense, sir. Aconitine doesn't leave gross traces for post-mortem, it's a job for the toxicologist, a chemical job. Since I knew Dr. Ginsberg would be working on it, I simply bore it in mind, prepared what he needed, and kept my eyes open. I can say under oath that I found nothing inconsistent with aconite poisoning having occurred shortly before the drowning. But the actual immediate cause of death was, in my opinion, asphyxia due to immersion, in other words drowning."

"Doctor, will you give the jury a description of the effects of aconitine in a lethal or near-lethal dose?"

"Frankly, sir, I'll be drawing on textbook knowledge, because this is the only case I ever encountered. Homicide by aconite is decidedly rare. So is suicide." Callista looked up, not to the doctor who dutifully faced the jury and would not look at her, but searching the rows of spectators. "Aconitine will cause numbness, tingling in the mouth, also in the fingers, possibly cramps in arms and legs. There's marked salivation, nausea, burning sensation in stomach and throat." Edith moved in her seat, and smiled, and tried to call in silence: *I'm here.* But Callista's eyes, searching, immense, drowned, passed over her. "A slow, irregular, weak pulse is characteristic, with rapid shallow breathing, muscular weakness, a general collapse. Nausea and vomiting are usual; sometimes there are convulsions. The poison depresses the medullary centers of the brain, but the cerebrum is hardly affected, which means the mind stays pretty clear until the coma that may supervene at the end." Callista's eyes found what they were seeking. It would not be her mother, Edith knew: Victoria Chalmers sat over at Edith's left. "Those symptoms I've described begin soon after aconite is taken. I believe death, when it occurs, usually comes in about four hours—but it can happen in a matter of minutes."

Edith wished not to turn her head; she felt instead an unwillingness, distaste, reluctance to learn what would be written in the face of Jim Doherty. But she could not help it. Knowing where he was seated, she was forced to turn until a sidelong look gave her the image of him, completing at that instant the sign of the cross, his eyes lowered, his lips moving. But the man beside him was watchful, interested, attentive, probably missing none of the testimony.

"What is the minimum lethal dose, Dr. Devens?"

"About a milligram. Some individuals might take up to five or six, and recover. More than six milligrams would likely finish anyone, unless there was immediate medical attention—you understand, those figures refer to a pure concentration of the drug."

Callista's lips were moving also. As Edith looked to her again, she saw them shape unmistakable words: "*Go away!*" There would be no sound, Edith thought, even for Cecil Warner, who had taken hold of her hand and was showing the beginning of alarm. "*Go away!*"

"Is the drug readily soluble in alcohol?"

"Yes, Mr. Hunter."

Callista, be quiet! He can't hear you. He can't hear anyone.

"Assuming a person had taken four to five milligrams of the poison, Dr. Devens, he could still be saved by immediate medical attention?"

The girl said something to Cecil Warner, quick and possibly sharp; Edith caught the faint note of her voice under the dry dominating noise of Dr. Devens, the words indistinguishable, blotted out by his: "Certainly, sir, the patient could probably be saved. Stomach pump. Tannic acid I imagine, to render the poison inert. You'd give heart stimulants, say digitalis. A healthy patient would have a pretty good chance."

"Thank you, Dr. Devens. Cross examination, Mr. Warner?"

"No cross examination." But Warner was up, for once urgently quick-spoken. "Your Honor, in view of my client's exhaustion, may we have adjournment at this time?"

In the abrupt hush that followed Warner's question, Callista's voice, not loud, not really a cry, was surely heard by everyone, even by Jim Doherty. "Go away, my love!"

The Judge winced, speaking hastily: "The Court stands adjourned until ten A.M. tomorrow."

Edith also observed the press tables, and the jolly excited scramble for the telephones.

IV

The pavements throbbed with a golden, sometimes iridescent flame, which could not deceive Cecil Warner, for he was not drunk. The time hadn't come and never would when two bourbons on top of an average dinner could make a fool of him. The dancing fire was nothing in the world but the reflection of headlights on sidewalks wet with the return of winter rain.

On his left a separate darkness kept pace with him, blotting out the fire-ballet as he moved. *I cast a shadow. It is the nature of a man to cast a shadow. This is done even by a few of the dead.*

No. 'Their works do follow after them'; but that's not shadow, except by ill-advised figure of speech. That is what I shall term—(BAR AND GRILL twenty paces ahead)—shall term the immortality of consequences, of continuing events. Shadow's different. Shadow is the occlusion of light rays by an impermeable mass, me for instance. Avoid all ill-advised figures of speech. Go away, my love!

He observed it was Hanlon's Bar and Grill, corner of Main and Willard, damned if it wasn't—interesting, since he'd thought he was three blocks further west. He advanced through the logical absurdity of a revolving door. Quiet here tonight. He read the others at the bar in a practiced glance: four nondescript males and a large platinum wench, all unknown. He fumbled past his damp overcoat, drawing forth and consulting his thin and ancient pocket watch of yellow gold. His inner vision recorded, as always, the florid inscription he would see if his thumbnail opened the hinged back of the case: *Ezra Allen Warner, 1880.* A gift from his grandfather to his father, on the boy Ezra's graduation from college at twenty-one. For the last thirty-odd years Cecil had not been able to look on this delicate artifact without some dark stirring of the thought: *I have no children.* The fantastically graceful hands declared the present hour to be ten-thirty; they had been truth-tellers for eighty years. "Evening, Tom. Bourbon and water."

"Sure enough, Mr. Warner. Raining again, isn't it?"

"A sprinkle. A certain piddling effort. Possibly the tears of the gods are running thin in this latter age."

Tom's patient face was acknowledging him as a Character. "You could be right." Tom would have absorbed every word on the Blake case that the evening *Courier* had to offer; adult, seasoned, sensitive, he wouldn't mention it unless Warner did. He had even spoken Warner's name in a soft tone that would not carry down the bar. He poured the bourbon, gave the mahogany a needless swipe or two for friendship's sake in case the Old Man wanted to talk, and drifted back to his post of command.

Two men, blurred by Warner's preoccupation, were discussing space flight across the intervening blonde. Beyond them two others carried on an argument that rose to audibility only now and then. The Old Man heard and did not hear them; heard and did not hear the deeper counterpoint within him.

Tomorrow, assuming tomorrow came, the attack would follow a different line. Callista's adultery and deception, illustrative details by courtesy of the neighbors and Nathaniel Judd, plus T.J.'s dreary assertions and reassertions that the girl was being tried for nothing but murder—perhaps T.J. could even manage to believe that himself, for the duration. Callista's atheism; yes, almost certainly some one of the State's witnesses would most casually drop in the word "atheist." Protest, uproar, the Old Man scolding, T.J. doing a baritone solo on religious tolerance; then the mockery (Terence himself would hate it) of striking an answer from the record when no means existed to strike it from the jurors' minds.

"It don't push against atmosphere up there, account there *isn't* any."

"All right, I know that, but how *does* it push, 's what I don't get?"

"No she didn't! She said, her exact words, 'you never knew what was ordinary for Callista'—exact words."

"Were you there?"

"Hell no, like I told you, I couldn't get off from work, but the *Courier*'s printing every word, so all you got to do is put two and two—"

"—pushes against itself, see? The satellite *itself* is the God-damn resistance, like you're shooting a pistol, and the recoil—you ever shoot a pistol?"

"Hate 'em. Sure way to get hurt."

Platinum said: "'S like this, Buck, what Sam's try'n'a tell you, you get up 'ere in shpace, you just be'r not fart."

"Now, June," said bartender Tom, "you want to watch the talk."

"I di'n' say single thing."

"O*kay*, June baby, just watch it is all."

"What I mean is, everybody figures the girl is nuts, that old woman Welsh and everybody. So what you're going to see, you're going to see an insanity defense. It always happens—"

"No sumbishn barkeep's telling me how talk."

"June baby, I keep telling you—"

"Happens every time. She'll be put away a few years, and then let out, do it all over again, like—"

"Only thing I'm try'n'a find out, what does it push against *behind?*"

"I'm beginning to think it's no use try'n'a explain it to you."

"Tom!"

"Hell, like a poisoner *always* does! You want to bet? Happened a million times. I read a book—"

"Tom!"

"Yeah? You better not have any more, June."

"Don't *want* any more—not why I called you. Just wanted say, 'm sorry 'f anything I said gave 'fense. None 'tended. All's I want's everybody be happy."

But the defense—

"Sure, June, that's okay."

"'S my whole life right 'ere, see? Ask anybody knows me."

"O*kay*, June!"

The defense never rests.

"Okay he says, he keeps saying okay, Jesus Christ, you ought to listen I'm telling you, not just keep saying okay, okay. Ever since I was little girl, honest, all's I ever wanted was everybody be happy."

4

... O how can Love's eye be true,
That is so vex'd with watching and with tears?

SHAKESPEARE, *Sonnet CXLVIII*

I

Thought of work had halted Edith's aimless wandering on the Christmas-spattered evening streets downtown. Now the drawing table and empty chair in her studio brought Callista poignantly close in absence. How arrogantly, like a beloved child, Callista had captured her life!

Window-shopping with no heart for it, necessary gifts already bought, she had become fed up with Winchester, noise, people, sidewalk grit flung by the wind; with gaudy lights desperately imitating good cheer, drizzle-nosed bell-ringers and Santa Clauses, carols once pretty now done to death, fed up with crowd faces till she recoiled from them as from a rat-race of tragic masks.

Getting off the bus—she seldom used her car downtown, hating the struggle of searching out a parking space—her skirt was twitched up by the breeze for the lech of a pair of whistling teen-agers. Edith had been dourly amused. *Try looking at the face some time, kids!*—and the mood kept with her as far as her third floor walkup on Hallam Street. The hour was nine-thirty, Papa Doorn just closing his delicatessen on the ground floor, giving her a gentle "Good night, Miss Nolan!"

No mail but a swatch of ads drenched in the season's gladness, and the janitor would never provide a wastebasket in the entry. She dumped the mess in the studio trash-box, glancing at the cameras, screens, props, at the dim end of the studio. A fantastic way to earn a living, close to the mainstream of human vanity. But at this end, with the north light, wall-shelves, drawing table, work could be done after survival was taken care of. Callista's work for a year, and Edith's own. The bread-and-butter end of the studio was already dusty. Edith had canceled portrait engagements for the duration of the trial, disinclined to hire a temporary helper: why knock oneself out immortalizing the fish-faced?

She touched the table, symbolic touching of a hardness-without-coldness that was one element of Callista Blake. *Stop it, Red! She's not here.* She took down a folder of Callista's drawings—some careful, some swift, all begotten of a mind that could see, laugh, pity, understand. Also in that folder was a letter Callista had written after Edith's last visit to the detention cell, Saturday, three days ago. Edith knew the drawings. She would find nothing new in them now, when she was out of temper and moved by a wish to start some work of her own. Glance at that abandoned wagon in long grass? Or the supermarket clerk, homely day's end weariness caught in a dozen lines with that compassion of Callista's (at nineteen!) which she could almost never convey in spoken words? Not now. Edith glanced at a watercolor on the wall, one she had taken from Cal's apartment for safety with Herb Chalmers' distracted consent and after the police had given leave. A mountain slope, a wind-ravished pine, shouting deep color against a storm sky intense with the power of two worlds, the world of life and growth and dying before Callista's eyes, and the world of Callista's most observing self.

Off in her living-room the telephone rang. Edith ran for it. The voice was slurred, uncertain. "Miss Nolan—Edith—all evening trying to get you. Jim Doherty—now please don't hang up."

"Of course I won't." She tried not to snap. "What is it?"

"Had to ask you something." He was rather drunk. "May seem unreason'ble, guess you hate me anyhow, but—"

"I won't hang up. I don't hate you. What is it, Jim?"

"Maybe wouldn't blame you. You feel I let her down. Feel I'm an enemy or something—sorry—not what I'm trying to say—" She waited, watching her thin white fingers play with a pencil from the telephone table, a pinpoint of perception somehow important, as if it kept her distressed and startled mind from swirling away down the telephone mouthpiece like water down the hole of a handbasin. She heard a beat of mechanical music; Jim would be in a bar, the booth shut against a squalling of radio or television. The large-boned, dark-Irish face would be pale with alcohol, filmed with sweat, black hair disordered, wide mouth talking against its own unwillingness. Dark eyes rigid, unfocused, behind them Jim's own image of a crackpot redhead who was Callista's friend. He was a tall man; the stingy crannies of the booth would bother his legs. An impressive young stallion: any woman felt that much, and one could (sometimes) see why Callista—"Edith, what happened there, before adjournment? I've got to know. I sort of lost track, then they were taking her away. What—"

"You didn't hear what she said?"

"No, that's it, I didn't. I was praying—well, for her, though I suppose that doesn't mean anything to you, no offense, anyway I—"

"Didn't your friend hear what she said?"

"My—oh, you mean Father Bland. No, he didn't."

"Is he deaf?"

"Yes, a little." She heard the righteous reproach; it must have done Jim good to put her in the wrong. "What did she say?"

"She said: 'Go away, my love!'"

He would be still there. She heard breathing, and the background noise, a hot trumpet squeaking up the summits of banality. She said: "Jim, do you still love her at all?"

But how could she know the color of the word in his language? How was he to glimpse the meanings of it in her own? If even Sam Grainger couldn't quite admit that divergence of language long ago (*my own language far simpler then!*) if not even Sam (*where are you?*) then how could poor Jim Doherty who had no wish to think for himself?

"What else did she say?" Hadn't Jim heard the idiot question?

It seemed to her the question had been divided, an echo-voice asking of another with another name: *Sam (where are you?) do you still love her (the name was Red-Top, remember?) or think of her at all?* Meanwhile—"She said nothing else, Jim, nothing I heard."

"Oh. I—look, I never told her—I mean—oh, *I* don't know. I—" Edith held the receiver further away with its wiry babble of misery: "I tried to make her understand—that part, all in her head—she—"

"She fell in love with what she wanted you to be."

"What? No, you're wrong, she *wasn't* in love with me."

"That's what I meant, Jim. She loved an image, not a man. Only, there was a—" (*Edith, stop! Don't say it!*)—"a tangible male involved in it too, who happened to get her pregnant."

"I—can't go for that psychological stuff. She's over eighteen. Well, I know, you can beat me over the head with the pregnancy if you want to, but since it wasn't God's will that it should live, what can I do?"

"What she said, perhaps." She heard her own voice electric, hurting in her ears. "If she were still carrying it, what *would* you do? That would be wages of sin, I guess? The way it was God's will you should try out a virgin for variety, or kicks? Or did you just feel that if an unconventional, unreligious girl wasn't a whore she ought to be?"

"I shouldn't have called. God forgive you."

Edith set the instrument down. The trembling would presently stop. Overcharge of adrenalin, stupid physical need to slash again, with claws. She fumbled a cigarette from the box by the telephone. Anyway Jim would not call back. He'd rest on the dignity of his last word, which Father Bland would have approved.

Sam Grainger was in the world, somewhere. Married probably, with one of the symphonies, teaching. His myriad hours of violin and oboe practice, piano, harmony, counterpoint, all had been aiming at that. The violin for preference, oboe because good violinists are numerous. With affection that had never perished, Edith thought: *What Sam wants, Sam earns and gets.* She noticed she was thinking in the present tense. Fair enough: it would still be true. Sam Grainger would still be a man dedicated and absorbed, immune to discouragement, too big for distractions. He had not been too seriously distracted by an affair with a redheaded art student. So what has become of the old brownstone front, shabby-sacred rooms, thready hole in the rug, genially silly print of "The Storm"—Mrs. Cardle considered that one real nice for anyone that was artistic-like—and the bed that mysteriously didn't squeak if you lay across it instead of lengthwise? What stills the music, and where are the green shadows of Arcadia?

The rooms would have accepted the whispering and secret laughter of a crowd of lovers in seven years, all giggling at sad, vague, moral Mrs. Cardle and that grayish lump of dough, her husband, whose thick delirium of hate for the antique coal furnace in the basement was very nearly a form of love. You saw the Cardles dealing with an ebb and flow of Boston lodgers world without end. But they could have been human and mortal; the brownstone could have yielded to a flat-faced office building. If it had not, though, the center flagstone of the rear yard would look the same in a sluice of rain, the crack in it like the junction of Ohio and Mississippi, seen by young eyes from the window of the third floor back.

One gray afternoon—Edith's room dim, the curtains adequate—they had stood naked near that window to watch Mrs. Cardle trying to teach her old round-bellied bulldog to roll over and play dead. Behind closed eyes and seven years, Edith felt again Sam's chin at her shoulder, shiver of held-in laughter at the dog's patient refusal to understand and its resemblance to Mr. Cardle; Sam's arm under her breasts moving, she turning then, clutching his black curls in mimic savagery, twisting free of him, racing him to the bed, caught with welcome violence and sudden entering thrust, violently held through a long course of love, an animal riot of pleasure carrying them together to the height, to the moment when the heart must break and die a little, the explosion of not-pain, the blindness and the quiet. And the quiet: summit of a hillside, also homely truth of two bodies in the aftermath of orgasm, each comic-serious detail of throbbing and subsiding organs felt, known, recorded in the mind's continuing life history with acceptance, tenderness, satisfaction, relief, amusement, wonder. Kissing him slowly in the quiet, kissing the hard-tipped fingers of his left hand, fine bony rib cage and knotty shoulders, the lifetime red mark printed under his jawbone by the violin, his other love. And—*"Time I should get back to work, Red-Top."*

Edith had been jealous, in a way, yet she had never knowingly desired to cut him down to size or usurp the government of his private world. And surely there had been cause to resent his indifference toward her own work, ambition, oriented dreaming. Not indifference: call it lack of awareness. As on that heartbreak evening when she had taken down Mrs. Cardle's "Storm" and replaced it with a darktoned watercolor, a Nolan original and, in her judgment, good.

He never saw it.

When he slipped into her room he had not seemed much preoccupied with his own studies; he just looked at the watercolor and didn't see it. Cheerful, until her darkening hopelessly unreasonable mood infected him. When the quarrel began, over something else, some damned side issue now blanked out of memory, he still didn't see the picture.

That quarrel was patched up the next night, in bed. There were others. The essential trust of two-against-the-world was gone: in the darkness behind daily perception two strangers still winced and glared, astonished at the wounds. Drift then, from radiance to near-commonplace, above the organ-point of things unsaid.

In the summer after the school year, Sam had written, once; Edith had answered, twice. End of affair. Yielding to a long assault of cancer, Edith's mother died that summer. An emptiness then, plus discouragement with art school that kept her from going back. Instead she had taken a commercial course in photography, her dazed but practical father approving and footing the bill. The following summer, a purposeful wandering in Amy the Model A (a cantankerously good little heap even now in 1959), remembering more clearly than any other conversation what her father had said before she left: "Look, Skinnay, you marry or work at something you like, or just loaf a while and raise hell, but don't turn into a dutiful daughter taking care of the old man." Shoving aside a heap of paper work brought home—the old man was a C.P.A. and a good one—and turning up to her the bald head, moon face, tenderly sarcastic eyes. "Don't do that, or I will turn you over my knee, and your fanny, dearest, is not fat enough to sustain the impact. The old man takes care of himself." A purposeful wandering, for that summer she had surely been looking for something more than a place that would do for a photographic studio; looking for maturity perhaps. Then Winchester, the investment paying off in adequate survival, plus a bit of freedom. No more letters to Sam: end of affair, diminuendo to an imperfect cadence dissonant with the organ-point, the only resolution silence.

What did we think we were doing? I was fighting to be a person? Or just to make Sam admit I must sometimes be person first, sweetheart second? A lot of the time I was just damn well fighting ... Deep inside, very likely, the daughter of earth had been weighing consequences, a simpler Eve murmuring of home, nest, security, advantages of snaring a good man when there was one to be had.

My first, my only, which for a warmblooded redhead is absurd, gentlemen, no argument. What happens? Why this other drift that for some of us, many of us, extends from months into years of accepting dullness and the erosion of daily demands, waiting for the rainbow blaze that may never appear, the heart knowing all the time that there's only one life and not much time to live it? Edith fidgeted, angry at the introspection itself, at the fatigue or laziness that held her in this armchair when some other part of her honestly wanted to get up and go to work. *O wind-sweet valley of Arcadia—remember me?*

She noticed the chill, and got up then with a flounce of irritation. Caught by Jim's telephone call, she had not yet turned up the heat for the Burrow. Maybe she wouldn't bother. Turn it up in the studio, leave the Burrow cool for bedtime. *Get to work! Or try to.*

Dust filmed the fireplace mantel. In a half-light beyond the bedroom doorway, yesterday's panties gaped lewdly from the seat of a chair. She must have been seduced by some clever idea when she was on the point of tossing them in the laundry bag. At least she had made the bed. *Too much alone, small Edith.* She remembered with a wrench of pain that early last August Cal had just about agreed to give up her apartment and come share this one. *August—* Edith carried her coat into the bedroom, hung it properly, stuffed the offending panties away.

If Callista and Jim could have spoken each other's languages? *Proposition absurd.* Callista groping out of the jungle of an ugly childhood, Jim living (till Ann died anyway) according to surface impulses and ready-made directives of social and religious authority—no, there could have been no conversation. *What ailed her, going overboard for that bundle of bad luck?* Call it chance. Swept away by need, nearness, charm of a prepossessing male; maybe unknowingly goaded in spite of herself by the dithering emphasis of American culture on sexual activity as the end, cure, meaning for everything: luv-luv-luv. And Jim no more "to blame" than she. As much an accident as falling downstairs.

A gust rattled the bedroom window and hummed across chimney-tops and died. *Go away, my love!*

Edith changed out of the green suit into a cherished dingy blue bathrobe. In the bureau mirror she glimpsed her own color and motion. Clear sky-blue eyes would hold that color a lifetime, though the irises would some day blur at the rims, the vision would not remain 20-20, lids would crinkle, brows turn sandy-gray, then white. Grooves in the forehead would deepen, and the brackets at nose and mouth. Red hair must whiten—quickly, one could hope, without streaks. That smoothness from small chin down a slim neck to the collar of Venus with no sag or wrinkle at thirty-one—well. Already crowding her luck a bit there; pretty Ann Doherty, for all her needless dieting, had been starting a tiny double chin at twenty-six. The bathrobe unbelted allowed a gleam of small breasts neat and high, jaunty and delicate, red-tipped like white peonies. *Fun for somebody, going to waste—are you listening, bitch in the manger?* Her finger tapped the unsmiling woman in the glass, and she was stricken by thought of another face, also far from the conventional norms of beauty.

They used a hood, didn't they, electrodes concealed by an intolerable obscenity of black rubber?

No thought is finished until the thinker dies, then only blotted out, the death rattle a throat-clearing for what's not to be said. Mother, the morphine not helping yet, certain she'd left something on the stove to boil over, couldn't convince her. For thought is action. What's this, Edith? Philosophy A, Radcliffe, Class of '48 and all that?

All the same, she reflected, it *is* action, and the hell with Plato the Father of Half-Truths. So why wonder that an earlier self becomes a creature of mystery? Where was the cross thin woman who talked sharply to Jim Doherty a few minutes ago? You say: It was one I who thought and acted thus and so; now I am not what I was, but I inherit any continuing good and bad and all responsibility: if I don't clean up after the person I left behind, nobody else will. That was the thorny passage, the truth too easily blurred.

Yet only a few, she thought, could endure the concept of mind-as-motion. By contrast, how apparently solid and comfortable are the absolutes, static symbols, devices of everyday talk to create the illusion of a stillness in time, so that we can draw breath and feel for a moment that we know who we are! In a ship you can stay below, avoid the portholes, ignore the long rise and fall as the vessel encounters a rolling of the sea, and pretend your cabin is a landside thing: fine woodwork, carpet, all that, and if now and then you do feel a throb of engines or tilting of the world, why, Captain God's on the bridge and will see to everything. And yet it doesn't take too much courage to go stand at the bow and discover the wind in your face: a child can do it; a grown-up can recognize the captain as skilled but humanly mortal.

Edith crossed the hall to the studio, where cool light on the drawing table waited like a reminder of courage. She took out Callista's letter, carefully as though the pages were drawings, and the large light handwriting did have some of that quality, Callista's hand refusing to waver at any disturbance of her thought:

Dear Edith:

It was good to be with you, though I was unpleasant, ridding myself of accumulated venom. I can't safely talk in my worst way to anyone else—Cecil is too vulnerable. And I miscalculated, thought we had more time, was about to shut up and hear you (what I wanted above all) but then time up, opportunity gone.

Don't try to cut the red tape for another visit after the trial opens. When I see you now I think too much, in spite of you, of what I may lose. The work, freedom, gaiety, good talk I never heard till I met you. I'd better keep my shell until this is over, I seem to need it. Stay away just because I do cherish you. Dear Edith, I'm sickened to remember how I talked this afternoon—but maybe it won't end the way my present mood says it will. A mood is only part of a journey—you said that to me once, now I keep the words with me.

Cecil came to see me after you left—he looks ill, Edith. Does poor old Mrs. Wilks really do enough about looking after him? Look—I tried to tell him more about Mother and Herb, and the Saturday night uproar with Mother that I described to you. Give him more of that, will you? I made a botch of telling him, I suppose because I love him, my mind wouldn't focus on my own mess. How does it happen (C. let it slip) that Herb is meeting so many of the incidental expenses when I said so damn plain it was to come out of my money from Father's estate? Please try to find out, will you?

I can't think straight any more tonight. I slop off into self-pity, lose track altogether. I don't believe human beings are *adequate* for this kind of thing, Edith, I know I'm not anyway. You heard me whimper once, only once. Alone, I do a good deal of that, friend, I can't help it—hermit crab's a soft blob of nothing-much inside the borrowed shell. I'm no Latimer sticking his hand in the fire. Not even jailed for a Cause, just want to live. I don't know what love is either, but now and then I wonder if anyone ever knew more about it than I do.

My love to you,
Callista.

II

Terence Mann stopped playing, tense with a dissonance of perplexity. A wrong time and mood for Chopin: his hands had been dull in the C-sharp Minor Impromptu. No music now, but an impulsive sorrow of December wind leaning against the building in the dark. *"Callista never cried."*

To Maud Welsh, that had been "real unnatural." Judge Mann did not find it so. Self-pity was not evident as a quality of Callista Blake.

He understood with almost amused distress that he *liked* the girl. That, plus old dislike for the representative of her accuser the State: how far can you go with such a bias before the judicial lid blows off?

He remembered doubtfully a talk with Joe Bass the evening before— anything more than a flurry of wishful thinking? Increase of humanitarianism in the last century and a half? Well, social history agreed, if you read it with some detachment from the immediate terrors of the decade. And the increase could hardly be ignored or dismissed except by someone bitterly in love with his own pessimism. Modern postwar pessimism, although a cult like any other, was persuasive, deceptively articulate. Something contagious in a comprehensive the-hell-with-it.

Social history made it clear that capital punishment had dwindled in frequency from a common public entertainment to something almost rare. The states still practicing it gave evidence of official shame, or at least of a schizophrenic need to serve two contraries, to appease the recurrent vengefulness of their multitudes but also to hide the dirty thing, tacitly apologize, soften its most visible nastiness in the hope that conscience would shut up and sleep again. Such a condition would be preliminary to change. Like tuberculosis and venereal disease, capital punishment was on the way out but going out in the manner of things legal, with dreary and creeping slowness. Wasn't that how he had reasoned two years ago, when his name was up in the election more or less unopposed? Or had he honestly faced it at all?

Hadn't he simply regarded a judgeship as mostly useful work and $18,000 a year? And hadn't he accepted, without enough examination, the doctrine that a judge is only an instrument of something greater than himself? An instrument of *what* something, greater than himself *in what way?* The questions projected themselves beyond the cloud-curtain of mysticism. But it seemed to Judge Mann that unless they could receive a daylight answer, the doctrine itself was solemn nonsense.

Imagining Society with a capital S to be greater than the individual—no answer there, only a more opaque mysticism. The mental construction

"Society" is an achievement of the individual brain, an organ that had better not be too dazzled by products of its own authorship.

The issue of capital punishment had been bound to arise. *I knew the laws. I knew that New Essex was no more free than any other state from crime and the balancing crime of punishment.*

From an unseeing stare at the carpet, his head jerked up as if at the entrance of another. *Balancing crime of punishment:* he had been thinking in specific words, talking to a half-personalized projection of the self, and the words had power to startle him.

It was a commonplace to Terence Mann that punishment itself is an archaic evil in the law. As special prosecutor, as defense lawyer on a few occasions, in the relatively clean region of civil law, he had tried to favor any reorientation of thought and action that might discredit punishment as a respected motivation and replace it by efforts at healing and reclamation. As a judge, familiar with the endless parade of minor offenders (most of them with no chance of redemption, for where in the modern state was there a sufficient will to redeem even the young, or the time, patience, money, wisdom, to implement it?), Judge Mann had been aware of no impulse in himself to punish, only of a desire to lessen disorder, and try for the long view. And then, Callista Blake. But—*balancing crime of punishment:* well, there it was simply his own unexpected rephrasing of the issue that had startled him. Apart from that, if that was significant, this self-castigation probably served no purpose.

Fashionable but without merit, to wail that we are all guilty. So we are, in a sense, and (unless one intends to do something about it) so what? Breast-beating is as solitary as any other form of masturbation. The modern spirit, he thought, for a long time before Hiroshima, had grown too fond of the wail, the masochistic acceptance of futility that ended in a downright enjoyment of it, a perversion as sterile as the antics of the louse-eaten monks of the Thebaid. Admit that two years ago he might not have been completely honest with himself. All right: what mattered now was that a slow broadening of reform might look very fine in the armchair perspective of a history book, but was no use at all to Callista Blake, nineteen years old. Capital punishment was on the way out, taking her along with it. Therefore in the very present specific instance: *What to do?*

Wandering to the other side of the room, fingering the stacks of sheet music and the bound volumes, Judge Mann reflected that a judgeship is a very damned comfortable thing, to the nerves of pocketbook and of vanity, until a moment of self-appraisal brings you the image of a bewildered monkey in a black gown. An image caught as though in multiple mirrors. No good turning your head aside: a mirror in every wall, and the monkey, poor puzzled well-meaning bastard, in every mirror.

He did not want now the fury or grief or laughter of Beethoven; not now the lofty tenderness or robust passion of Johannes Brahms. He took down his one-volume edition of the *Well-Tempered Clavichord* and glanced at a memory-stirring litter of pencil marks made long ago in the curly script of his teacher Michael Brooks. Mr. Brooks had died before the war, very old and partly blind. He might live another hundred years in these marks, far longer in the spreading influence of his fifty years of teaching, the impetus he gave to other lives continuing beyond any knowledge or measuring. *Very good, Terence!... More slow trill practice absolutely essential!! Andante does not mean Adagio. In this Prelude schmaltz is possible but I do not like it. Excellent but you could do better. Bring out the inner voices.*

Mr. Brooks grew vivid in memory, speaking with difficulty and panting breath because of age and the burden of fat that seemed (till you learned better) as though it might block his pudgy improbable hands away from the keyboard entirely. He had been seventy when Terence at age eight began lessons; he went on teaching twelve years thereafter. Terence remembered the gray eyes, tiny-appearing, sometimes inflamed, in folds of drooping lids and fat, the completely hairless skull rising to a peak, the wondrously ugly features that after the first impact of astonishment left the word "ugly" without meaning. "You think the Fugues are dry, Terence? Bring out the inner voices.... See, Terence, all the composers have something for you. But when you are unhappy—" blinking, sighing, coughing; and Terence recalled a child's botheration, dread of giggles, at an old man's prolonged throat-clearing, guttural noises, conversational spray, habit of patting forlornly at the air when a needed word was gone from him—"or when you have discovered that happiness is only a sometime thing at best, not too important, then try Bach, Terence, try Bach. Because he will let you enter a place where you become bigger than sadness or happiness. And bring out the inner voices."

He set the old book on the piano. Hands and brain were tired, the hour late, though the neighboring apartment-dwellers were tolerant and often kept their mechanical music perking until after midnight. For a while he was in that place: *Well, Mr. Brooks, "container and thing contained": aren't we always bigger than what stirs within us? All the same it was a good way to talk to a child.* But the very facility of his hands betrayed him, leaving his mind too free. Good at first, to continue private thought while Bach was speaking, but then only another troublesome dividing of the self.

Terence's father, not a patient man, would have said at this point or sooner: "God-sake, Terry, make up your mind!"

He would have said that, before 1928. In that year Father changed. And maybe the gray and harassed man could have entertained doubts earlier in his life on such an issue as capital punishment. He didn't have a closed or ungenerous mind; he couldn't afford to, a small-town doctor with two skittish growing boys and a wife who came to believe herself in deep other-worldly communication with Mary Queen of Scots. But many of Father's opinions were formed when he was a young man in the era of Teddy Roosevelt, and he didn't always remember to speak softly. Unlike his older brother Uncle Norden, who must have early learned the advantages of speaking softly at great length—anyhow Uncle Nord built up that accomplishment into a thundering good law practice.

Father (before 1928) would likely have said if you asked him that criminals so hardened as to commit murder—oh, put 'em out. For the good of society. Human failures: the unfit—odd word much loved by the nineteenth century, used apparently in a sort of gentleman's agreement that no one was going to ask: unfit for what? Father would not have spoken so out of vindictiveness or lack of human feeling: just the impatient judgment of a busy man with troubles of his own, who accepted a number of antique notions because he grew up with them. That few hardened criminals ever commit murder, that most murderers have acted on a blinding impulse unlikely to recur—such facts would have been outside his mental territory, and unacceptable. Knowledge of what Father would have said was for Terence a bloodstream thing, no longer traceable to any remembered words. Like most people including doctors, Dr. Carl Mann had never witnessed an execution, nor known anyone well who wound up in jail. Gentlemen don't.

After Elinor Mann's final breakdown and commitment, Father no longer announced his views with much positiveness. In that year 1928 the bottom fell out; Dr. Mann couldn't even get positive about Al Smith, in spite of a long-standing rage at the imbecilities of Prohibition. When not meeting the heavy demands of a country medical practice, he was beating out heart and brain in a private crucifixion, asking himself the wrong questions: *What could I have done differently? Where did I fail her?* As though a clarification of his own past might even then help to restore Elinor's mind, that had never really tolerated the difficulties of living before it made permanent retreat into the smoke of paranoid fantasy.

Terence's hands fell away from the piano, leaving the third Fugue unfinished. How had he arrived at contemplation of that time-eroded grief? The subject was Callista Blake, not Elinor Mann.

Who still lived, if you could call it that, in the curiously ordered world of yellow brick and manicured lawns that was Claiborne Hospital. She was seventy-eight this year, clouded by senility along with the psychosis. She recognized Terence on his visits, listening or seeming to, usually with patiently closed eyes, as he toiled to create a conversation.

Jack, successful in his own psychiatric practice, had more difficulty when he drove or flew from Boston to see her. Thirty-one years ago the cobwebs of her delusions had wrapped themselves inextricably around the life of the elder son, four years older than Terence and at that time in his Junior year at Harvard. Her voices (many others along with that of Mary Queen of Scots) had informed her that Jack was increasingly involved with gangsters and women of ill fame. The college authorities and, for some never-explained reason, Mayor Jimmy Walker, were all in it together. When she was on the point of going up to Cambridge to deal with all that, Dr. Carl Mann, goaded at last into understanding, said no. She flung an inkwell in his face and gouged it with a pair of scissors; though he was fairly muscular and she was not, it required the help of his office nurse to restrain her. Most of that was over, the dust settling, when Terence, sixteen years old, got home from school. Now in her antiquity the sorrows, fantasies, and angers of the past were still preserved for her by the specialized, selective memory of the schizophrenic, flies in amber. A year ago, Terence and Jack visiting her together, she told Terence that she could easily have forgiven poor Jack if he had lived. Then it came out, in a natural, pleasantly quiet conversation, that the slim gray-haired man sitting over there was nothing but a body, stolen for no good purpose by the unclean spirit of Henry VIII. Later, at the airport, Jack remarked: "Psychiatrically speaking it may be a poor symptom, but don't mind it, Terry. I'll make out all right as hell-fire Harry Tudor. Less of a strain than some of my other roles."

"Beyond psychiatry, isn't it?"

"If you mean beyond effective therapy, yes, boy." "Boy" from Jack was acceptable—always had been. "It was beyond existing therapy thirty years ago." Jack also counted years. "We just don't know the score on paranoid schizophrenia. We know approximately what to expect, which is something maybe. Mental disease could be the last holdout among medical enigmas, Terry. We may be sweating out cases like Mother's when there's a pill or a shot for cancer. It's the—oh, the inaccessibility of mental action." Jack had been tired, but not remote; fatigue never dulled a shining quality of his alertness. "Wait till you get some big case in court with a borderline paranoid as a star performer."

That conversation of a year ago had been hampered, Jack waiting on the start of his plane flight back to Boston; no leisure, bustling strangers, time pressure, uproar of loudspeakers and warming engines. Was it relevant now? Callista Blake a borderline paranoid? Rather urgently and emphatically, Judge Mann thought: *No, she's not.*

Psychiatry more or less stood in the wings, in *People vs. Blake.* The State's man called her legally sane. If he hadn't, the State would have had no trouble shopping around for someone who did. Warner had had the girl examined by a Dr. Coburn, who might or might not testify; so far Warner had dropped no hint suggesting an insanity defense.

Inaccessibility of mental action: that was relevant. Dominantly. For wasn't that the very essence of the principle of "reasonable doubt"? And was there any rational formula anywhere in the law, except the principle of reasonable doubt, at all likely to save Callista Blake?

Must see Jack again, soon. He looked out on the city's darkness past a false curtain of window-glass reflection; a city of magic under a lens of illusion, as long ago in the creaky white-pillared house in Emmetville where he grew up he used to look out from the bedroom he shared with Jack, at images that would not live by day. Especially on rainy nights the vacant lot on the other side of Maple Street became for the boy transfigured, a garden of living shadows; sometimes, under the lash of wet wind, even the sea as Conrad and Melville had given the sea to him. In winter, leaves fallen, one could look past the few naked trees at the back of the lot, to a gleam of water a mile away, Walton Pond reflecting the motion and glitter of the railroad yard on its far side. Every night at 9:25, the ghostly passage of a fourteen-car express (to Terence and Jack, The Express)—one of the great trains that couldn't be imagined as stopping at Emmetville. You did not hear its thunder, only saw the silent gliding of windows; then thirty seconds after the vanishing came the desolate splendor of the whistle crying for a grade crossing, the night imperfect until that music had fulfilled its mission and died. *See him again; and bring out the inner voices.*

The once vacant lot was now occupied in front by a filling station, in the rear by a drive-in theater; as a passion-pit, that probably served on a mass-production basis the same purpose once served by the vacant lot, where he and Jack occasionally discovered and snickered at the discarded rubber, stained handkerchiefs, and other detritus of hasty lechery. As for the gracious white house, where Terence had once known every spot, every squeaky board and dim hideaway in closets and under the eaves, it now belonged to someone who had made it a Tourist Home with noxious plastic animals on the front lawn, and called it Tumble Inn. So perish treasures of the spirit, to be born elsewhere in other guise, perhaps.

And he remembered the evening after his mother's commitment was made definite. Jack had been home for several days, his presence helpful in the confusion, the curious desolation like and not like a death; Jack would be returning to college in the morning. Terence had gone to bed; Jack was about to, lazily delaying. "How honest shall we get, Terry? Are you, inside of you, relieved? I am." Half undressed, Jack stood over Terence's bed, smoking, in ever-observant kindness.

"I guess I am."

"Bad, the last few months?"

"Each day a bit stickier. The moods. No—no way of *talking* to her. Every remark turned upside down. Like trying to see a room in a twisty mirror.... Jack—"

"What, kid?"

"Does it mean we shouldn't marry?"

"No." His brother's quiet hand waved away smoke from between them, and the question too. "It's probably not hereditary. Anyway your children get half the endowment from *their* mother. Marry a mattress type, Terry, brains optional. No, come to think, you couldn't get along with a clothhead. Make it a mattress type *with* gray cells; they do exist. Might have to hunt around a little. Testing mattresses." Jack sat down and spread his left hand light and warm on Terence's chest, frowning off at the window, saying to it: "Got a kid brother with social conscience yet."

It was, at sixteen, the first time Terence had encountered the full revelation of love for another, seeing that other as a complete human being all the more beloved for his separateness. He said only: "Not hereditary—how can you be sure, Jack?"

"Nobody's sure—just the best educated guess. I saw this coming more than a year ago. Had to study into the thing for my own sake, Terry: books, talk with one of the Psycho faculty up there who seems to be able to tell his ass from a barrel of flour, useful accomplishment. I had to answer that question you asked, and others. Like for instance asking a character I saw in the mirror: How about you, Jack, you going that way too one of these days? Studying it seemed to be the only method of meeting it head on."

"That why you switched to premed courses this year?"

"Partly. Would've anyhow, I think. Mother's brains began to get hurt and kicked around when she was small, I think—but not by the genes. Wish we'd known Grandpa and Grandma Kane. They seem to have been a lovely pair of pious frauds, probably started raping her wits as soon as she could talk. Uh-huh, Terry, I've got every intention of marrying and plowing a few seeds into that interesting furrow. You will too, my guess."

Terence had felt then a hunger to talk bawdy and blow the lid off in words; wondered also if he would cry, because of the secret inner fire that held no name in the language: happiness was not the name, and the new-discovered love for his brother was only a part of it, an opening of a door. "Got something all lined up?"

"Nope—playing the field. A premarriage elective. Technical studies, how to tease down the most drawers with the least squawk." He said that with no leer but a mild pagan amusement already far removed from the idiom of Emmetville. (As it turned out, Jack went on playing the field quite a while, not marrying till he was thirty-nine; in his terms that probably made sense too.) "You haven't tried it yet, Terry?"

The sixteen-year-old Terence flushed unhappily and shook his head on the pillow, wishing there had been a hundred experiences, suppressing an impulse to invent a few. But Jack wasn't dismissing him back to childhood. Jack said: "I hear tell, and ancient memories within this senile bosom do confirm, that in every well-conducted high school there is at least one—how shall I put it with utmost delicacy?—at least one kitty with an available pussy. Or two, or three." He grinned and took his hand away. "Relax, boy. There's no rush." As he finished undressing with his unfussy neatness, he asked: "Remember Cassie Ferguson, in my class?"

"Cassie—black hair, skinny, lot of eyebrow. Well well."

"Did the quiet, you-be-damn manner fool you? The ones who put out for the joy of it don't make much noise about it. Cassie was very very good for me. More tricks than a monkey on a greased flagpole." Jack turned out the light and sat on his own bed for a final cigarette; he said softly, recalling childhood: "We missed The Express. Did she blow?"

"She blew, she blew ..."

"Good night, Terence Mann."

He turned from the window, from the lights of Winchester. He ran the blunted tip of a thin finger along the edge of the piano's raised leaf, a motion of affection: another friend. A friend not exactly left behind when he went to law school, but—

It seemed to Judge Mann that his present way of existence, compared to that of, say, Michael Brooks, was not very successful, important, or useful to others. A majority of his countrymen would assess it differently of course: Mr. Brooks, never a concert performer even when young—poor health, no presence, no glamor—why, the old boy probably did well to make three thousand a year, if that. Obviously the bitch goddess wouldn't have looked twice.

He wondered (not long) why the thought of another face, familiar and vigorously detested, should have crowded away the cherished ugly features of Mr. Brooks. This face was a handsomely carved block of chilly pink meat under white hair. High falcon nose, flexible lips that squeezed a manifest delight out of elaborately precise diction. Words did not simply pass through the lips of Judge Cleever: they were escorted out, by a pair of busy pale red snakes, the only organs of the man's face that ever knew emotion. The lips writhed, twisted, enjoyed, were sickly passionate: "that you be taken hence to the place from which you came, and thence, at the appointed time, to the place of execution, where—" but give the dreary old cannibal credit, the apparatus under that raptorial beak would squirm with the same enthusiasm when it was ordering a poached egg. The pallid blue eyes of this pillar of society were astonishingly dull. Cleever was an earnest prohibitionist: no drink, no smoking, no cussing, likely hadn't been laid in thirty years, yet you could observe similar eyes whenever the drunk tank yielded its human load to the courts and hospitals. To learn of an original thought behind those soggy irises would be nearly as incredible as to learn of a generous one. Cleever had been a judge since the days of the political machine preceding Timmy Flack's, into his present miasmic twilight of senility. Automatically, in a new trial, if Terence Mann were for any reason disqualified, he would sit in judgment on the life of Callista Blake.

Thanks, Judge, thanks to your obscene simulacrum for reminding me of several things I must not do. Terence Mann flexed his hands to relieve a tension; then he played the third Fugue, to completion this time, and well enough. Mr. Brooks would have rubbed his fleshy nose and said: "Mmm."

Then he was compulsively searching through a pile of long unused material, until he unearthed the beginner's book, the first-grade instruction prescribed by Michael Brooks. He remembered insisting, eight years old, that he must pick out the book personally, so off to Simms' Music Store in Winchester with the tickled, slightly bumbling Doctor, who knew everybody and took occasion to introduce him to the lantern jaw and slow-motion smile of Hubert Q. Simms; and embarrassed the toe-twisting bejesus out of the boy with some well-meant cockadoodle about "latest threat to Josef Hofmann." Then four blocks down Court Street to (Terence hadn't quite believed it) Judson's Piano Store. This same piano now standing here thirty-nine years later, rather old as such things go but good as new. The Doctor's way, taking such a plunge out of nothing but faith in a small boy's dream. Probably that year he'd been just barely able to afford it. *He should have lived another forty.*

But Dr. Carl Mann, in the early winter of 1930, not drunk for he never was, a blue ugliness of ink still visible in the long seam of scar tissue across his face, his financial affairs well in order—in fact very little hurt by the smash of 1929, for country people still got sick and still paid for it as well as they could—and the night cloudy, yes, but no rain or ice on the roads, happened somehow to drive his car into the concrete abutment of the railroad overpass at Pritchett. His only unkindness the matter of uncertainty. It could easily have been a syncope as the coroner decided, or a mechanical failure of the car concealed by the total smash. Or the Doctor might have been uncertain himself, up to the last blind instant of no return.

Here anyway was the instruction book, pages gone brown at the rims, and with the script of Michael Brooks. *Eyes on the notes! Get rid of that shoulder-arm tension!!*

Judge Mann carried it to the armchair, with a go-to-bed glass of brandy. Not all those careful fingerings had been written in by Mr. Brooks. The last half of the manual (he had forgotten) had quite a few figures in an eight-or nine-year-old hand (correct too!) placed there after he had got by the first few hurdles with his enthusiasm still afire. The book would be more or less out of date, Judge Mann reflected: modern pedagogy had new notions, some good, some not.

He wondered if he was examining this relic from a middle-aged need to get nearer somehow in time to the mind of Callista Blake. Partly, maybe. Certainly the dignified black notes before his eyes, the passages of the third Fugue remembered, The Express, the first discovery of *Huck Finn*, *Moby Dick*, Beethoven Opus 57, the embrace of a Filipino girl whose body was a little golden candle flame—certainly none of all that had the effect of shutting away Callista Blake. She was very present. ("*Which is the Clerk?*") But more than anything else, here at the frayed, tired, lonely end of the evening, he was wondering—practically too, and with the special fascination of such practical problems—how he would go about helping a child beginner to free the fourth finger, strengthen the fifth, accomplish the small-immense passage from the five-finger cage to the wide-open country of the octave. And he found that he meant just that: how *he* would do it, he, Terence Mann, age forty-seven, not merely Judge of the Court of General Sessions in and for the County of Winchester, but also a pianist of more than decent competence.

If in the habit of speaking aloud in loneliness, he supposed he could have said reasonably to the imagined presence of Callista beyond the bright amber of the brandy: *Not now, not while your life is proposed for burning, Callista. But afterward, maybe. Afterward. Possibly a letter to the New Essex Bar Association, explaining how for me the law has been an interlude of a quarter-century, and interesting, but now I would rather attempt something that I find more important. Which would annoy the holy hell out of them, Callista, but all the same I may write it.*

A curious thought which he took to bed; sleeping quite soon, to encounter the inner voices of sleep, with moments of tranquillity.

III

She saw it behind her eyelids, a small cloud but deep, suddenly come, suddenly gone. The light strengthened; there was the rock, and a whiteness in the water. *How could you know, Callista, that she was dead?*

She had, as usual, dared to move her cot nearer the wall with the barred door and the graffiti, so that if she crouched at that end of the cot a triangle of shadow protected her from the glare of the naked bulb in the corridor. Matron Kowalski on night duty had a habit of turning that light off and on at chancy intervals after midnight. Regulations probably said it should burn steadily, but Kowalski was a zealous screw when not deep in a comic book, and doubtless hoped to catch her charges in bottomless wickedness by playing cute with the switch. Short-sighted as well as thick-witted, Kowalski had apparently never caught on to Callista's crime of moving the cot. Callista generally tried to retrieve the sin before Matron Flannery came on in the morning, though whenever she forgot, Flannery just looked sad and grumbled: "Now dearie, we gotta put that back where it belongs or it's my arse." And sometimes even shoved it back herself with a heave of a massive thigh.

Interesting but maybe unprofitable, to contrast that kindness with the satisfaction Flannery had shown a week ago in disciplining a shouting and clawing wench who didn't want to go downstairs. Flannery had caught the girl from behind with an arm like a side of beef, in the pattern of rape, a stiff block of finger jabbing at nerve clusters here and there, leaving no mark. And if Callista Blake the Weird Woman, Cold Callie the Monkshood Girl, were to create a disturbance, Flannery would be ready, would spread her flat feet and grunt in the same way, like a boar in rut, in the interest of law and order.

"I want more heat, I want more foodibles. I want more heat, I want more foodibles." The old woman down the corridor had been silent a while, the interval like the recession of a toothache. Hearing her resume, Callista dropped her face on her knees, listening more or less. Listening is an act of living. Listening, the human unit can at least say: I am not dead, I am here, I can prove it, the current of life is dancing in the delicate nerves, the brain recording, comparing, remembering—understand, I am not dead!

"I want more heat, I want more foodibles." She sounded plaintive at the moment, harping on a single string, a note in it much resembling enjoyment. The name was Watson; the nearly baritone voice brought the image of a body shriveled and small, crowding seventy perhaps. "I want more heat, I want more foodibles." Watson must have been picked up Sunday as a D&D, Callista supposed, raising hell somewhere in the chilly streets until somebody called the wagon. She couldn't be drunk now, two nights later, but the noise continued unchanged. She didn't belong here of course. "Ya-*hoo*! Kiss my cold aching ass, you dirty-dirty-dirty—all rise! All rise! I want more heat, I want more foodibles." Sooner or later the fumbling dustmop of the law would pick her up, shake her out into a different sort of institution. Or back to the streets and whatever dim hole of a room she lived in—with small possessions? Old photographs? Sewing-basket? Rocking-chair? "All rise!"

"You Watson, you shaddap." The voice of Kowalski.

"Fuck you, Polack, I want more heat, I want more foodibles."

"Listen here, you don't shaddap, I'm coming in there again."

"Yah!" Weary, diminuendo, but not actually a sound of yielding. Silence followed, as dust settles after an eddy of wind.

Callista tried to review the course of the day, long in retrospect. Maud Welsh all morning. Sergeant Shields, sober, exact, not unkind: four bobby pins and a paper clip. Sergeant Peterson a bleached mechanism for the production of not very good photographs, including one of the rock and the pond by daylight, not the light of a troubled and hazy moon. Trooper Curtis, plaster casts and fingerprints and so what? Sutherland R. Clipp who did everything. Trooper Carlo San Giorgio the nice boy. And Dr. Devens. None of them except Maud Welsh had remained very long on the stand; Cecil who understood the nature of the conflict had let most of them pass by with little or no questioning. Callista found she was remembering too mechanically; names and faces would not coalesce to any rationally useful larger pattern. Yet at some point—she thought it was during the testimony of Cousin Maud—something had been done or said that had lessened the opacity of the Blank, like a hint of dawn or false dawn beyond a dirty window.

Or was it anything done or said? Cousin Maud of the Plum Jam understood nothing of the interview with Ann at Covent Street, a happening far outside the cage where the life of Cousin Maud fluttered and squeaked. Perhaps this was the way of it: during the examination of Cousin Maud the Blank had thinned temporarily, of itself; a coincidence in time, maybe nothing to do with any word spoken. Probably during the cross-examination, when Cecil was questioning Maud about the Saturday night, the bedroom scene—*A sorry Hamlet I made!*

"Fuck your stinking jail too! We got rights, Polack. You ain't saving the taxpayers nothing, we all die of pee-neumo-nia, they gotta pay for a box.

Listen, I been flang out of better jails before you was old enough to shove a finger up it. I want more heat, I want—"

Callista winced at the smack of Kowalski's feet passing her cell. She heard the clash of keys, clang of the iron door, high anticipatory whimpering (still that note of enjoyment?) broken off by the crack of a flat hand against flesh, repeated and repeated, Callista's body clenching in misery at each repetition of the sound, her scream of protest choked into silence by a bitten lip. *They can't! Stop it!* But it had happened the same way last night, would happen again and again, maybe always, here and there in the world, throughout the extent of foreseeable time: how long is that? Callista's fingernails were hurting her legs. Her mind held firm somewhere, listening.

Watson wasn't yelling much. She hadn't last night either, only a small rhythmic outcry. Mouse in a trap. "You gonna quiet down now?"

"Uh-huh. I'm sorry, Kowalski."

"Mrs. Kowalski."

"I'm sorry, Mrs. Kowalski. Gi' me a butt."

"This ain't no charity ward." Anger spent, Kowalski probably just wanted to get back to her comic book. "Nor you ain't no psycho, you're putting on to get attention, beat the rap for what you done wit' your busted bottle. All the jerks on Mullen Street, you had to stick it into plain-clo'es cop. That was crazy, but now you're crazy like a fox. You know that t'ing punt'red his intestyne? Still in hospital, and that ain't good news for you, Crazy-like-a-fox."

Watson giggled. "Couldn't he'p it, he wasn't nothing head to foot on'y one big turd. Gi' me a butt. Just one, huh, please?"

"God give me patience!" That noise of Kowalski's was mechanical, a kind of breathing, blurred by the iron clang. Callista was standing by her own cell door. "Matron—"

Kowalski's square bulk swung about, her flat face slipping into shadow as her head turned from the light. "You, huh?"

"Will you take her a pack of mine? I don't use 'em much."

"Got plenty, huh?"

"Yes." Callista held the pack through the bars. Kowalski made no move to take it. "I'd like her to have it."

"You'd like.... You feel pretty big, don't you, *Miss* Blake? You feel real big wit' them cigarettes. I t'ought we was just dirt, now everyt'ing's okay, you can bend low 'n' give an old woman a pack of your butts." She held her voice down; Watson was mumbling and crooning to herself, perhaps not listening. "Maybe it wouldn't occur to you, *Miss* Blake, but that old trot's got pride. She ain't lickin' up no at'eist prisoner's dirty leavings. Me neither. Miss Blake, I wouldn't touch you not by a ten-foot pole." Callista saw thumb and forefinger of the woman's hand pinched in a circle at the shelf of her breasts. Her soft tones had lost distinctness, slipping back into the vaguer argot of a South Winchester childhood. "Ain't comin' in 'ere, not 'less Sheriff or somebody gives me direc' order, you can drop dead. You ain't human, you're a stinkin' t'ing, you can hang yourself I won't go in, leave you for Flannery to find by the morning."

Callista put the cigarettes away and sat on her cot gazing at interlaced fingers, trying (as if the time allowed were not short but the need urgent) to grasp the nature of hatred, especially in this new guise. Kowalski had not displayed it before, had seemed only an indifferent mechanism busy with her job. It occurred to Callista that she herself must have been shamefully unobservant. Did others unsuspectedly ache with this kind of loathing for her? T. J. Hunter? Cousin Maud? Jim? *Why?*

"I guess you don't talk, you can't be bod'ered."

"No, Mrs. Kowalski, I'd rather not talk."

"Oh, you'd rather not. Much too good to talk to a dumb Polack. Let me tell you somet'ing, Miss Blake, what they do after they pull the switch in that little room—what they do, they take out the heart, doing the oddopsy, understand? No matter you got lots of money, 'r' gonna be buried fancy somewheres, they take out the heart. They got a reason. All right, you don't talk."

Kowalski stood there a while longer, exercising great courage perhaps, or having faith in the cold iron of the bars. Then Callista sensed that the woman had gone away. *I will think about the night of Saturday, the 15th of August.*

Cousin Maud must have been telling the truth about that episode on the front porch. Callista could not remember seeing or hearing Ann then, but Cousin Maud would not have lied.

How unmistakably the bedroom was Mother's! Nothing there of Herb, who slept at the far end of the upstairs hall in a room Mother indulgently called "his den," as one might refer to a cat's favorite basket. Well, the entire house merely tolerated Herb Chalmers, who after all did nothing except own it, pay taxes and upkeep, and exist there. *Poor Herb! If only he wasn't so inclined to agree with that estimate himself!* By contrast, the spook of The Professor, the great Malachi Chalmers so respectably dead, was quite at home. Cousin Maud liked to behave as though all major directives were announced jointly by The Professor and Victoria.

The room smelled of Victoria, a scent resembling dilute vinegar now and then penetrating the ordinary flavor of sachet and face powder. That night, without asking, Callista knew her mother had been sitting for some time at the antique secretary desk, dealing with correspondence of the Thursday Society of Shanesville. And Victoria, after her absent-minded greeting, would go on sitting there preoccupied, long enough to make the point. "I'm sorry I didn't know you planned to come out tonight, dear."

"No plan—impulse. I wanted to talk to you, Mother."

"Oh, something terribly important? Well, dear, just make yourself comfortable till I'm through here and we'll have a nice little visit." Callista stood near the desk, where Victoria must at least be aware of her. "I wish you would sit down, Callista. It is a little trying to be stared at when one is attempting to concentrate."

"Sorry. But I wasn't staring at you, Mother." That was true. Her mind, too swiftly to be caught in the act, had generated an image perhaps well worth staring at: a thing approximately sixty days old (for it must have been conceived in the deep middle days of June) possessing a bent head larger than the blob of body, stubs with a blind intent to become legs and arms; a thing charged with the strain and pressure of life, and yet finger and thumb (if they could reach it) might pinch it out of existence like a soft bug: *Mrs. Chalmers' grandchild.* Callista's hand, driven by involuntary thought, dropped to rest at the level of her womb where the thing sheltered inaccessible—whether a motion of hostility or protectiveness or both, impossible to say; and Mother would never notice. "I was staring at something that happened a long time ago. You may not remember it. I wanted to find out if you did."

Resignedly, Victoria capped her pen and laid it on the unfinished letter; took off her amber-rimmed reading glasses and retired them deliberately to their case. "Callista, I must say that for anyone so young this habit of mulling over past events is not healthy, not the way to become adjusted to reality."

"I know, Mother. I'm not in tune with the times, am I?"

"If you realize it, I dare say that's a step in advance."

"What," said Callista, "is the virtue of being in tune with the times when the times are corrupt?"

"Callista, I am rather tired. Must we have one of your—your rather naïve philosophical discussions? All part of the process of adjustment I dare say, but frankly I am not up to it."

The big questions, Callista thought, always break the line and swim away. Too big, and a weak line; who wants the great dangerous things anyhow?

Not Mrs. Chalmers nor the Thursday Society. "Mother, do you happen to remember the time I spilled that nitric acid?"

"Happen to remember! Callista, that passes belief." Large gray upturned eyes filled with tears. "I am not a monster. Am I?"

"I'm sorry, I spoke clumsily. I meant, do you remember the details? I was going-on-five—it's difficult—"

"What details? Naturally I remember them all perfectly. What do you want to know?" The sharpness was excusable; yet Callista wondered whether she truly regretted the cruelty of that blurted question. Hamlet, Act III, Scene 4—she had reread the play in the afternoon. A catalytic action, although it had been a seemingly random choice, a turning to Shakespeare for relief, illumination, distraction, and something more, in a time of trouble, as another might have turned to music, or physical exertion, or the warmth of a friend. Her thought still rang with it, reverberated, and she understood now that the choice had not been random at all: "*Let me be cruel, not unnatural: I will speak daggers to her, but use none.*" "Your father was drunk, Callista, otherwise I don't suppose even he could have been so heedless as to leave that bottle where a child could knock it over. Is that what you wanted to know?"

"No. That's only what you've told me before. Drunk?"

"Of course."

"It keeps coming back to me that his face was burning."

"What?"

"His face was burning. It was the malaria. Wasn't it? You've told me yourself, he brought that home from New Guinea, latent but never cured."

"Oh, he had that, yes. A mild form."

"Mother, malaria is not mild if it gives you recurrent fevers and collapse. I've read up on it. I had to, trying to understand."

"You're very full of book knowledge, certainly."

"I've found more truth in books than in people. A mild form—why, two years later he *died* of it, didn't he?"

"Now, my dear, your father died, and I think you know this perfectly well, of pneumonia. The doctor informed me that the malaria was at most a—a complicating factor. The pneumonia was induced by exposure, and that in turn was caused by his passing out, as they call it, on a January night, in a drunken stupor, on his way home from a bar."

"A drunken stupor, or a blinding fever. I was seven; I remember hearing you answer the telephone—the hospital, I suppose it was, where they'd taken him. I'd been put to bed long before, but wasn't sleeping. You were having drinks or something with Cousin Trent, after Aunt Cora and Uncle Tom Winwood left. I even remember hearing Aunt Cora say good night, and then your voice going on a long time, to Cousin Trent. I don't suppose I heard many of the words, but I knew the tone, the one you always used when you were explaining Father's shortcomings."

"Callista!"

"Wait! I must tell you what I remember, but not about this; I mean the earlier time, two years earlier. Let me tell you what I remember of that, and then I'll go. I remember running into the studio, dragging my red fire-engine. Father was on the couch. He'd been working, the big table was littered with his things. He sat up and smiled and held out his arms to me. I climbed into his lap. When he kissed me his face was burning, his hands shaking. I know he talked to me, but the words won't come back. Except 'Draw me a big horse and a little horse.' Then I remember lying belly-down on the floor, working with crayons—the horses, I suppose. And he went out of the room, for quinine probably—he had an allergic reaction to atabrine in the Army, didn't he?"

"Something like that. Callista, I can't see—"

"It was morning, Mother. Sunlight in that east window. Shining aslant across the things on his work-table. From what I've learned, what I can remember and piece together, I don't believe my father would have been drunk in the morning."

"Callista, is this your time of the month?"

"No, God damn it."

"Really! Callista, I must ask you to control yourself."

"I was never colder. I think I must have a fuller memory than most. It comes back, how serious I was about the drawing, at going-on-five. Precocious. I still possess some talent that way."

"Callista, as you know, you have a quite considerable talent that way, if you would learn to discipline it, and—well, and outgrow your taste for the unpleasantly morbid and erotic subjects that seem to attract you so much. I have never understood in fact why you chose to be so childishly disagreeable a year ago when I ventured to show some of your—your less controversial drawings to the Thursday Society. Very well, I should have asked your consent, being merely your mother. Now Mrs. Wilberforce, who is after all an art teacher of somewhat wider experience than yours, to say nothing of having written and illustrated a number of altogether charming children's books, Mrs. Wilberforce felt that one or two of those drawings showed distinct promise. Distinct promise."

"Yes, Mrs. W.'s a nice lady. O Mother, so much comes back! Spring of 1945—he was invalided home a whole year before then, wasn't he? 1944? Didn't I have him a whole year before my face was burned? Why are you crying? Wasn't it 1944?"

"1944? Yes, he came home that year. And to think, she even offered to let you try some illustrations for one of her own books, was willing to instruct you, help you in every possible way!"

"Who?—oh, Wilberforce. Yes, she's nice—what a pity the books are garbage. Why are you crying? Cousin Trent? That little man?"

"Trent—why, I never—Callista, you are hysterical."

"I was never colder. 'Mother, you have my father much offended.'"

"What? What are you saying?"

"I'm not thinking of Cousin Trent—that doesn't matter. It couldn't matter if you sneaked into the sheets with him a hundred times—"

"Callista!"

"It doesn't matter, I said. The real infidelity was in the way you treated my father, day to day, the nagging, belittlement, the wearing down, little needles of disparagement, mental castration—but I don't think you ever managed that, I think he stayed a man. I was seven when he died—you think I couldn't feel what you were doing to him, and can't remember it? I do. Even more I think of how you've gone on since then, trying to destroy him for me—why, in your view nothing he ever did was good, or wise, or even honorable. Isn't that why you cut me off from Aunt Cora Winwood—because she knew better? Mother, he was one of the gentle ones—a fault if you like—is that what you held against him? That he couldn't black your eye when you needed it? Mother, I have three paintings he did to please himself, escape from commercial work. Just three. He must have done a great deal that was never sold. There must have been sketches, unfinished things, portfolios put aside. I never asked you this before, afraid of the answer I think: what became of that work?"

"I simply will not endure any more of this."

"What became of my father's work?"

"Oh, if you mean—well, when we moved here from New York, and there was so much—"

"I was right then. You threw it away?"

"If you will control yourself and listen reasonably: yes, your father did leave certain drawings and paintings which were very obviously done to please himself, as you put it. They were—I am sorry, Callista—they were vile. No one could call me a prude, but there are certain limits—"

"Now it's out."

"Callista, I must ask—"

"They were all destroyed, all his visions? Everything beyond the level of, say, the Thursday Society—destroyed? Everything? You didn't save one charcoal sketch, one line drawing, one bit of a doodle on scratch paper? If you did I'll stay, to beg you for it—or steal it if I can. I want nothing else from you, ever, but for one scrap of my father's work I'd go on my knees."

"Callista, you are out of your mind."

"'Mother, for love of grace, lay not that flattering unction to your soul, that not your trespass but my madness speaks.'"

"Oh, this morbid dramatizing, this neurotic—quoting 'Hamlet' at me as if I—are you *laughing*?"

"Not very much. I was thinking how neither poor Herb nor Cousin Trent fits the picture very well—it doesn't matter. There's more than one way to pour poison in the ear of a king. You did it with words, millions of little nibbling words, all the years he lived with you and—and for a final dirty joke of the fates, begot me—but I think he knew I loved him, as much as a child's capable of loving, maybe it gave him something, after all he couldn't see ahead. And I was thinking: I must write to Aunt Cora, I think she'd remember the crazy brat who adored her and then couldn't come to see her any more, because Tom Winwood d-r-rinks! She might have some of his work, and might send me to friends of his, people you never knew. I was thinking, Mother, how differently you'd feel if his work could be recognized, now that he's been safely dead for twelve years. What a change! Then you'd be—what, his inspiration?"

"Callista, don't! Stop it! Do you have to break my heart completely? What have I done?"

"'Such an act'—oh, poor Mother, nothing, nothing at all. Maybe that's the worst of it. You've done nothing, just lived inside the shell of your own vanity—as everyone does, I suppose. I'm sorry, Mother. It's all right, I'm going, and I won't come back. My own vanity tricked me into saying too much, but you'll forget, and go on in your own way. I haven't changed anything. 'Assume a virtue if you have it not'—remember? 'Forgive me this my virtue, for in the fatness of these pursy times'—you don't have one little scrap, a three-line scrawl on the back of an envelope?"

Callista's mother, weeping with her head on her arms, did not answer that. To Callista, standing in the doorway not yet able to turn and go, it seemed as though all hatred and resentment had drained away suddenly from within her; including the old dark aching hatred for herself, which until then had seldom released her except at certain times in the warm presence of Edith Nolan. She would have liked to cross the room, try for some physical contact implying comfort and forgiveness with that stranger over there who still made strangled sounds of self-pity and other kinds of pain, all of them real. But having no confidence in her skill at such gestures, no illusion that a relation thus broken could ever be repaired, and fearing to lose the new-found inner quiet, Callista only said: "Good night, Mother." Downstairs then, pausing on the landing, her hand tightening on the rail as she waited on the passing of a curious nausea. Too early for the sickness of pregnancy, wasn't it? Nothing else wrong, and the nausea did pass. "*My pulse, as yours, doth temperately keep time.*"

She wondered, standing there still faintly sick, how the self of a week before could possibly have knelt in that wild garden, pulled up those innocently wicked plants, broken off the roots to be dropped in her handbag, and thought: *This way would solve everything and hardly hurt at all.* Yet the self of a week before had done that; the self of a few hours past had glanced at the brandy bottle, death dissolved and waiting, and had thought: *Have it out with Mother—there could be some of his work, maybe buried in the attic where my searching never uncovered it—and then, then probably—*

The self pausing on the landing, hand letting go the rail and moving again softly, shelteringly, over the secret life in the womb, had thought practically and sensibly: *Throw away that stunk-up mess as soon as you get home.* And the self of twenty minutes later, arriving at the apartment with a burden of abnormal fatigue and drowsiness, had forgotten—(*is there any true forgetting this side of death?*)—forgotten all about bottle and canister, everything except bed.

The self on the landing thought: *It's all right, Funny Thing, look, it's all right, I'm going to bear you. I'm going to take care of you. I can do that. I will.* Had wondered, incidentally, if the small bra wasn't already a bit tight. The girl on the landing ran a finger lightly along the column of her neck—wasn't there slightly more fullness, softness? *Should go to a dentist too—and—oh, lots of little chores. Never mind anyhow, Funny Thing, never mind the details, it's going to be all right for you and me.*

The self seated on the cot where Kowalski had left her stood up uncertainly, with a sense of listening, although she knew Kowalski was gone, Watson was keeping quiet, the night also was in a deep hush with no longer that occasional whine of wind beyond the barred glass. No one had spoken. *Unless I did.*

She glanced at the window, uneasy as though the blank of winter night beyond it had paled, and might show again some light or color if she stared patiently enough. No. Not that window. Not that blank. And no true sound of speech.

She stood with eyes closed and hands pressed over her ears. Waiting; and hearing at least the dull noise—muffled, as it ought to be on the other side of a closed door—of a bottle, heavy glass, drawn across resonant wood from the back of a shelf. Faint pop of a cork and clink of glass, and tap of high heels: "Callie, come on now! I poured a little drink for you." And that fool lying frozen on the bed down there—why, how long had that fool held herself frozen, knowing everything?

How long before that fool was telling herself: *I didn't really hear her, I couldn't make out what she said*—how long? Whining maybe before the Blank shut down complete: *It wasn't anything I did, I wasn't there, I couldn't move, anyway how could I know she'd drink it herself?* Saying later (O the Blank!) in righteous innocence to Mr. Lamson: "I don't know, I can't remember." Screaming in the secret heart where not even Cecil could hear it and understand: *I don't want to know! I don't want to remember!*

Eyes open, hands fallen, she noticed by the cot the handful of trifling possessions allowed her. She fumbled through it, unsure what she sought until her fingers held the lipstick pencil. To the wall then, dizzy and obliged to lean against the cool plaster while her hand labored, but the effort was interesting; she could feel wryly, justifiably certain that no hand had ever written *these* words on *this* wall, ever before. She stood back, dizziness gone, and saw how the red letters in the dim light took on a magnificence, a glory like tranquillity:

I AM GUILTY.

IV

Edith Nolan pressed her fingertips over eyes grown tired from work. Possibly when she opened them and looked again at the broad sheet of drawing paper on the table, she would know whether her curious urgency of the last hour, the sense of good achievement that had driven her to this exhaustion, had been something more than self-deception. A glance at her wrist watch before she closed away vision had told her it was past one in the morning. Time to quit, if she was not to arrive for the next courtroom session hopelessly unintelligent from weariness and lack of sleep.

She lowered her hands, looking very briefly down. The faces, hands, shadows of the big drawing did leap astonishingly into life; but she said half-aloud: "Not yet." She got up without another look at it and crossed the room to stand, huddling in the blue bathrobe stiff and a little cold, before Callista's watercolor of a pine tree on a windy hill. She could not quite see Callista's vision, or not as much of it as she wished; she resisted a while longer the pull of what waited for her back at the drawing table. *It may be*, she thought. *This once I just may have done it.*

In the past, no work of her own had ever pleased Edith Nolan enough to give her a complete sense of belonging by natural right in that small company who can now and then draw from the confusion of the world's raw material a new synthesis, a work of disciplined imagination worthy to last a while. She knew the company, in books, music, painting; and in at least one other person: Callista, who belonged there so inevitably that the girl had probably never even wondered whether she had a "right" to call herself an artist. In need of hard work and long study, yes, but Callista knew it, and while she had struggled and learned and enjoyed the struggle, she had still been drawing and painting as naturally as a robin sings in the morning.

Sam Grainger had considered that he did not belong. "I'm a performer," he said once, "so I may get well-to-do some day; and a performer, as of course you've noticed, Red-Top, can be an awful nice guy, *but* ... but God damn it, I can't compose, and I have a most un-American impulse to get down and lick the boots of anyone who can."

She remembered saying: "Why, you're creative." Sam had just grunted, inarticulately annoyed. In those days Edith had not been fully aware of the dismal condition rapidly overtaking that once honorable word, and Sam had been surprisingly insensitive to words and the rich changeable life of words, as if he could hear only one kind of music, or believed other kinds irrelevant. Nowadays Edith's skin crawled when the corpse of the word "creative" was being kicked around. It gave off a squashy noise; was almost as offensively decayed as the corpse of "heritage." Today everything's creative, including beauty culture, business letters, and the application of new superlatives to old laxatives. There was, Edith had heard, an operation known as "creative selling." We wait perhaps, she thought, for the day when the market will offer a creative toilet as an aid to positive thinking.

Reluctant, not quite frightened, Edith returned to the drawing table and looked down at twelve pen-and-ink faces. They returned the gaze, with intensity, with the force, savor, complexity of an authentic life that no exploration could ever exhaust. *But—my hand—My hand?*

Certainly no other. Technique of course; that much, after long effort of years, Edith could take for granted. But this—wasn't it beyond technique?

For the first time that evening—it had been nowhere near her while she was deep in work—Edith recalled Daumier's "The Jury." She took down the volume of his work, not trusting memory. After the comparison she could say *No*: a round, unworried, satisfying *No*. This curious thing of her own, this hating-fearing-loving-pitying distillation of the jury in *People vs. Blake*, owed no more to Daumier (or to Callista) than any work should honestly owe to whatever the artist has encountered in the past. Conception, development, fulfillment—unmistakably a Nolan original. Perhaps the first.

The drawing frightened her then in a different way, grown temporarily larger than her mind's resistance. These people were all looking at her, as the twelve faces of flesh and blood had seemed to for a moment in the afternoon, when someone in the row behind her had a loud coughing spell. They looked at her now, bloated Hoag and ancient Emerson Lake and cloth-brained Emma Beales and kindly Helen Butler, and by a trick of her exhausted mind they made her no longer Edith Nolan but a woman at the defense table, whose life would end or begin afresh somehow according to the will of those twelve imperfect beings. Who meant well; who wanted to "do the right thing," whatever that was; who (except maybe Hoag) wouldn't dream of turpentining a dog or pulling the wings off flies or starving a child.

She forced herself out of that illusion. Well, the illusion was at least fair evidence of power in the work. She warned herself: *Discount everything: tired; the illusion is strong because of personal involvement in People vs. Blake; by morning the pen-and-ink may be ashes.* But leaving it, turning out the light, Edith almost knew that it would not.

And she marveled, with something like the wonder of a child to whom all discovery is fresh and nothing worn down to the stale and bromidic, at the stubborn power of life to draw out of mold and decay an oak tree or a flower; out of confusion or sorrow a work of enduring good.

5

It is indeed some Excuse to be mad with the greater Part of
Mankind.

ERASMUS, *Colloquies*

I

Answering T. J. Hunter's inquiry about her occupation, Mrs. Phelps Jason of
Shanesville replied in her own time and manner: "I am a widow with a limited
private income, not employed in the usual sense, certainly not unemployed
in the sense of idle. I manage my Shanesville property as a wild life sanctuary,
and am Secretary of the Winchester County Anti-Vivisection League."

Judge Mann exhaled. One of those; human, however. In the minute-book,
belatedly, he entered the date, December 9, and the witness's name. On the
pad he sketched a dour bluejay cuddling field glasses.

"Mrs. Jason, how did you spend the afternoon of Friday, August 7th?"

She made no fussy business of verifying the date. "On that day I attended a
picnic given by my neighbors, Dr. and Mrs. Herbert Chalmers."

"Who were the others present, if you recall?"

"Besides Dr. and Mrs. Chalmers, there were Mr. and Mrs. James Doherty,
Mr. Nathaniel Judd, and Mr. and Mrs. Thomas Wayne of Shanesville with
their two children. Also Miss Maud Welsh and Callista Blake."

"Are you well acquainted with the defendant, Callista Blake?"

"Reasonably well. I met her first in 1951, when she was eleven. That is eight
years." Mann sighed and relaxed. Eight years ago, law practice at Mann and
Wheatley already routine: 1951 was the Forman will case; and spare-time
reading in constitutional law with old Joe Wheatley, Uncle Norden a dusty
memory; and creeping up on forty.

"You've been continuously acquainted with Miss Blake all that time?"

"Yes. Of course I saw less of her after she moved to Winchester."

"At that picnic, August 7th, did you have any talk with her?"

"No. We waved or nodded I suppose, when I arrived. Those picnics are quite
informal. The fact that I had no talk with her was accidental; I was engaged
with the other guests, and she was spending her time with the Wayne
children."

"All her time?"

"Why, yes, until about 3:30 anyhow."

"Did anything noteworthy happen then?"

"I don't know if I can judge what's noteworthy, Mr. Hunter."

Mann's attention sharpened at the hint of hostility. Was this State's witness by any chance intending to pull the rug out from under Hunter?

"I'll rephrase my question. At 3:30, did anything happen important enough so that you now remember it and wish to tell it under oath?"

"It's not a question of my wishing to tell it, Mr. Hunter. I do not. If I may use an old-fashioned and unpopular word, it's a matter of duty. At 3:30 Callista went alone into a wild garden back of the lawn."

"Are you yourself familiar with that wild garden?"

"Yes."

"I ask you to show the jury, on this map, the location and extent of the wild garden. And describe it in your own words, if you will."

Tense but self-contained, Mrs. Jason stood by the map, her hands moving intelligently, her voice firm and rather pleasant. Mann recalled that she had given her age as forty-seven; his own age; more weathered than himself in the face, but an outdoor type, possibly better preserved, her figure attractive and graceful. "The wild garden area is roughly square, about a hundred feet on a side. It's closed away from the lawn by a mixed hedge of forsythia and lilac. There's only one break in that hedge, an angled passage about two feet wide. It's marked here—"

"Angled—you mean the opening is on a slant?"

"Double slant, zigzag. The hedge is ten or twelve feet thick—that forsythia will take over everything. I understand the little passage has to be pruned out fresh every year."

"If it's a zigzag, then you can't look through from the lawn area into the wild garden—is that correct?"

"Correct. From the lawn it looks like an unbroken hedge. Well, the wild garden itself is just a patch where everything's been left more or less natural. There's an old paper birch. Hardy perennials."

"In earlier testimony, the plant monkshood was mentioned in connection with that wild garden. Have you seen it growing there?"

"Yes." She spoke reluctantly, returning to the witness chair.

"After 3:30, when did you next see Callista Blake?"

"About quarter past four, getting into her Volkswagen."

"You didn't see her come out of that wild garden?"

"No, I didn't happen to. I think I'd gone indoors for a while."

"You're quite certain she went into the wild garden alone? The children couldn't have gone with her, or perhaps ahead of her?"

"No, they didn't. Shortly before 3:30 Doris Wayne—she's ten—started an argument with her younger brother Billy. Mrs. Wayne reproved them, told them to sit by the picnic table and restrain their voices. They did." Mrs. Jason glacially smiled. "The origin of the argument—"

"Well, that might lead us too far afield. Just—"

"If the Court please—" Cecil Warner cleared his throat with sudden but stately sonority—"I submit that, to appease the curiosity of all present including myself, the *casus belli* between Doris and William Wayne, though doubtless not part of the *res gestae*, should be made known." Cecil was even standing, making a production of it, announcing with eyebrows and twinkle that all he wanted was to have a bit of ponderous fun and relieve the tension: what could be more innocent?

Risky, but Mann wanted to play along. He said: "Mm, yes. The rules of evidence should not debar us from ascertaining the gravamen of this ancillary conflict." *How'm I doing, Cecil? Gravamen, ancillary, each five dollars, please.* Hunter looked uneasy, not prepared with any elephantine humor of his own.

"Well, your Honor, Callista had been showing Doris Wayne how to make a squeak by blowing across a grass-blade held between the thumbs. The effect on neighboring eardrums is impressive. The argument I mentioned arose when Billy wished to perfect himself in the same peculiar art and was informed by his sister that he was not old enough."

Mann let the courtroom rumble while Cecil Warner sat down poker-faced. Now the jury could never quite forget that this was a girl who could play with children; that the children must have liked her; that children are often "judges of character" and so—maybe—

Callista this morning was looking different. Since she first appeared Judge Mann's gaze had been repeatedly drawn to her as he tried to discover the nature of the change. No make-up, dressed the same, the white blouse more wilted. But her cheeks showed faint color; her mouth was not set in such a bitter line. Once or twice when Warner whispered to her she smiled, a flash of light almost shocking in its unexpected sweetness. And when her thin face was relaxed, perhaps the only word for it this morning was—peacefulness.

With no change in the circumstances, with the troubled honest woman on the stand obviously about to do a little more toward destroying her from a sense of duty, what had Callista Blake to do with peacefulness? He noticed also that redheaded Edith Nolan had managed to get a seat one row nearer the arena, and her candid blue eyes seldom left the face of her friend.

"Mrs. Jason, did you notice Callista Blake talking with anyone but the children that afternoon?"

"When she was leaving, I saw Dr. Chalmers standing by her car talking with her, and the children ran over to say good-bye."

"No one else?"

Mrs. Jason shrugged. "Everything informal—acquaintances of long standing, no occasion for formal gestures."

"How was Miss Blake dressed that day?"

"Brown skirt, green blouse, very nice with her color."

"Did you notice a shoulder-strap bag?"

"Yes."

"Were you aware of any constraint, or hostility, between Callista Blake and any of the guests at that picnic?"

"Conclusions of the witness."

Mann said: "I'll rule it admissible. But limit yourself to the single question, Mrs. Jason."

"The answer is no, I wasn't aware of any such thing."

"Early this year, before the first of May, did you learn—by direct observation—of anything unusual about the relation existing between Callista Blake and James Doherty?"

"Objection! Leading the witness. No relevance established."

"The relevance is direct, to the question of motive."

"Objection overruled."

"Exception."

"Shall I repeat my question, Mrs. Jason?"

"You needn't. The answer is no."

"What about after the first of May?"

"I learned on the 12th of May that there was a love affair between Callista Blake and Jim Doherty." Her brusque answer, shoving aside legal caution, came on a note of regret that Mann thought could not be false. Her mind precise, somewhat fanatic, Mrs. Jason would be a truth-teller at any cost. Never knowingly unjust according to her own standards, she might wish to temper duty with kindness, but her habits of self-rule would not allow much of that. "Shall I tell of this in my own words?"

"Yes, please."

"Very early on the morning of May 12th, about two o'clock, I was walking up Summer Avenue toward the junction with Walton Road. I take walks at night sometimes, to observe the activities of wild things, also because I sleep poorly. A short walk is sometimes helpful. I knew Mrs. Doherty was away for a visit of a few days with her parents in Philadelphia, by the way. As I walked down the road toward the Doherty house there were no lights in it. I was wearing tennis shoes, walking quietly. Near the Dohertys' driveway I heard the voices of Jim Doherty and Callista, both very individual voices and of course familiar to me. They were standing together in the drive. Jim's car was there, pointed toward the road. Moonlight—I was partly hidden by roadside bushes—I'm sure they didn't see or hear me. As I was about to retreat, they sat down on the grass near the car and were then turned more toward me, would almost certainly have seen me if I had moved. The—the situation was such that I could not let them know I was there—too painful for all three of us."

"But I must now ask what if anything you saw or overheard."

"Oh—Jim said: 'What are we going to do?' And Callista said: 'There aren't so many solutions, Jimmy. Find a little strength anyway, it isn't the end of the world.' And he—I did not hear his answer."

"What else was said?"

"Callista said: 'The only real solution is one I'm not ready to face, Jimmy.' I heard nothing else that she said."

"They were just sitting there on the grass?"

She frowned. Judge Mann saw her lips move.

"I'm afraid the jury didn't hear you, Mrs. Jason."

"I said, she was holding his head to her breast."

"Your witness, Mr. Warner."

Warner stood by the defense table, one hand maintaining contact with it. "In that overheard conversation, Mrs. Jason, the name of Ann—Mrs. Doherty— was not mentioned by either of them?"

"No, sir. I've repeated everything I heard."

"Did they learn of your presence there?"

"No. I slipped away. I saw the car—well, if it matters—"

"Go ahead."

"When I was nearly to my house, I saw the car come out of the drive and go toward the Walton Road junction."

"All you learned, actually, was that some sort of love relation had evidently developed between these two?"

"Yes, sir, that's all I learned."

"Mrs. Jason, I take you to be a literate person and a lover of truth. As such, I ask you to consider the thing you've quoted Callista as saying: 'The only real solution is one I'm not ready to face.' Would you agree that such a remark, made under the conditions you have described, could be interpreted in many different ways?"

"Yes, certainly."

"For example, whatever it was she referred to may have seemed, at the time, to a nineteen-year-old girl, like 'the only real solution,' and yet the words don't give another person any actual clue as to what she meant?"

"That's true."

"As a lover of truth, would you also agree that you do not know, at first hand, one single fact, or group of facts, which would justify an inference that the love relation between these two people was responsible for the death two months later of Ann Doherty?"

T. J. Hunter was examining his fingernails with labored disgust. Mrs. Jason said at last: "That is true. I know they were in love with each other for a while; I know Ann died. So far as genuine knowledge is concerned, that's all I do know, Mr. Warner."

"Thank you. No further questions."

If he had been defense counsel, Mann was thinking, he would probably have gone too far with the woman, perhaps losing everything in the hope of winning a little more. *For a lawyer I'm not the damn type.* And Mann reminded himself that there is no type. You recognize a few general patterns, but the simplest human individual is not to be duplicated in a billion centuries.

A ruddy gray-haired man was being sworn in. Paunchy, scant of breath, his prominent eyes had the directionless belligerency of a man in some habitual dread of being laughed at. "Nathaniel Judd, sir, senior partner in the firm of Judd and Doherty."

"The junior partner is Mr. James Doherty, correct?"

"Yes, sir. Since 1955."

"Your business is real estate and general insurance?"

"Yes, sir." Judd spoke breathily on a while about that. Overweight, poor and changeable color, slow motions when his body's natural habit should have been a jerky aggressiveness—maybe what he feared was not only laughter. Jack, with his comprehensive doctor's glance, might have seen Nathaniel Judd as a candidate for a coronary, if the man hadn't already suffered one. Judd was telling how his only son, killed in action in Korea, had been a close friend of James Doherty's overseas. Doherty had written when the boy died, and had looked up Judd after his discharge. "Much as anyone could," said short-breathed Judd, "he's been like another son to me. Took him into the firm, 1955. Fine head for business. Good boy. Sixty-one myself, not too active nowadays."

"Did you meet Mrs. Doherty also that year—1955?"

"Yes, sir, soon after they settled in Shanesville, they invited my wife and me to dinner. Very nice. Met her then. Played bridge."

"Did you meet the Chalmers family then too? And Miss Blake?"

"That summer anyhow. Miss Blake was fifteen." For a lumpily modeled face, Judd's was expressive. When he mentioned her, the blobby features sagged.

"You went to a picnic at the Chalmerses', 7th of August, this year?"

"Yes. Can't add anything to what Ella Jason testified."

But Hunter fussed at it a while. Mann's attention wandered. No individual like another, no one replaceable, not vague soft Judd for instance or any other. A commonplace: why go on worrying at it, insisting that no one is expendable? *Expendable*—the stink of that word lingered from a war already part forgotten, obscured by a more vast and quiet terror. Under the new terror the politics of 1959 had been squirming in a fantastic display of the passions of a disturbed ant hill. *Expendable*: well, the first to express this obscenity must have been some thick-browed operator of prehistory, who found his fellows could be manipulated by appropriate grunts and chestthumpings into doing a concerted job of skull-busting and rape on those Bad People with a better campsite and interesting females. As the original inventor of advertising was the one (man or woman?) who first got the idea of tying a rag on the genitals.

Mann remembered how in the war years most people, having gagged a bit at the gnat of that word *expendable*, had then swallowed the camel of the fact with no great strain. *How does it happen that a man who transferred to the Medics mostly out of distaste for carrying a rifle is now a judge of General Sessions, in a state that keeps the death penalty on the books?*

"Have you met Miss Blake often since she moved to Winchester?"

"No, sir, hardly at all. We—hadn't much in common."

"I see. No ill feeling between you, was there?"

"No, sir, not that. I get along with people—try to." Judd looked more unhappy; perhaps he felt the prosecutor's silence pushing him. "Well—when I thought about it at all—guess I supposed she'd outgrow that cynical attitude, atheism, all that stuff."

"I object!" Warner spoke quietly and, for once, coldly. "Again the prosecution allows a witness to express loose, incompetent opinions."

"Objection sustained."

Hunter elaborated a patient smile. Judd looked bewildered and dismayed: what had *he* done? Warner said: "My thanks to the Court. I will express the hope that religious bias will not again be injected."

Hunter's face flamed. "There's no religious issue injected!"

"The witness has chosen to call my client an atheist. The statement is incompetent: Mr. Judd has never actually learned Miss Blake's opinions on religious matters. Why should he? And since the question of religion is totally irrelevant here, what was the purpose of that remark if not to inflame prejudice? What was the purpose?"

Callista Blake—white, cool, unreasonably peaceful—did not look up, remaining in the country of her own thoughts.

Mann said: "Mr. Warner's objection has been sustained, because the Court agrees that the witness's remark was out of order. But Mr. Warner, you are out of line too in suggesting an intent to prejudice the jury. The witness spoke carelessly, as he should have been instructed not to do. It must not be supposed that he did so with malice. If it should later appear that a religious issue *is* relevant, then let discussion of it be carried out in the closing arguments of prosecution and defense, not in the course of testimony, which must deal with facts. Counsel to the bench a moment, please."

Callista Blake did look up then, as Warner left her side. Mann felt the puzzled study of her eyes as the lawyers leaned to him, T. J. Hunter starting to whisper some comment on the clash, which Mann shut off with a wave of his hand. "Not that. T.J., your witness isn't looking good. Has he ever had a coronary, do you know?"

Hunter was startled. "Don't think so. Never said so."

"Was he that short of breath the last time you talked with him?"

"Sure. Just out of condition, I think, Judge."

Warner unobtrusively appraised Judd, and said nothing.

"All right. Watch it, both of you. Can't have him conking out."

"Mr. Judd, as a friend and business partner of James Doherty, have you often visited at his house in Shanesville?"

"Oh yes. Real often. Pretty near every month."

"Did Miss Blake ever call there when you were present?"

"No. Wait—I do remember one time. Before she moved to Winchester. Not a call exactly. Mrs. Judd and I had stayed with the Dohertys overnight, the weekend. Remember now, the girl came over Sunday morning when the four of us were getting into Jim's car to go to Mass. The Chalmerses wanted to give Jim and Ann some maple syrup they'd made on the place, and it was Miss Blake who brought it over. Spring of last year. Come to think, that was the last time I saw Miss Blake before she moved to Winchester."

"And after that, you say, you saw her hardly at all?"

Judd flushed and paled. "To be exact, sir, just once."

"Can you give us the exact date?"

"Friday, June 19th."

"And the place, and the time of day?"

"My office in Winchester. About ten in the evening."

"Please describe this occasion in your own way."

"Well, my secretary Miss Anderson had been out sick several days, so Jim and I were swamped with work. I left the office my usual time, took home some stuff. Jim said he'd stay and work late. Evening, found I'd forgotten something, drove back for it, near ten o'clock. Light on in Jim's office, door of the outer office braced open way I'd left it, for fresh air—guess that's how I came to go in so quiet, wasn't trying to, certainly. Passed doorway of Jim's office, saw Miss Blake was—in there." Judd swallowed and coughed. "Compromising situation."

"Do you mean they were embracing, something like that?"

"Call it that. Divan. Jim's office. Wouldn't've believed it."

"Was an innocent interpretation possible? She'd felt faint, or—"

"Nothing like that, sir. Slacks, underthings, arm of divan."

"Are you saying Miss Blake was nude?"

"Wearing a—a blouse."

The listeners were too intent to snigger.

"Was Doherty also undressed?"

"Part—partly."

"Were they, to your knowledge, engaged in sexual intercourse?"

"They—yes, they were."

Short of breath, the courtroom sighed.

"What did you do, Mr. Judd?"

"Stepped back—got papers I wanted—left."

"They didn't learn of your presence, so far as you know?"

"No," he said, his breath still a burden to him. "No."

"You can be certain they didn't see you in the doorway—how?"

"Their eyes were closed."

"Your witness, Mr. Warner."

Warner remained by the defense table, standing, his hands pressing heavily on the back of his chair. Callista looked as though she had heard some dull distasteful gossip about a neighbor. "Mr. Judd, did you speak of this episode later to James Doherty—or to anyone?"

"To Jim, yes." Judd's face showed unhealthy mottling. "Following Monday. Only right, I thought—had to have it out."

"You told him what you had inadvertently seen?"

"Yes. Felt I owed him that. Said—you want what I said?"

"I think you might give the substance of the conversation."

"Well, I—said it wouldn't do. Said, what about Ann? Jim was perfectly frank, honest. Told me he realized—whole affair—terrible mistake, shouldn't't've started. Said he was breaking it off. Of course I—only too glad to leave it at that, trust Jim's conscience, religious upbringing and so on. Least said, soonest—and so on."

"There was no question of dissolving your partnership with him?"

"Dissolving—heavens no! Never entered my head."

"You could find it in your heart to forgive him?"

"Not the way I'd put it, sir. You just can't condemn a man for—for one moral lapse. Could happen to any hotblooded young man."

"You are describing James Doherty as hotblooded?"

Callista Blake lowered her face in her hands. She was not weeping; her breathing was slow and regular. Perhaps, Judge Mann thought, she needed to shut away the voices, the faces, the nearness of her accusers. He noticed the newsmen scribbling busily a moment, and heard among the spectators a rustling, shifting, sighing, as if they were in some manner bound to her and could not move till her motion released them.

"I don't know. Jim's a good boy. Just sort of slipped."

"The woman tempted him?"

Hunter protested: "Counsel has strayed far from the matter of direct examination, and is trying to put words in the witness's mouth."

"Rephrase your question, Mr. Warner."

"I'll withdraw it." Warner was speaking gently, absently. "Mr. Judd, you were deeply concerned for James Doherty?"

"Of course. Terrible thing, specially if Ann—"

"Yes, you were concerned for Mrs. Doherty too, weren't you?"

"Of course."

"For anyone else?"

"What? Why, if you mean myself, I suppose—oh, I don't know."

"You weren't concerned for anyone else?"

"I don't get your drift."

"If you don't understand that question, I have no others."

"I—I—"

"I have no other questions, Mr. Judd."

Disturbed, not immediately certain of the cause, Judge Mann asked: "Do you wish to make a redirect examination, Mr. Hunter?"

"No, your Honor, not necessary. I—"

Judd's right hand groped toward his left arm and sagged away. He looked not exactly frightened, more as though shocked by some astonishing news. He said: "I wish I—" As if meekly, apologetically, he tumbled out of the witness chair in a slow sprawl.

II

The clock said half past one. Callista watched Judge Mann hurry into the courtroom, all business, dark pucker of a frown, the black robe too priestlike. It seemed to her that all present including herself were distorted by the magnifying power of ritual. As Father Bland, in the back row beside (*my late acquaintance*) James Mulhouse Doherty, would appear deceptively beyond life-size if he were wearing his magic vestments and saying a Mass.

"This Court is now in session." *Mr.-Delehanty-which-is-the-clerk.*

When did judges start wearing black robes, and why black? How long has the office of judge existed at all? How about the wig—(O the opportunity for mice!) and why did the American States do away with it?—unfair to bald American lawyers. Subject for a thesis—relation judiciary to priesthood—ecclesiastical courts—modern veneration for office of judge—has judiciary ever become really secular? In fact could it, ever? My ignorance—

"Members of the jury," said Judge Mann, "your attention, please. I have just been talking on the telephone with Dr. Garcia at St. Michael's Hospital, where Mr. Judd was taken after his collapse this morning when he had finished testifying." (*Talking-to-Edith, compare ignorance to an unplowed field.*) "It was a heart attack, as you probably realized, and the outlook for him may not be good. In Dr. Garcia's opinion, Mr. Judd's condition has probably been developing for quite a long time." (*The soil itself is ready, indifferent, to produce flowers, nice fat potatoes, or stinking weeds.*) "The attack occurred, please remember, when his testimony was done. Legally the situation is this: Mr. Judd's collapse has no bearing on the case you must deal with. He had completed what he had to say; Mr. Hunter had announced he didn't intend to make a redirect examination. During this long noon recess I have talked with both counsel; neither side felt there would have been any occasion to recall Mr. Judd. While he testified, I think you'll agree, Mr. Judd was in full command of his faculties, so far as anyone can tell. Give his testimony the same weight, no more and no less, that you would if his breakdown had not happened; simply try to shut it out of your minds. To my certain knowledge, neither counsel was aware of the bad state of Mr. Judd's health. Both counsel believed him as well able to stand the emotional strain of giving testimony as any other witness. Mr. Judd undoubtedly believed this himself. Dr. Garcia tells me Mr. Judd had neglected medical attention for a long time and was unaware of his heart weakness. I charge you now, and will again: remember this thing happened outside of the trial."

The Judge was laboring, Callista understood, laboring too much perhaps, to defend Cecil Warner and through Warner herself, against the chill poison of unspoken words, illogical notions. If Nathaniel Judd died, no one would blame Mr. Hunter for summoning him, but many would recall Cecil Warner's words: "If you do not understand that question, I have no others." For certain minds it would be no strain to argue: *Judd died, therefore the Blake girl is guilty.*

It could be true that Warner's words might have helped to topple old Judd, by making Judd sense for an instant some failure of charity and of perception in himself. Ill, embarrassed, he might not have rallied self-justifications quickly enough, so Warner's words might have caused a brief stab of conscience, enough to send him over the edge. *But if he dies the chief fault is mine. I am guilty. To live is to destroy—true or false? I am small; my only real quarrel with Hunter is that if he has his way I shall never grow. How stubborn the life that can't desire to die!*

Last August she had desired it, or thought she had, until a moment of that Saturday night, on the stairs, her mother weeping in a room left behind, her mind visited strangely by Victoria's grandchild the Funny Thing. She had begun to desire death earlier—in July, after Jim's letter, the only one he ever wrote. Stilted, timid; needless doubletalk; the awkwardness and misspelled words not endearing or funny but rather shocking, evidence of the blindness of her love.

I will not say part of me died when I read that dismal thing. We die and regenerate with every breath. All that happened (I-would-say-to-Edith) was that my journey had taken me beyond the region where I met Jimmy and learned some aspects (not all) of a passion called love.

Notice also (am-I-still-talking-to-Edith?) how the laughing-crying devil-angel that Jimmy woke up in me has not died, but rouses me even in the prison night, stinking bare-light-bulb night, starved for the pressure, the almost-anger, furious crescendo, meteoric release. Oh, in an enlightened society I could have been a splendid high-class whore!

"You may call your next witness, Mr. Hunter."

"Sergeant Lloyd Rankin!"

Callista heard Cecil Warner's short involuntary sigh, felt his hostile stiffening and alertness. Detective Sergeant Lloyd Rankin of the Winchester Police came down the aisle and held up a flat hand for the oath, the slab-faced sober man. His gray hair under the cold light glinted like dull steel, his eyes a lighter gray but opaque, oyster gray. *Draw him as a bulldozer—Cecil might like it.* She ran her fingers softly over the wrinkled hand, lifted away the idle pencil and drew his scratch pad toward her.

A bulldozer has its own squat dignity. If it's directed to knock over some little house loved by generations, that's no fault of the dozer. The blade advances, the Diesel bellow swells to the roar of a caged hurricane. Old timbers—nobody wants them—crumble like dry cheese. And look!—the picture grew in swift lines and leaping shadows—look, a doll! Left behind maybe under the eaves years ago. It had tumbled into brief light in front of the caterpillar treads, which would of course move on. Too bad, but no time to stop.

She knew idly that the small brilliant drawing was good. Light lived in that doll, the rest a melancholy gray, a darkness. And turning the sketch face down, she wondered if she had done right in telling Cecil Warner of Sergeant Rankin's curious lapse on that afternoon last August when the world fell apart. In the Old Man's steady glare at Rankin—maybe he hadn't even felt her take the pencil—she glimpsed a blaze that would have suited the eyes of a male tiger about to drive another way from his mate and if possible gut him to ribbons. Her own half-welcomed excitement, private elemental anguish akin to the neural riot of approaching orgasm, was just as irrelevant, just as far from any notion of discovering truth—in a courtroom, of all places! For what after all did Rankin's moment of rutty brutality have to do with the truth or falsehood of her story? Accused of it—(*he will be!*)—Rankin would flatly deny it, the word of a respectable policeman against that of the Monkshood Girl.

Gravely, to the prosecutor, he was admitting twenty-two years of service with the Winchester Police, twelve of them with the Detective Division. An honest policeman, Rankin, an up-to-standard product of what must be a tight, hard school; a product chipped at the surfaces but wearing well. *And what is honesty?*

She supposed that for Lloyd Rankin it would mean being no more dishonest than a majority of his peers. It would mean: don't take *big* bribes, and don't be an unpopular holy joe about the percentages from bookies and pimps and what-not: that's sort of like a tax, see? No compromise with major crime, but don't stick your neck too far out except in the obvious line of duty. There, in that clear line of duty, be ready to risk your life all the way and maybe lose it. Certainly give him that, she thought. He had all the earmarks of what is called a brave man, who could probably say with a bullet lodged in the bone: "It's the job." To Sergeant Rankin honesty would mean that obeying orders comes first; the top brass is paid to think, so when in doubt follow the rules. And Sergeant Rankin would believe (this she knew) that all criminals once caught are somewhat outside the human race, no longer protected by the common laws of charity and fair play. The professionals among them are The Enemy; the nonprofessionals, the one-shot wife-stabbers and other grown-up first offenders—his mind would balk at those, fretful and baffled: why couldn't they act like other people? Or perhaps he would be wedded to some one of the superficial formulas, substitutes for thought, derived from religion or popular psychology. Sensing no contradiction, Rankin would also believe in his heart that the world is more or less a God-damn jungle where every man (including this man Rankin) has his price.

"What is your present assignment, Sergeant?"

"Attached to Homicide Bureau, sir, the last four years."

"I ask you to recall the events of Monday, the 17th of last August. Did anything happen that day in the line of duty that had to do with the defendant Callista Blake?"

"Yes, sir."

"Give your own account of it, please."

Sergeant Rankin slipped on his reading glasses, appearing in that owlishness no less a cop, and consulted his notebook. "Late on the morning of August 17th of this year, Chief of Detectives Daniel Gage directed me to go to the apartment of a Miss Callista Blake at No. 21 Covent Street, this city, in response to a telephone call that Miss Blake had made to the local precinct station. The station had passed on the substance of her call to our headquarters, and Chief Gage relayed it to me. Miss Blake had told the desk sergeant she wished to give information to someone in authority concerning the death of a Mrs. James Doherty in Shanesville the previous night. She had said further that she was ill, and gave this as the reason why she did not wish to come to the police station herself. Chief Gage had communicated with the State Police, and he passed on to me what he learned from them about the death of this Mrs. Doherty, who had been found, apparently drowned, in a pond at Shanesville."

"All the persons involved—Miss Blake, Mrs. Doherty, and others you may have heard about later—were at that time unknown to you?"

"Yes, sir. Routine assignment to follow up information received."

"Go on, please."

"I reached Covent Street around noontime. I was in plain clothes of course. Miss Blake admitted me, and before looking at my identification remarked: 'Fast work! I've only been waiting an hour.' I don't know if this was sarcasm. There had been no unnecessary delay."

Wanting to soften the intensity of Cecil's glare, she whispered: "It was a noise to crack the silence. He stood in the door like a zombi, the dear man, so's to make me speak first." She won from the Old Man only a start, and a drowned look. He wasn't quite with her.

"Go on, Sergeant."

"I asked for her name, gave her mine, entered the apartment at her invitation after showing my credentials. I inquired how she came to know of Mrs. Doherty's death, and she said, first, that her stepfather had telephoned her about it, but then immediately, and without questioning from me, she said: 'Oh, I knew it, I knew it last night.'"

"Did you inquire what she meant by that?"

"Not right away. I first asked about her stepfather's call. I wanted to get the identification and relations of these people clear in my mind. She gave me the name Dr. Herbert Chalmers, said he had called her about eleven o'clock and told her Mrs. Doherty's body had been found in the pond. I engaged her in some general talk: who Dr. Chalmers was, and what was her connection with Shanesville, with Mrs. Doherty, how long she had lived there at Covent Street, things like that. She said she had called the precinct station right after her stepfather hung up—which checked, as to time. That first remark of hers—"

"I think we'll come back to that later. You say that in her call to the precinct station Miss Blake had said she was too ill to go there. Did she appear to be ill when you saw her?"

Rankin frowned. "I wouldn't say so. Dark under the eyes. I noticed a tremor in her hands. Nothing that couldn't be explained by—oh, nervousness perhaps."

"In that general talk, were her answers clear and satisfactory?"

"I learned nothing later to contradict them."

"I see. Well, did she then tell you what information it was she wished to give—what she had in mind when she called the precinct?"

"Yes, sir. When I inquired, she said Mrs. Doherty had come to the apartment the evening before. I asked what time; Miss Blake said Mrs. Doherty had come at about quarter to eight and left at eight-thirty."

"Did she give the occasion, the reason for Mrs. Doherty's visit?"

"Miss Blake said she had telephoned to Ann Doherty, asking her to come. I inquired the reason for this, what it was she wanted to see Mrs. Doherty about, and she refused to tell me."

"Did Miss Blake explain her refusal?"

"No, sir. Just said: 'I won't tell you that.' I didn't press it. I wanted to get on to other facts, facts she was willing to tell me."

"And she did give you other information?"

"She did, sir, freely enough."

"Just summarize it, please."

"She began by saying that since some time in July she had been under the influence of what she called a suicidal depression, that she had some poison in the apartment, and that she was afraid Mrs. Doherty might have drunk some of it by accident. Miss Blake said she had become ill during Mrs. Doherty's visit, had gone into her bedroom and shut the door—'to get away from her,' as Miss Blake put it—and that while she was there, in the bedroom, Mrs. Doherty must have poured a drink from the brandy bottle which contained the poison. Miss Blake said she had been still in the bedroom with the door shut—locked, in fact—when Mrs. Doherty left the apartment. Then, according to her account, Miss Blake came out, found the bottle had been moved, and became alarmed for Mrs. Doherty's safety." The slight drawl and falling cadence of Sergeant Rankin's voice was effective, Callista noted; good theater; something to admire as a work of art. "She got her car out of the garage and drove to Shanesville, to the Doherty house, found the Dohertys' car in the driveway, found Mrs. Doherty's handbag fallen in the path, house dark and door locked. Miss Blake said she then followed the path toward her mother's house, assuming that Ann Doherty must have gone that way, and presently discovered her, dead, in that pond. At that point, Miss Blake said, she panicked, and was also ill again, and—drove home. You understand, sir, I am merely summarizing, as you requested. Actually in that preliminary talk with her, a summary was all I got—with, as I later learned, some omissions. As soon as I had a general idea of the situation, I called Chief Gage, using Miss Blake's telephone. Chief Gage himself arrived at Covent Street at about ten of one, with a fingerprint man—Sergeant Zane I think it was—a photographer, and yourself, Mr. Hunter."

"Did you inquire, before others arrived, about this poison Miss Blake said she had?"

"Yes, sir. She said it was aconitine, and said she had prepared it a week before, by steeping monkshood roots in alcohol—brandy. I asked where she got the roots. From her mother's garden in Shanesville, she said. I asked whether she still had the stuff on hand. She said: 'Of course.' Mr. Hunter, maybe I ought to say at this point that up to then Miss Blake appeared to have no idea at all that she might be accused of anything. I don't pretend to understand it, but that was my distinct impression. Well, she took me out to the kitchenette, and showed me a half-full bottle labeled brandy, which she said contained the poison, and also an ordinary kitchen canister with some chopped-up mess that she told me was monkshood roots. She herself remarked that the brandy bottle probably had Mrs. Doherty's fingerprints. I took these items back to the living-room later, and from then on they weren't out of my sight until Chief Gage arrived and had them sent safe-hand to the Department's toxicologist Dr. Walter Ginsberg, after a fingerprint check. Miss Blake was very composed, I'd say sort of indifferent, about all this. When she had shown me the brandy bottle and the canister in the kitchenette, I asked her: 'Miss Blake, what did you have against this Mrs. Doherty?—you might as well tell me.' She didn't answer, just looked at me as if the question was— well, foolish or surprising. I said: 'Why did you do it?'" Sergeant Rankin turned over a leaf of his notebook. "She replied: 'That's how it is? I've told you the truth, but it's going to be like that?' I told her yes, of course it would be like that, and I asked her who she thought would believe the kind of story she'd given me. Miss Blake then said: 'Who knows what anyone believes?' And she asked: 'Are you going to arrest me?' I said that would be a decision of my superiors. Then I—told her to go back to the living-room and remain in my sight while I used her telephone. She did so."

Callista felt the Old Man lean close. He was muttering at his mouth-corner: "Is that when he—?"

She nodded. "He's deleted five rather long minutes. Why not let it go? My word against his, nothing much happened anyway, and it hasn't any bearing." Warner growled indecisively. "Partly my fault too—should've remembered my skirt might be transparent against that sun." Warner's hand tightened and fell slack. She noticed Rankin's oyster-gray glance flick her lightly and pass on, for the first time since he had taken the stand.

"Before Chief Gage and others arrived, did Miss Blake do or say anything else you remember as significant?"

"Well—one thing—I don't know how significant. There was a fancy aquarium thing in her living-room, with fish, tropical fish I guess. When I'd finished my call to Chief Gage—well—should I take up the Court's time with this?—I don't know if it's relevant at all."

Surprisingly to Callista, it was Judge Mann who said: "I think, having started, you may as well tell it, Sergeant. We can stop you if it's too far afield."

"Well—when I'd finished my call, Miss Blake said: 'I'm getting something from the kitchen, I suppose you want to come with me?' I did so, and stood by while she got a pitcher and emptied the ice-cube trays from the refrigerator into it. I inquired about it, and she said: 'Don't worry, it's just ice.' She carried the pitcher back to the living-room. She pointed out where an electric cord from the aquarium was plugged into a wall socket and asked me to disconnect it. I did so, mostly to humor her, saw no harm in it—I don't know anything about aquariums, nice hobby I guess. Anyhow before I knew what she intended she had poured the whole pitcher-full of ice cubes into the tank, and lifted out a gadget—a heating-coil in a glass cover—and rapped it real sharp against the leg of the table so that the glass broke and scattered over the carpet. I asked her what on earth she did that for, but she didn't explain the action—that is, she said the fish were beautiful, said it as if that explained something, but I don't know what she meant. Then she just stood by the aquarium watching them die. Two or three of them were dead almost right away, anyhow a matter of a few minutes. She pointed one of them out to me, a very small red fish, said it was a—a live-bearer I think she called it, and she gave me the scientific name of it too, but I don't remember that— platy-something. She said that one was a female ready to give birth. I'd thought all fish laid eggs, but seems not. I asked her again what she wanted to go and do a thing like that for. She said: 'They were beautiful and I loved them. Now watch them die.'"

Again it was Judge Mann who asked: "Those were her exact words?"

"Yes, your Honor. I asked her then if she took pleasure from killing beautiful things, and she looked at me—rather strangely, I must say—and said: 'No, Sergeant, this is the only time I ever killed anything beautiful, or anything I loved.' I don't know why a person would do a thing like that."

Tight-voiced, dubious, like a man groping through uncertain country, Judge Mann asked: "Was she, in your opinion, overexcited—exalted—anything like that, Sergeant?"

Hunter just watched. Callista thought: *Hunter isn't liking this.*

Sergeant Rankin's voice echoed something of Judge Mann's perplexity; a true echo probably, for Callista sensed that Sergeant Rankin had never until this moment entertained the notion that the Monkshood Girl might be of unsound mind. And the notion might be, to Sergeant Rankin, interesting, without regard to the tender feelings of the District Attorney's office. For an accusation of physical coercion and threat of rape would be far less convincing from a psychopath. Cecil would be noticing the Sergeant's tentative nibbling at the idea. Cecil might be wishing that the Judge would make more inquiry along that line—for to Cecil, she knew, an insanity defense might still be a sort of last-ditch possibility in spite of her total refusal to go along with it. While she herself rather hoped the little man in the too priestlike gown would shut up and mind his own business. *What's it to him? Perhaps it will be to him, and not to Cecil whom I love, that I'll find the courage to say: I am guilty.*

Sergeant Rankin picked his way among words like a man stepping from hummock to hummock through a marsh. "I would say, your Honor, that there was, maybe, something like that about her—general behavior. But—a vague sort of thing—I don't know if I should express an opinion, just a—a layman's opinion anyhow—"

"Well," said the Judge crisply, "did Miss Blake become abusive, or scream, cry, talk irrationally or too loud or too fast, anything like that?"

"No, your Honor, none of those things, not at all."

"Did she seem confused, inattentive to what you said or unable to understand it?"

"No, your Honor. Very cool and self-possessed, really. I had—if I might put it this way—I had an impression that she was deliberately talking over my head—that I didn't understand some of the things she said because I wasn't meant to."

"Do you mean her answers were unresponsive, unconnected with the questions you asked?"

"No, not quite that, your Honor. Well, I recall one thing, after she broke the aquarium heater and we exchanged those remarks about—about killing beautiful things. I said to her: 'Look, Miss Blake, if they decide to arrest you, surely you've got some friend who would have looked after that aquarium for you while you're away.' Now it's my recollection that I said that in a perfectly friendly, kindly way—I certainly had no wish to make things hard for her—but Miss Blake said: 'A spring morning can't be warmed up in the oven.' Well, I wouldn't know whether a head—whether a psychiatrist would call that an irrational reply or not. I just didn't think it made much sense."

"I see. Go on, Mr. Hunter."

"Did anything else significant happen before Chief Gage arrived?"

"I think not, sir. Nothing I remember. I didn't think I was getting anywhere trying to talk with her, so for the last five or ten minutes we just sat there waiting for the others to come."

"Yeah," Callista said under her breath, "we just sat there." She leaned a little against Cecil's shoulder, weary, suddenly desiring sleep above all things, yet touched and curiously disturbed by the Old Man's harmless, rather pleasant smell of shaving lotion, soap, tobacco. Drowsily she thought: *He's really nothing like my father.*

"What happened, in your presence, after Chief Gage and the others arrived at Miss Blake's apartment?"

"Well, Miss Blake was briefly questioned by Chief Gage and yourself. It covered the same things I'd talked about with her. She was asked by Chief Gage about a photograph and a couple of letters that I found in a desk in her bedroom."

"She was not at that time under arrest, was she?"

"No, sir, she was not. I recall that Chief Gage quite formally asked her permission to look around the apartment, and she gave it."

"Please describe those items, the photograph and the letters."

"The photograph was a snapshot of a man in swimming trunks, taken at some beach or other, and the name 'Jimmy' was written on the back—just the name, nothing else. One of the letters, dated July 5, 1959, was signed 'J', and Miss Blake, when shown it, identified it as one written to her by Mr. James Doherty of Shanesville. The other one, bearing no date and not signed—in fact not finished—was identified by Miss Blake as one that she had started to write to Mr. Doherty, but had never mailed."

"Was Miss Blake questioned about those letters, there at her apartment?"

"Not much then, sir. She identified Mr. Doherty as the husband of the Mrs. Doherty who had been found dead in Shanesville. Chief Gage asked her to explain the relation between herself and Mr. Doherty, and she said without any show of emotion—with a shrug, as a matter of fact—she said: 'Oh, he was my sweetheart for a little while, a summertime amusement.'"

She saw T. J. Hunter, relaxed and thoughtful, walk to the prosecution's table and spend a weary time standing there, brooding at the small papers he had taken up. Callista closed her eyes. "If it please the Court, I will offer these two letters and photograph for admission in evidence, but, if they are accepted, I will have the letters read to the jury somewhat later, to make a more orderly presentation. For the present I merely wish to establish their identification by Sergeant Rankin."

The deep voice by her shoulder remarked: "I will ask to see them." *Do you have to go over there, Cecil?* Then Callista was aware of a small but unaccountable lapse of time, for Cecil was already by the prosecution's table glaring morosely at little scraps of paper, his bushed eyebrows in a clench, while T. J. Hunter stood by politely, hands in his pockets. Had she fallen asleep sitting up? Was it possible for an accused witch to do that in a court of law? *Oh, likely had something to attend to, and took off on my broomstick—well, sure, a mission, three times around the Shanesville house casting a spell to curdle Cousin Maud's plum jam, and high time too—it merely slipped my mind—how'd I manage without a cat?* She saw the Old Man's shoulder sag and stiffen. It was cut and dried, he had told her: the letters would go in, mostly because he hoped to gain more than lose by them, when there was a chance for the defense to interpret them. This present show of examining them was what he called legal window-dressing. She saw him make some quick *sotto voce* comment, his face savagely disgusted, an aside that no one but T. J. Hunter could hear. Hunter flushed all the way up his bald forehead; the flush passed, leaving no sign of anger. Then Cecil spoke in his courtroom voice, smoothly, a tone of indifference close to contempt: "The defense will not protest the admission of these documents."

How could I have slept? Cecil was returning. *Apparently no one noticed—a minor accomplishment of necromancy—I just toss these things off, you know.* Some mumbling and talking over yonder, as she felt the return of Cecil's warmth, and took hold of his hand, though he was really nothing like her father. Yes, Rankin, identifying the silly things. *Poor Jim, spelled "relinquish" r-e-l-i-n-q-u-e-s-h. E for effort.* "Cecil, what did you say to the rising young lawyer that turned him pink?"

He looked at her doubtfully, not smiling. "I said the prosecution must be running out of keyholes."

"Maybe you touched a childhood trauma."

"His childhood be damned," the Old Man grumbled. "He's still a snotnose pulling the wings off flies, as a profession."

"I decline to be compared to a house-fly."

"Shut up, dear. I've got to listen again."

"Sergeant, after Miss Blake's admission that James Doherty had been her lover, was she questioned any further, there at her apartment?"

"No, sir. Chief Gage informed her that she would be detained for questioning. She made no protest. Accompanied by yourself, Mr. Hunter, I took her in a police car direct to Mr. Lamson's office, in this building."

"Was she questioned there, in your presence?"

"Yes, sir, mainly by Mr. Lamson. My recollection is that the others present were yourself, Chief Gage, Miss Wallingford—that's Mr. Lamson's secretary—who made a stenographic record of the interrogation, and Sergeant Shields of the State Police, who was present only a part of the time, a few minutes."

"Did Miss Blake sign anything during that interview at Mr. Lamson's office, while you were present?"

"She did, sir. The stenographic record of the interrogation was typed by Miss Wallingford. Miss Blake then read it, and signed it—signed the written statement that the answers given by her and recorded in the transcript were true to the best of her knowledge and belief. Her signature was witnessed by Mr. Lamson and yourself, and Mr. Lamson requested me to read and initial the pages of the typescript, which I did."

"If it please the Court—" and Cecil was gone again, looming over yonder, examining the pages, large ones this time, impressive legal size. More window-dressing. But discussion was longer; she grew inattentive in her drowsiness. She heard Hunter remark that the transcript would be read after cross-examination of Sergeant Rankin—if, said the bald polite man with the shovel chin, Mr. Warner elected to cross-examine. Cecil grunted. A side-bar huddle followed that. Some of the time she knew her eyelids had drooped, hiding her in a murmurous partial darkness; some of the time she was watching, with an abstract friendliness and faraway approval, the thoughtful and still puzzled features of Judge Terence Mann. *I can't explain it either, Judge. According to my own biased notions, I'm not mad, at least no more than my old buddy Hamlet, who also had a mother. Gets complicated there, because Hamlet was decidedly male, I think, any side up, while I'm every inch a wench. Ask Rankin. You see—*

It disturbed her, to reflect how little any of those present would ever know about her. They looked at her; anyway their eyes did. In a few days they would hear her talk from that dizzy isolation of the witness stand; anyway their ears would register certain sounds. Already through the testimony their mental vision (imperfect, cloudy, variously preoccupied) had watched her squeaking grass-blades with the Wayne kids, snapping at poor Cousin Maud on the front porch. They had seen her (through the fogs and excitements of their own scrambled sexual histories) caught in that slow frenzy—(*wearing a blouse*)—on the divan in Jim's office, under the glazed smirk of an "art"-calendar nude. *Who were you then, Callista?—what were you then?* They had seen her, guilty or innocent, standing by black water, under hemlocks, under a hazy moon.

But they did not know her.

They could not communicate with the inner spectator-participator. It had needed nineteen years to create the Monkshood Girl, a short time, yet to the jurors, the Judge, Cecil, even to Edith, the nineteen years amounted to an infinite complexity never to be explored. They could not watch the golden kitten Bonnie, nor Aunt Cora. They could not learn of the young discoveries: language, music; endless expansion of the visible world as her hand acquired certain powers of dealing with line and color and mass or began to acquire it. They had no vision for the dreams of her sleep, or the waking dreams.

Ann Doherty, inarticulate Jim, mysteries quite as obscure. *What do you think you know about Ann, gentlemen? Cute, blonde, and married: isn't that about as far as you go?*

We are not what you see, we people who look at you out of clever photographs in the paper at your breakfast tables. When you burn the image you have created you burn the true self also, but you cannot know that self. I am here with you, and captured, and maybe you ought to fear me as you do, but I am not what you suppose.

III

He met the flat patient stare of Sergeant Lloyd Rankin, which indicated a readiness like that of a dog who will not attack unless provoked. Say a Boxer: Rankin was built like that, and would fight in a Boxer's style, with single-minded courage closely akin to stupidity.

He saw T. J. Hunter seated at the prosecution's table and turned partly away from the witness chair, making a show of rereading that transcript of Callista's ordeal. T.J. would be listening to the cross-examination, and sharply; but Cecil Warner had to admit that the show of bored indifference was quite as expert as anything he could have managed himself. This silence had lasted long enough, or too long; he heard fidgeting in the back rows; he could not spend any more time gloomily viewing Rankin's Boxer jaws.

"Sergeant Rankin, when Miss Blake realized she would be under suspicion, you asked her—I think these were your words—you asked her who she thought would believe a story like hers. Correct?—that's your recollection of what you said?"

"Yes, sir, I think I put it that way."

"Meaning, I suppose, that you didn't believe her story yourself?"

"No, sir—I mean no, I didn't believe it."

"Did you suggest that she ought to change her story?"

"Oh, I told her—more than once, I guess—that she ought to tell the truth about it, that she'd get a better break if she did."

"A better break. Those were your words, 'a better break'?"

He noticed a dim flush on Rankin's heavy cheeks, some flicker of doubt or uneasiness in chilly gray eyes. Rankin could have no way of knowing how much Callista might have told. "Yes, I think that was how I put it, Mr. Warner. She seemed to be expecting me to believe it, and—"

"But she replied: 'Who knows what anyone believes?'"

"Yes."

"And asked then if you were going to arrest her?"

"She did, and I told her that would be up to my superiors, not me."

"This conversation took place in the kitchenette, after she had taken you out there and shown you the brandy bottle, and volunteered her account which you preferred not to believe?"

"It wasn't a case of preference, Mr. Warner. I—"

"All right, never mind that. The conversation took place in the kitchenette?"

"Yes."

"And you told her to go back to the living-room, and she did so?"

"Yes."

"She went ahead of you?"

"Ahead of me?"

"My words are plain, aren't they?" *Give him no time—Boxer hates to be pushed.* "She stepped out of the kitchenette and walked ahead of you down that little hallway toward the living-room, did she not?"

"Really I don't remember. I suppose—"

"Don't *remember!* In direct examination you showed an excellent memory for details. Let me just check your memory a little. What way does the front of that apartment house face, 21 Covent Street? East?"

"Why—yes, east, or south-east anyway."

"Was it a bright day, August 17th?"

"Yes, bright sunny day."

"Hot?"

"Very hot."

"Sunlight in the living-room windows, was there? Remember?"

"Yes."

"In the hallway?"

"I guess so."

"Good memory. Let me check it just a little more. What was Miss Blake wearing that day?"

"A—oh, just a dress, I don't know what a dressmaker would call it."

"Well—color?"

"White."

"Good. A simple white dress. Now look, Sergeant, I think you can remember whether she went ahead of you into the living-room. I'll help you out—you wouldn't have left her alone with that brandy bottle when you'd as good as told her she was under suspicion, would you?"

"Oh—well, that. Yes, if it matters, I remember she went first."

"Did you again tell her she ought to change her story?"

"I may have."

"Sergeant, I point out to you again, your memory under direct examination was excellent. You referred to your notebook, you repeated several remarks verbatim—to some of which the defense might have justifiably objected, if I had seen fit. Now—did you tell her a second time that she would get a better break if she changed this story which you say you didn't believe? Did you, Sergeant?"

"Yes, it's my recollection that I did."

"Did you suggest any other thing she might do that would, in your words, give her a better break?"

"Any other—I don't know what you mean."

"Then let me help your memory again. This conversation, when you repeated that she ought to change her story—did this conversation take place while you were going back to the living-room?"

"I—oh, I guess so."

"I'm asking for testimony, not guesswork. Did it, or not?"

"Yes."

"What did Miss Blake say?"

"It's my recollection that she—I don't think she said anything."

"She didn't? You remember how she *looked*, don't you?"

"Of course."

"Of course. Simple white dress, you said—correct?"

"Yes."

"Walking down the hall, between you and the sunlight in the living-room. Didn't she say, or rather cry out: 'Take your ugly hands off me, you fool!'— have you forgotten that?"

He heard Hunter jump up, and waited motionless for the angry blast: "Objection! This is outrageous. There has been nothing—"

Judge Terence Mann said: "There has been a good deal." Warner looked up quickly then; if his astonishment showed for a second, probably no one but Terence saw it. There was time to wonder how much of a surprise it was to T.J.—complete, very likely. And Terence Mann himself looked astonished at the swiftness and sharpness of his own words. "If there is any suspicion that a police officer has acted in that manner toward the defendant, the defense is well within its rights to pursue this line of questioning. The objection is overruled." *But Terry must know we can't prove it.* "Answer the question, Sergeant."

Staring at the Judge, T. J. Hunter said slowly: "Exception."

"Answer the question, Sergeant Rankin."

Rankin too had gone quiet, no visible motion in him except a rhythmic twitch at the corners of his Boxer jaws. "Will you repeat the question, Counselor?"

"I will. I ask whether Callista Blake said to you: 'Take your ugly hands off me, you fool!'"

"She did not."

"I quote to you these words: 'Look, I can give you a lot of breaks if you'll put out.' Did you say that to Callista Blake?"

"Objection."

"Overruled."

"I did not."

"You have no recollection of that?"

"It didn't happen, that's all. I never touched her."

"No? You didn't, a few minutes later, strike her across the face with the flat of your hand?"

"Objection!"

"Overruled."

"I certainly did not. The whole thing is imaginary."

"Did Callista Blake, while you had hold of her, tell you that she was ill, that she had had a miscarriage the night before?"

"Objection!"

"Overruled." *So Terry sticks his own neck way out, his own feelings involved, his judgment slipping, and where does that take us?*

"Exception."

"She did not tell me that, Counselor. She had no occasion to tell me that. I say again, the whole thing is imaginary. I know my duties, and my position as a police officer. Nothing like that happened, and if the defendant says it did, she is lying." Except for that twitch, and the high tension of his blocky hands gripping the witness chair, nothing in Rankin's solid front suggested he might himself be lying.

"You say the whole thing is imaginary. Really! Is it imaginary, just a bad dream cooked up by the defense—what do you take us for, Sergeant?—is it imaginary that you shoved Callista Blake down on the couch in the living-room, that she then told you she was ill, that in spite of that you went on trying to force her, that you exposed yourself, that she then said a certain thing which frightened you, so that you let her go, after first striking her across the face with the flat of your hand?"

"Objection of course. Whole question improper and fantastic."

"Overruled."

Terry, I don't know—

"Exception."

"Nothing like that happened. I deny it absolutely."

"In that view of it, I won't question you further about this, or anything else, I think, since the only thing of service to my client is the truth. I dare say, in redirect examination, you'll have opportunity to repeat your virtuous denials—"

"That's outrageous."

Warner swung around. "Something else is outrageous—"

"Mr. Warner!" But that was Terry, and he must listen. "We cannot have this. Please control yourself."

"I am sorry, your Honor. My apologies to the Court, and to Mr. Hunter— who, I am sure, knew nothing about any improper conduct on the part of his witness. That's all."

Warner sat down, with a sudden breaking out of sweat on his face, a dizziness and blurring of vision. Callista's hand slipped over his, easing his fingers out of their involuntary clench. She was repeating his name softly: "Cecil— Cecil—are you all right?"

"Yes." He covered his mouth to speak to her. "I couldn't break him. I thought I could break the bastard."

"Never mind. Relax. You bent him, but good."

"Not enough. You'll have to take the stand, maybe."

"But I must anyway. Relax."

Concerned for me. He noticed the courtroom was quiet, Hunter delaying. Judge Mann's gaze was on him too, worried and speculative. *Do they think I'm going to fold like Judd? Judd—I said to that man Judd: 'If you do not understand that question—'* He wiped his forehead. Maybe Callista had helped him get that handkerchief out of his pocket. He would not fold. Let them take their eyes off him. *Let them get on with it.*

Hunter was getting on with it—neutrally it seemed. "Sergeant Rankin, I'll merely ask you: is there any foundation in fact, anything at all, to support this suggestion of misconduct on your part with the defendant Callista Blake?"

"None whatever, sir. None whatever."

Hunter was pausing another long time. Warner now helplessly understood that he was giving Rankin time to think, time for the man's rather slow wits to come up with the obvious countercharge. Hunter said at last: "In summary, then, you simply questioned Miss Blake about the story she had told you, you took charge of the brandy bottle and so on, you called Chief Gage, and then there was this episode of the fish-tank—when Miss Blake, you say, was composed, sort of philosophical and all that, hardly the way a girl would act, I guess, if she'd just been threatened and pushed around. That's a correct summary?"

"Yes, sir, I think that about sums it up. Well—" It was comic enough, to observe the slow grimace as Rankin caught on to what Hunter would like him to say.

Hunter asked mildly: "Something you wish to add?"

"Well—I guess not. Of course I'm very much surprised that the defense should see fit to make a charge like that against me, but there seems to be no way of proving anything—Miss Blake's word against mine—and if I say anything about—about her own conduct in that respect, it's the same situation, so I would rather ignore it, let it go."

Warner sickened inwardly with self-blame. *I underestimated the brains in the son of a bitch*—no, hardly even that, for a cub lawyer should have seen it coming, the obvious countercharge by innuendo. Rankin had done it cleverly, though; he could hardly have said anything better calculated to make Callista seem a whore. *I should sell apples on a streetcorner.*

A sober workman driving in finishing nails, T. J. Hunter said: "I understand your reluctance, Sergeant, and I think we might as well leave it at that. Recross, Mr. Warner?"

Cecil Warner remembered how, long ago, on childhood occasions when he had been goaded into fighting, he had often been struck by a crying spell in the midst of battle. It had become a sort of distinction: "*Cecil's all right till he goes to bawling—then watch out!*" It would not happen now. But he knew his voice was shouting, too loudly, and cracking absurdly in the shout: "Are you being humorous, Mr. District Attorney? I am concerned with establishing the truth, and questioning that man will not serve any such purpose."

Judge Mann started to speak but checked himself, watching Sergeant Rankin step down and stride away. *Terry will not look at me. Take my hand, Callista.* Hardly wondering at the coincidence, he felt the cool pressure of her fingers renewed. *I shall not survive the conclusion, win or lose, but that hardly matters, Old Man—*

"If it please the Court, the prosecution is ready to read the transcript of the interrogation of Callista Blake on August 17th, which has been admitted in evidence and which I have here."

Judge Mann said drily: "It will be read by the clerk of court."

Something accomplished anyway, in that side-bar huddle before Rankin's cross-examination: the transcript would not be read with baritone sound effects. Hunter passed the pages to Mr. Delehanty with good enough grace, having no choice. To the hearers, Warner knew, much of it would be dull, a repetition of what had already been said. A welcome dullness, allowing time to rest. Mr. Delehanty would begin smartly, then fall to droning as the question-and-answer rhythm caught hold of him. The duller the better. *Keep my hand, Callista.*

Cecil Warner drifted into bewilderment, a sense that at some point there had been an illogical reversal of roles. Must he draw on the strength of this girl who in a few months might be butchered by the State, as if there remained in him no power at all, not even the power of wisdom? As if it were natural, and right, that in her danger and misery, in her green youth too, it should be Callista who possessed a power to heal and save? *The defense never rests, but—*

Can anyone save another? Maybe, with good fortune.

Or help another? The heart says yes. Keep my hand, Callista.

He came alert with a frightened start. Mr. Delehanty's voice had already sagged into a singsong monotony, and might have been burbling on a long time.

QUESTION (by Mr. Lamson): Can anyone support your statement that you were experiencing what you call a suicidal depression for a month or more, from early July to the middle of August?

ANSWER: No, I never spoke of it to anyone.

Why not to me? I might have—

Near his eyes, Callista's face took on a momentary immensity, like a great image on a softly brilliant screen. She must have had her teeth clamped a while on her underlip. It looked swollen as though from a bout of love.

QUESTION: Was anyone aware of your taking those monkshood roots?

ANSWER: No one.

QUESTION: Not even James Doherty?

ANSWER: I have had no communication with James Doherty since receiving that letter of his you took from my desk. In that time I've seen him only once—at the picnic when I got the monkshood. I didn't talk with him then, he did not talk with me, he knew nothing of what I was doing.

"You'll come to see me tonight, Cecil?"

"Yes."

"Something I must tell you."

"What, dear?"

"Not now. Tonight."

QUESTION: You had these roots, this poison, a week ago Friday. What about the suicidal depression?—change your mind?

ANSWER: I don't know how the mind works.

QUESTION: Now, Miss Blake! Anybody knows if he's changed his mind.

ANSWER: Does he?

QUESTION: All right. I can assume you gave up the notion of suicide?

ANSWER: Not a notion. An uncompleted decision, perhaps. Which did lose its importance after a while.

QUESTION: Did you, or you and James Doherty acting together, intend that poison for Mrs. Doherty?

ANSWER: Must I answer that again? James Doherty knew nothing about any poison, or my possession of it. I intended it only for myself.

QUESTION: But kept it there more than a week, where I suppose anyone might have stumbled on it?

ANSWER: Not exactly. Back of a shelf. Nobody visiting me was likely to go get a drink from a back shelf without invitation.

QUESTION: But you say that's just what Mrs. Doherty did.

ANSWER: Why, I think her idea was to get the drink for me. Then I guess she understood I'd locked myself into the bedroom. With the drink in her hand, and upset by what I'd been saying, I suppose she just tossed it off, maybe not even knowing she did. It would be natural.

QUESTION: Didn't she knock? Call to you? Try the door?

ANSWER: I don't know, Mr. Lamson.

QUESTION: Don't know. I can't accept that.

ANSWER: It's the truth, and all I can say. Partial amnesia.

QUESTION: Do you have any idea how many professional criminals try that amnesia thing? Everything went black—yeah. You're not a professional criminal, you're a very intelligent girl. How do you think that amnesia stuff is going to sound in court?

ANSWER: Bad.

QUESTION: Well? Don't you care?

ANSWER: I can't invent for you. I don't know. I can't remember.

QUESTION: All right. Mrs. Doherty was upset by what you'd been saying. What had you been saying?

ANSWER: I told her about my affair with her husband.

QUESTION: Just like that?

ANSWER: Yes. I think I was very stupid. I hoped to persuade her to allow a separation. I knew her church doesn't allow divorce, but I thought she might permit us that much. I wanted my baby to have a father, married or not. It's bad, trying to grow up without a father. Mine died when I was seven. I wanted mine to have a father.

QUESTION: Yes, that was in the letter you wrote him.

ANSWER: Wrote but never mailed. I should have destroyed it.

QUESTION: Why didn't you mail it?

ANSWER: I'm not sure I can explain that. An obsession is a strange thing, and so is suicidal depression—and so's pregnancy. You don't just sit quiet and work out the mathematics. Your mind shifts and struggles like a thing in a web, tries to decide what matters most. The answers don't always stay the same. The day after I started that letter, I didn't go on with it because then I didn't even want Jimmy to know I was pregnant. I saw it wouldn't work out even if he were entirely free. Too different. We couldn't possibly have lived together. Then later I was trying again to think it might work—and so on.

QUESTION: Go on, please.

ANSWER: How? Mr. Lamson, I know ten million more things about myself than you ever could, but you're asking me to explain things that even I don't know. How can I? Well, the night before Ann came to see me, Saturday, I had a time when everything looked possible. I wanted to have the baby, I was almost happy, I wasn't thinking of suicide—I even forgot about that poison. Next day, Sunday, I was imagining again that Ann might permit a separation so that he could be with me. Crazy, but that's how I had it lined up that day, that's why I telephoned her, that's how it looked right up until I began to talk with her. Then—card-house fell down.

QUESTION: You told her you were pregnant?

ANSWER: No, I didn't even get that far. I saw it was no use, waste of time. We had not enough words in common.

QUESTION: Not enough words?

ANSWER: Oh—oh—whatever I said meant something else in her mind, the way everything I say now means something else to you, heaven knows what. No such thing as a common language. We all talk in the dark. If a bit of light breaks we're frightened and try to blot it out.

QUESTION: I don't follow you.

ANSWER: Don't try. I'm not going your way.

QUESTION: This isn't an occasion for humor, is it?

ANSWER: People will tell you I laugh at the damnedest things.

QUESTION: If you didn't say you were pregnant, how much did you say?

ANSWER: All she understood was that we'd had an affair.

QUESTION: Did you quarrel?

ANSWER: No.

QUESTION: She wasn't angry?

ANSWER: No, very forgiving. That's when I was sick to my stomach.

QUESTION: Really, Miss Blake! Are you saying—

ANSWER: I don't know what I'm saying any more.

QUESTION: Yes, I realize you're having a bad time. I'm not intentionally cruel, it's merely my job to enforce the laws of this community. Naturally your pregnancy entitles you to every consideration, but—

ANSWER: Mr. Lamson, didn't I say I *was* pregnant? I had a miscarriage last night.

QUESTION: Oh. I'm sorry, I don't think you did tell us that. When did it happen?

ANSWER: Out there, after I'd found her in the pond.

QUESTION: A result of shock, or—exertion?

ANSWER: Shock maybe. Is this the fourth time I've told you I didn't push her in the water? I found her, I knew she was dead, I came away.

QUESTION: The miscarriage—I'm sorry, but I must ask—

ANSWER: Why, frankly, Mr. Lamson, it hurts.

QUESTION: You know very well that's not what I meant. Where exactly were you when it happened?

ANSWER: First pain, there by the pond. I went back to my car because I thought I might be able to drive home somehow—

QUESTION: You mean to your mother's house?

ANSWER: I do not, I mean my apartment. But it was getting worse, and at the junction I did turn that way on Walton, because I remembered the woods across the road. I left the car by the pines, and got over there, into the woods. It was over pretty soon.

QUESTION: You must have a good deal of courage, Miss Blake.

ANSWER: Enough, I hope.

QUESTION: I hope so too. By the way, Miss Blake, you might glance at this folder, if you will.

"That's where he flashed the morgue pictures at you, Cal?"

"Uh-huh. I was a—what's the term?—a cool customer. Oh yes—he's reading my intelligent comments now. Not bad for a beginner, don't you think? Like Lizzie Borden."

"Hush, dear."

"Well, Lizzie was a beginner too. What's more she had to operate on a breakfast of mutton broth."

Cecil Warner could wonder then whether it had been Callista's wry and thorny humor that saved her during the moments last August—there must have been such moments—when she had drawn that dark bottle forward on the shelf and perhaps set out a single glass.

IV

As Joe Bass emptied the ash tray and made gentle needless motions with a dustrag at the bookshelves, Judge Terence Mann glanced at the handful of doodle scraps he had taken out of their temporary shelter in the minute book at the close of the day. None of them pleased him now, except possibly his sketch of the fingerprint technician Sergeant Zane scratching the lens he wore in place of a head. Drawing the toxicologist Dr. Ginsberg with his smooth face modified into a chemical retort had not turned out well. There was no comedy in solemn Dr. Ginsberg, unless it might be in his very self-conscious aloofness, his volunteered declaration on the stand that he never listened to anything about a criminal case except the facts immediately pertinent to his specialty. He had said in effect: "*That* for your emotional involvements!"—but it was a valid attitude if you happened to be Dr. Ginsberg, and not very funny.

"Did you stick it out, Joe?"

"No, I wanted to tidy up in here, so I slipped out after Mr. Delehanty finished reading that statement. Did I miss anything important?"

"Not much. Fingerprints. Mrs. Doherty's and Callista Blake's on the brandy bottle. It should even help the defense slightly, showing that Mrs. Doherty handled the bottle and that no attempt was made to wipe it or dispose of it. Callista Blake had all night and next morning to get rid of anything incriminating, if she'd been so minded. Then we had Dr. Ginsberg. Nothing new, he just made it official. Four milligrams of aconitine in the organs he studied, and they say one milligram is enough to kill. Wound up the day with Mr. Lamson; he testified to receiving those three other letters of Miss Blake's, direct from James Doherty. It seems Doherty simply walked in and dumped them on Lamson's desk, following the advice of his priest. I hadn't known it was quite like that. Lamson seemed to imply it was an example of civic virtue. No comment, Joe. I'm unhappy. Well, Lamson identified the letters, and they went in without protest, but won't be read till tomorrow, which will wind up for the State, I guess. Defense ought to open tomorrow afternoon, or sooner. Oh—you would have liked this. When Mr. Hunter asked if Mr. Warner wanted to cross-examine Lamson, the Old Man said: 'I believe I will decline the privilege.' But nobody laughed."

"Do you think Mr. Hunter will put James Doherty on the stand?"

"No. Not needed, and too likely to blow up in his face. Doherty couldn't testify to anything but the affair, so far as I know, and that's been proved and admitted."

"I was watching Mr. Doherty a little this afternoon, Judge. One of his knuckles is bloody, from biting it."

"Another casualty of the case. Nobody will be the same after it, not even you and I."

"I, Judge? I'm too old to change much. I already knew the world's full of sadness according to where you stand."

"I suppose I knew it too," said Judge Mann, and watched Joe's small crinkled hands spread out on the other side of the desk resting on the fingertips, and felt not only uncertain but immature. *Bring out the inner voices.*

I should have taken another road, Mr. Brooks—other roads. I should have married, maybe.

Where does anyone find the vanity to become a judge? No, that's not it. I have vanity enough, or too much. But in me, I suppose other forces balance the native vanity, cancel it out. There was never anything in Judge Cleever to make him doubt he's God's own right hand man.

Exercising a privilege of age and kindness, Joe said softly: "Relax, boy."

"Yes, when it's over, I must do that. Do we ever know where we're going?"

"Not to say know, maybe. Just the present road, and good or bad guesswork."

"And crossroads?"

"Same thing, Judge. You try to make the right guess, with whatever good judgment you've got at the time. I've always been alone at my crossroads—I guess everyone is. Or if there was a crowd, I didn't see how they could know where I was going. I was better off trying to puzzle out the signposts myself."

6

Nox est perpetua una dormienda.

CATULLUS

I

"In the prison house are many mansions. This one looks very nice—thank the good Sheriff for me, for us, Cecil. Is it wired for sound?"

"No, dear, it's just an office. Sheriff's working late down the hall—records room—and said we could have this. Nobody'll bother us."

"May I sit at the desk and judge humanity?"

"Why not?"

"Or I'll be a lady of the Abbey of Theleme, where the law was 'Do what thou wilt.' No—can't have anything like that going on in the Sheriff's own office. And still—flowers on the desk?"

"The explanation is anticlimax. Sheriff's good-looking, has a devoted secretary, her brother-in-law runs a florist's shop."

"Like that. Never mind, I hereby make-believe the flowers are for me, the blood-red roses and the little white ones, sweet hot-house children. Not quite real, are they?—no black-spot, no bitten leaves, sheltered children, I guess they don't understand. But I'll make-believe. Am I occasionally beautiful, Cecil?"

"To me, always."

"I've always loved words, you know. It amounts to a fault. I can't make them do as I wish. I could never write. I don't know enough about people, maybe never shall. But I know the power of words. You say I'm beautiful to you, and that makes me so, I believe it, the words shut away everything foreign to the Abbey of Theleme—no, that's not where we are. But isn't it strange what words can do? Comfort and terrify, heal and kill. Make out of nothing, something, and another word can send the something back to a nothing. It was my father's gift, that love of words. I was reading precociously at least a year before he died. Mother (who is definitely literate and past president of the local PTA, no kidding) felt it wasn't quite right at such an age."

"What's that paper? Are you tearing it?"

"Just a blank sheet the good Sheriff left on his desk. I hope he won't miss it. Not tearing, love, building. It's my crown, Cecil. I need a pin. Is that a pin in your lapel?"

"Yes—here."

"Thanks. That'll do it. Ouch! Well, nothing created without pain. How does it look?"

"Royal."

"Does it suit my complexion?"

"White and ivory—yes, not bad."

"Is it all right for a queen to suck a pin-pricked finger?"

"Rank has its privileges."

"Good. So, not a lady of Theleme but a mere queen, I'll do my best while I have authority. This object shaped like a ruler is my scepter, and this apparent ink-bottle—no, if rank has its privileges, we'll omit the orb and you give me a cigarette. You may light it for me, and remember you have the right at any time to be seated in my presence. My lord, do you have any defense to set forth in favor of this mewling monster, this three-billion-headed lurching mooncalf humanity?"

"Your Majesty, I must first know what specific charges have been made."

"Item, he stinks of shrewd stupidity like his father Caliban."

"A fault that might be remedied by going to school a few thousand years more; at least there's manifest intelligence."

"Latent, you mean, don't you?"

"Mostly latent, but a good deal of it overt, liberated."

"Item, his fears are inconsistent: he's afraid of the dark but quite ready to play with matches."

"Another trait of childhood."

"Also of masturbating monkeys. Item, he talks a great deal about truth, but in the end, what he believes is what he wishes to believe."

"At that point I must draw your Majesty's attention to an essential point in the original indictment, namely the admission that this monster possesses roughly three billion heads. And three billion bodies. In that view of it, it's good law as well as necessary charity to insist that each head-and-body unit of the monster be tried separately."

"There isn't time, sir, there isn't time. Are you implying that not everyone is snotty?"

"Something like that."

"But then we can have no trial. No trial, no justice, no fun. Ah, damn it, I was looking forward to a hanging, with a bang-up speech from the platform and not a dry eye in the entire public square except for a few pickpockets and sellers of soft drinks."

"Callista—"

"Sir! No—fair enough. I'll put my scepter down. Maybe I'm tired of being queen. But may I keep my crown a while?"

"You've always worn it."

"No. No. Bring your chair—no, take this one, Cecil. I'd like to sit on the floor with my head on your knee—not that you're like my father at all. My crown—oh, put it away somewhere, keep it, I don't care. I don't hear that wind any more. Is it turning cold?"

"Yes, it's quite cold tonight. Callista, the prosecution will finish tomorrow, with the reading of those letters. We'll probably open after the noon recess.... Is there anything, anything at all, you haven't told me?"

"Yes."

"You said, in court today, you said there was something."

"Yes. Why did you stop moving your hand over my hair? I loved it. That's better. Cecil, I am guilty."

"The—blank?"

"Yes. Haven't you almost known it all along?"

"No. But I've been afraid you might remember something, or convince yourself that you've remembered it, and so come to believe yourself guilty."

"Oh, Cecil, this isn't belief, this is knowledge. You're trying to give me a way out before you even hear. It's like this: it came back as a clear auditory memory, the dull noise of that bottle being pulled forward on the shelf, and the cork, and a clink of glass, then the tap of her little high heels outside the bedroom door. I remembered what she said, each word very clear in that high sweet voice of hers: 'Callie, come on now!—I poured a little drink for you.' That's how it was, Cecil. And I lay still. I didn't speak. Knowing what might happen. I won't say, wishing for it to happen, but knowing, Cecil. Oh, sure enough, my mind squirmed around a bit trying to imagine the drink was from an innocent bourbon bottle, but knew all the time that the bourbon had been emptied the week before and the bottle thrown away. I'm no split personality, Cecil. Call it a paralysis from conflicting drives, if you want to. The self that had no wish to murder was the same self that—that hated her guts and wished she was dead. So I lay still. And my brain began generating the smoke-screen, first the useless fraud about a bourbon bottle that wasn't there, then the amnesia."

"I don't believe you hated her guts, Callista. She was a frustration, someone in the way, as T.J. would insist on saying, has said in fact. But I don't think you hated her as a person."

"Not for long, but long enough. I killed her."

"That was a thing that happened. You did not will it to happen. You were sick, bewildered, temporarily unable to prevent it from happening. If you'd been out in the living-room with her—do you remember that bronze paper-knife you kept on the table, a handsome thing with a sharp point? She was small, slight, your arms are strong. You know you could never in the world have taken it up against her."

"Why, dear apologist, you're only saying that I'm a coward about physical violence. I killed her by lying still. She's as dead as if I'd taken that knife to her. I say the guilt is greater. Seeing red might have excused me, or so most people would say. My very cowardice, weakness, retreat—that's what killed her. Cecil, I killed her by a failure in simple decency and common sense. If I'd been decent, sensible, I'd have run out there the moment I heard that bottle move on the shelf."

"Callista, if the good, the righteous, the respectable were half as stern in self-judgment as you are—"

"Oh, there'd be no living with them at all. Mother's a Colonial something-or-other because some worm-eaten ancestor was a Saint in the Bay Colony. I think Father must have laughed at it, but I was too young to get the point. The Puritan in me gives many a squirm. But the point is, my self-judgment serves no one now—she's dead. Well, it seems to be a jury of the righteous and respectable, more or less, who are stern enough in judging others, I've noticed. Cecil, will you give me a sharp honest answer to a question you don't want me to ask?"

"I'll try."

"Do you think we have a chance?"

"Of course we have a chance. Today was bad. They'll go on feeling Judd's collapse, in spite of common sense, in spite of everything. The poor guy couldn't have done us more harm if he'd been trying. T.J. will manage to drop in some apparently inadvertent reminder of it, no doubt in his closing speech when I'm done talking—hell, mere mention of Judd's name in a baritone tremolo would be enough, and there's no legal barrier against that. Terence will charge the jury again to forget it, and most of them will honestly try to, which would mean something only if people knew how to watch their own minds. And today was bad because this was the day when they laid out the heavy circumstantial stuff, proving your episode with Jim, making it official on the aconite, all that. But now, dear, so far as evidence is concerned, T.J. has finished, done his worst. Those letters to be read tomorrow aren't evidence. T.J. just thinks they are. He'll try to interpret them as indicating premeditation as well as motive; I know better, and I think I can make that fly up and hit him in the face, in my own closing speech or sooner. I'm not painting it bright for you, Callista. It's not bright. But we have a chance. There is this: with your story clearly told—as it has been already, really, in that Lamson interrogation—it passes my understanding how anyone in his right mind could find first degree."

"Mr. Lamson had the answer. Remember?—'the fact is, my dear girl, we just don't believe your story.'"

"Hell with Butch Lamson—he's not the jury."

"You think they might find second degree?"

"That could happen. The only just verdict would be involuntary man-slaughter."

"My love, can't you hear me? I've told you, I am guilty. Twenty to life. What do people feel when they cry out 'O God! O God!'—does the sound do something for them?"

"I don't know, Callista. I was never religious. Were you, ever?"

"Not for real, I guess. Away back, soon after Father died, I think the fluff and tinsel mythology of Sunday school had some hold on me for a short while. But I kept remembering a few of Father's comments, spoken when I was too young to get the point. They fell into place finally, made sense. When I was thirteen I told Mother I wasn't going to make the motions any more. Stuck it out, too, with a bit of surprising help from Herb. One of the rare times I've seen him lose his temper—popped half-way out of the armchair while Mother was lecturing, and said: 'God damn it, Vic, let the kid do her own thinking! She will anyway.' I could've loved him for that, if he hadn't lapsed back into being Herb Chalmers—if he wasn't a stepfather—if I wasn't a crossgrained bitch who never knows how to make advances at the right time. Well, that time Mother was so startled the artillery just didn't function. She went meek, maybe to see what Herb would do next—which was nothing. But also she never bothered me about it again, much. I suppose because her own religion is pure social conformity. If she'd had any serious convictions I might have had a battle on my hands. Twenty to life. What happens tomorrow?"

"The letters first. We sit quiet and hear them. I can't ask you to display anything you don't feel, Callista—as an actress, my dear, you're nowhere. But if you feel—well, indifferent about those letters; if it seems all far away and irrelevant, don't let your face shout to the jury that you feel that way."

"I'll be thinking of the briers. They'll read no indifference in me then, I think."

"The briers—"

"Where I lost my baby, Cecil. Some little tree whipped me across the face when I was leaving there—a birch, I think. I remember I was superstitiously grateful, glad of the sting. A primitive game, Cecil, the mind snatching at notions of punishment and atonement. We're still savages, and I suppose some of the time there's no harm in it. As if the birch tree—the whole dark place, and the thorns—had accomplished enough of the punishment so that I could meet the rest well enough. And maybe the savage, the poor greasy primordial Eve down inside, would say that I have, so far. After the letters, the State rests?"

"I expect it. Hunter doesn't bother much with surprises—not his method. The State rests, and I move they dismiss the case, and Terence will deny the motion because he must."

"Part of the ritual?"

"In a way. We open then, probably after an early noon recess. The defense is going to be brief, Callista. It's better that way. We have only a few things to say. Reiterating them too much might turn the jury against us. They've heard the essence of the defense already, in my remarks, the cross-examinations, the Lamson interrogation. We mustn't repeat ourselves too much, because— well, heaven help any defendant if the jury is bored. What's happened is that, in effect, we're required to prove a negative. In the sense of tangible proof, on the same level as—oh, say Peterson's photographs—the thing is impossible. Proving a negative usually is, and that's fairly common knowledge among people who think at all. I'll bear down on it when I talk to them in closing, and before then. We must also insist on the element of reasonable doubt. I can see that Terence is very much aware of that aspect, and you must have noticed how he's given us every break he possibly could. Including some that surprised me. I shall open the defense by calling Edith. She's prepared to say anything at all that might help you, and if T.J. tries to get tough with her in cross-examination I'm sorry for him, that's all. She'll make a monkey out of him, and I believe she'll remember the jury every minute while she does it. In her direct testimony, the thing that will help most will be her emphasis on that suicidal depression."

"Haven't I already told Mr. Lamson that no one else knew of it?"

"Yes, but Edith did know, don't you think?"

"She knew I was unhappy."

"She's told me that you gave her the story about Jim, after that damn letter of his."

"Yes, I went to pieces too, that once. But at that time I wasn't even quite certain yet about the pregnancy. As for the suicide thing, why, I wasn't consciously thinking in those terms until the day of the picnic. It was all over, you know, but I'm female enough so I didn't enjoy watching Jim the tender husband and Ann acting like a new bride, Jim all braced to speak to me politely but hoping to God he wouldn't have to—and also wanting to—yes, I could feel that. So I wandered off into that part of the garden. It wasn't till I noticed the monkshood plants that I started telling myself how that way wouldn't hurt. Then I was digging up two or three, just to look at them. I nibbled at one, and spat it out."

"You saw Edith every day that week, didn't you? Went to the studio as usual?"

"Yes."

"Oh, she knew you were in the depths. She loves you. Your moods aren't the mystery to her that they are to most people, Callista. As for her factual knowledge—well, you might as well be prepared to hear her exaggerate that a little, even lie some about how much she knew if she thinks it will help you."

"I'm strangely rich and fortunate. I have two friends."

"I wish we were stronger. Well, after Edith testifies, then you, if you will promise me one thing—two things."

"One, that I shall not say I am guilty."

"Yes. The other is that when Hunter is attacking you, as he will, without mercy and with every trick he knows, you'll remember that you, and your friends, desire you to live."

"That I can promise. The other—"

"Callista, look up at me."

"Not yet. In a moment."

"Tell me this: is there any virtue, any rational good, in declaring a literal truth when misinterpretation is inevitable, when you know to a certainty that your hearers cannot grasp the whole truth nor keep the partial truth in proportion, nor even guess at the background, the related truths?"

"Virtue—rational good—I'm too confused, Cecil. Other thoughts. I don't know. I suppose not."

"You call yourself guilty—of a momentary lapse that happened to end in disaster. But if you say that much, the jury will inevitably charge you with a different sort of guilt. They will say: she brooded and planned to murder her lover's wife, the old story—let her burn! But is it right, reasonable, is it anything but insane, that for such a lapse, when you were sick in mind and body, you should be strapped in a chair and the life burned out of you?"

"You can frighten me, Cecil. It's strange. I don't think the brute fact has really frightened me before, not completely. It wasn't real."

"It's real. I was trying to frighten you. You must not say on the stand what you've said to me tonight. I know it to be truth, because you've said it to me. Telling it to the jury will not serve truth, because their minds will make a lie of it. Look up at me now."

"I'll promise it, I think—for a bargain. I'll lie by silence, in return for a promise from you."

"A promise—what is it, Callista?"

"Promise me that if I am acquitted, I may come to you, live with you—in marriage or not, it doesn't matter—love you and care for you so long as I can have you. Give me that, and then I will lie, I'll swear anything to save my life, I'll be such an <u>actress</u>—"

"Callista, I'm sixty-eight, old and fat and ugly and tired."

"Hush. Understand. It's you, you, you—the self in you, not old nor young nor anything but *you*. Promise me. My promise for yours. No other terms."

"I promise it."

"Now I can look up at you. Now I know that what Edith said is true: living is journeying, and love's a region we can enter for a while."

"Yes, a region that changes if only because we do ourselves. Some try to prevent that, I suppose. They want it to be a closed room thick with perfume and curtains drawn against all weather, against night and day."

"But when I come to you—you've promised it—I'll make it a region of summer, of morning and summer evening and every star at night."

II

COURT OF GENERAL SESSIONS
OF WINCHESTER COUNTY, NEW ESSEX

December 10, 1959

Action: *People vs. Callista Blake*; Justice Terence Mann presiding.

Court in session at 0956.

JUDGE MANN: Do I understand, Mr. Hunter, that you wish to have read to the jury the letters that were admitted in evidence before adjournment yesterday?

MR. HUNTER: Yes, your Honor. I am prepared to read—to go ahead with that right away.

JUDGE MANN: Let them be read by the clerk of the court.

MR. DELEHANTY: Your Honor, I have a—not laryngitis exactly, but a sort of cold. I'm perfectly ready to do as the Court directs, only I'm afraid that with this cold or whatever it is, maybe my voice won't be too clear to the jury.

JUDGE MANN: Well ... Yes, Mr. Warner?

MR. WARNER: Your Honor, the defense will not object to a reading of these letters by Mr. Hunter himself. I am certain my learned colleague would never take any improper advantage of his dramatic ability, admittedly great. Very often, however, written words are capable of conveying different meanings according to where the emphasis is placed, not because of any willful misconstruction, but simply because our language is not always a precise instrument. Therefore I would only stipulate, request rather, that if there should be any doubt in my mind, or in my client's mind, that the meaning of the letters is being correctly conveyed, we may have the privilege of interrupting the reading at that point, to indicate what we believe is the right interpretation.

JUDGE MANN: Is that agreeable to you, Mr. Hunter?

MR. HUNTER: Yes, your Honor, so long as the interruptions have to do with important points, not trivialities.

MR. WARNER: Sir, there are no trivialities in this case.

MR. HUNTER: Subject to the limitation I mentioned, the request of the defense appears reasonable, and I will not argue it.

JUDGE MANN: You may proceed, Mr. Hunter.

MR. HUNTER: The first of these letters, acknowledged by the defense to have been written by Callista Blake to James Doherty, is dated the 10th of May, 1959. Members of the jury, my dramatic ability is not, as Mr. Warner has described it, great. Any drama here is provided by the force of events, not by me. I must simply ask you to remember, while you hear these letters, that they (that is, the first three and the fifth) were written by a girl nineteen years of age, in the summer of this year, under the influence of a love affair which the testimony of witnesses has established and the defense has not denied. The first letter reads as follows:

"Jimmy—

"Tonight I cannot see you—that was really all I understood over the telephone, though I know you gave me the decent sensible reasons why you cannot come—something about work at the office, wasn't it?—for as soon as I heard you say that, I thought, Oh, bang goes the whole batch of cookies. You see, I was going to be domestic for you tonight, and I had just taken some cookies from the oven when you phoned—the airy egg-white kind, a sort of culinary idiocy because no damn good the next day, like letting air out of a tire. Therefore if I were a weeping wench they would now be soaked in brine and serve you right. But I never weep, Jimmy. Never. Remember that. So, since you cannot come, I will only count over the times I've had you with me, a miser adoring the sparkle and fall of jewels through her fingers. While you are submerged in the honest dreadfulness of whatever you do at the office—what the devil is it anyhow?—do you convey subtle conveyances and do dark deeds (these are puns) or just sit with your feet up and brood over Deals?—think of me playing with my pretties and having a better time than yourself, because this is all I can wish to do when you're away from me. Because I love you.

"It occurs to me, I never wrote to you before. You may not like me on paper. I sprawl and ramble, Dearest. Don't mind my doodling either—see the border I drew around your true name while I daydreamed and my pen was thinking for me? I'm only surprised it wasn't a tangle of Cupids, an out-of-season Valentine, and maybe it will be yet. In my here-and-now mood I would draw them saucy, I think (most of them), strutting and romping and showing off their little male apostrophes—all, I suppose, with a sneaking resemblance to you. Because I love you.

"No, don't say it's reckless and foolish of me to write at all—I know it. I can't care, not now. I tell you, Jimmy, what we have (is it possible it's only ten days?) is something that could not happen with Ann. Or anywhere in her world. I tell myself, I am not she, she is not me, my love (you know it) is nothing like what could happen for you with anyone but me. And there's my cure for jealousy—if I could apply it, if I could make my head rule me a little more, my crazy heart a little less. I want you, I'm empty and dull in your absence, tonight this is the only way I can talk to you. So let me talk, and think me foolish and reckless, and destroy this scrawled thing if you think best. It's me, though. Remember when you throw it away, it's me. And perhaps (because I love you) I wouldn't like you to burn me.

"More than you have already.

"Yes, I will type the envelope and mark it PERSONAL, lest the chaste eyes of Miss Anderson be stricken unto confusion and dismay. Damn 'em, why hasn't the Postoffice a Bureau of Hollow Oaks? Ooh—now I think of it, there is—not an oak, but a big maple with a hole in the trunk about seven feet above ground, on the path between your house and Mother's, near the pond. I saw a squirrel in residence there last year, stuck his head out and told me with the usual fuss that it was his'n. No good, I guess, because he's probably still there, and would think poorly of anyone dropping a letter into his living-room. He'd eat it or use it for nest-lining. That's how Nature is, you know, not a bit cooperative with the frills of romance, only with the essentials—but there, how cooperative indeed! As if, so far as Nature cares, every atom, every motion of life were aimed at nothing but the mounting of female by male and the begetting of young. Well, it comes to me that you with your long legs could reach that hole in the maple, though I'd have to stand on something. It comes to me that a letter could be squirrel-proofed in a metal box. Let us reflect on this."

Members of the jury, I might say in passing that because of this mention in the letter, the maple tree in question was examined. It does have a hole in it, nearer eight feet above ground than seven. Nothing was found there except an abandoned squirrel's nest; no sign of any previous disturbance by a human agency. [*Laughter by the defendant.*] I see Miss Blake is amused, which is her privilege I suppose. [*Disturbance at rear of room, a man (James Doherty) leaving his seat for the exit; Mr. Hunter waiting for quiet.*] The letter resumes:

"I love you as a sleeping seed in the earth must love the rains of spring, blindly, thoughtlessly, responding because it must—the shell breaks underground from the inward pressure, the outer warmth and fertile moisture. Shall I one day become a flower for you and know the sun? I am still in the dark, and rather blind, and yet happy to be living. You my awakener, it seems to me you're finding no such happiness. Am I too much for you, Jimmy? Too weird and different? Poor Jimmy, did you want only that May-day moment, and then discover the dryad had caught you fast and would not let go? There are thorns in my branches, I suppose. I never wanted them to wound. Oh, I must write no more like this, or I'll be needing you too much to sleep.

"Don't look distressed, as you did last night, and ask me, what are we to do? I don't know yet, Jimmy. There's an answer and we'll find it somehow. Likely it will be you that finds it, and not myself. I don't know. Maybe I'd never try to tell you what to do, even if I were inwardly certain what was best. May-day, it seemed ridiculous to me that anything about this could be a solemn Problem—no more a problem than the romping of animals. It is, of course—I merely had to shove that aside (without regrets) for the sake of May-day. It is, and I—(here comes a truth, my darling, that may be unwelcome or distressing; if it is, just set it down to my weirdness and forgive me for it)—I am, in many important ways, a much more civilized human creature than you. So civilized—so wide a gap between the cool life of the mind and the violence of that primitive part which never grows civilized in anyone—that I can never hope to explain myself, or be anything but a stranger to the easy routines of existence. My mind looks down on both of us, Jimmy, sees well enough that we are foolish lovers running into the jungle blind—(running, I will not say driven)—and inviting disaster in everything we do. But if now I only glimpsed you or heard your voice—why, away with all thought, the self you roused up on our May-day would be mad for you, throw away all sober knowledge, bite your throat, dance like a maynad and burn your flesh in a blaze of love."

DEFENDANT: The word is "maenad," if it matters.

MR. HUNTER: I stand corrected, I suppose. May it please the Court, my understanding was that any interruption of this reading would be made by counsel, in an orderly manner, not by the accused who is not at present under oath.

JUDGE MANN: It must be so ordered. I hope you understand the legal necessity, Miss Blake. If any other point comes up, please draw your counsel's attention and let him deal with it. That is the method required of us here. Incidentally, if anything during this reading makes it desirable for you to confer at any length with Mr. Warner, a short recess can always be requested, and the Court stands ready to allow it. Go ahead, Mr. Hunter.

MR. HUNTER: Well, the first letter is nearly finished. It concludes with these words:

> "Understand, Jimmy, that I fit no pattern. No one can own me, no one can make me over. I was born a heretic and so live. No one can catch me except if I will.
>
> > "I love you.
> > "Callista."

The second letter, also from Callista Blake to James Doherty, bears no date except Thursday, but it is in an envelope marked PERSONAL, addressed in typing to Mr. Doherty at his office at Judd and Doherty, 12 Somerset Street, Winchester. The postmark on this envelope is June 18th. It reads as follows:

> "Dear—
>
> "More than a month ago I wrote you a letter, and I remember that although you didn't say so, you weren't exactly pleased at my doing it. So I am reckless, but look, love, the heavens didn't fall, the grass is still green and soft (as we should know) and so here I go again, because I want to take advantage of an evening when I seem to be fairly clear-headed, or as near it as I ever am. Anyway, darling, you told me Miss Anderson is out with a cold, so this is sure to pass through no hands but yours, isn't it?
>
> "Jimmy, I can almost wish that Ann did know. Don't blow your top—caution will prevail. I'm just wishing. The fact of secrecy I don't particularly mind—what business of anyone else is it that I love you? I don't care about parading you before the world in a proper woman's look-what-I-caught manner—that's nothing, to me there's even a kind of indecency in public possessiveness. But I do mind the

- 161 -

limitations and humiliations of secrecy, the haunting by social fears, enforced furtiveness—can't go alone into a restaurant with you, where some friend of yours and Ann's might notice you together with that screwball broad with the limp. That I hate. It's a spoiling thing. I wonder more and more whether we are big enough to stand much more of it. And yet if you tire of me, or if the dreary social pressure forces you away from me—I swear the world's turning into one big God-damned suburb—I don't know what will happen to me. I don't know if I'm big enough to take it. I suppose I am. I just don't know.

"Please tell me: is your own religious feeling so strong that you do actually feel sinful when you're with me? I hardly dared write that. Do you realize how badly you hedged when I asked you almost the same thing two nights ago? I wasn't asking about Ann's views, blast you—I know she'd condemn the whole thing without a moment's pause for thought—I wanted to find out how it was with you, but all you could talk about was how Ann would feel. Well, I picked the wrong time of course. A real feminine trick, to cross-examine you with your head on my breast and only a few minutes after the little death. Bitchy of me, I suppose I was going by instinct, and when I do that, bitchy is my middle name. But see, dear, everything's calm now, I'm not whispering in your ear, I'm only fumbling for words on paper. I suppose you do know, don't you, that if you had to be free of me I would let you go? The dryad's thorns would scratch some—that I couldn't help, couldn't help your bleeding a bit—but they couldn't hold you, and would not. I don't want you as a prisoner. You are already a prisoner, and I wish I might set you free.

MR. WARNER: I will call the jury's attention to the fact that there is no actual break in the letter at the point where Mr. Hunter stopped reading. The thought there is incomplete, and Miss Blake went on to complete it in the same paragraph.

MR. HUNTER: I will call the jury's attention to the fact that I have been reading a rather difficult handwriting for several minutes, and am slightly hoarse. I would also point out that it is the end of a page, and the indentation at the beginning of the next page looks to me very much like the beginning of a paragraph.

MR. WARNER: Mr. District Attorney, you must have noticed that Miss Blake's writing does not make a very precise left-hand margin, but the paragraph indentations are characteristically quite deep.

MR. HUNTER: Very well—I don't want to argue a point like this—it's all one paragraph if you like. May I continue?

MR. WARNER: By all means, finish the paragraph.

MR. HUNTER (reading):

> "... No, I don't hate Ann, I was not thinking only of Ann when I wrote that.
>
> "Another thing, by the way, that I hardly dared to write.
>
> "Jimmy, I need to know: if Ann would allow a separation, and if we went somewhere—no matter where, so it's a long way off—would you be mentally, emotionally *able* to live with me? Look into yourself. Tell me, if you can, what would happen inside you, supposing the situation was like that. Make it far away—Arizona, Tahiti, island of Capri, who cares?—and I am with you, in your bed at night and with you in all the long bright days. Would you see me still as a human woman who loves you and who would be happy to bear you children?—that could be, you know; a doctor assured me of it a couple of years ago, the little deformity is no obstacle. Or would I become the whore who 'led you astray' and 'wrecked your life'?
>
> "You know, Jimmy, it hasn't seemed to me (but I could be so damned wrong!) that religion goes very deep with you. Isn't it mostly a matter of being brought up in a certain way that automatically shuts out other views without seriously examining them? I'm trying to suggest that unlike Ann, you're really not embedded in religion like a fly in amber. I've made no secret of my own agnosticism with you— wouldn't have occurred to me to do so—and that hasn't appeared to trouble you particularly. You do shy away, you don't like the topic, I suppose you feel the way so many people do nowadays, that religion is all right but talking about it is not quite nice. But I can't imagine that you condemn me in your heart (do you?) for relying on my own reason, being unafraid of doubt, interested in proof, critical of all self-appointed authority?

"So I'll even dare ask you: just where is the mercy, the rationale, the loving-kindness, in an ethical-religious system that makes me a whore bound for hell because I love you and welcome intercourse with you and want to live with you?

"I want to see you tomorrow, Jimmy. You spoke of having to work late because of Miss Anderson's being out sick—may I come there in the evening, just to see you for a few minutes? I'll be well-behaved (I hope). There are one or two other things—things even I don't care to scrawl on paper. If you call and say I mustn't come, of course I won't, but—please?

"For the first time in our experience I shall be listening for the phone and hoping you don't call. 'How do I love thee? Let me count the ways'—I can't, I can't.

"Callista."

The third letter, members of the jury, is again from Callista Blake to James Doherty. It is dated June 25th, just a week later than the one I last read, and was addressed, like the other two, to Mr. Doherty at his office. It reads as follows:

"Jimmy—

"Didn't you say you would call me Monday evening? What happened? I remember you said you would be tied up over the week end—if only my silly hungry arms had been the rope to tie you!—well, so I counted the hours to Monday evening, and glued myself to the phone, but no Jimmy. I know I mustn't call your house—you needn't have reminded me of that, last Friday! Tuesday, though, I did try to call you at the office—I'm sorry, Jimmy, I know you didn't want me to, but I was miserable, I had to try to reach you somehow—but you were out, anyway Mr. Judd answered the phone and said you were, and he sounded so chilly—am I a black cat across his path or something?—I didn't know he disliked me. What's happening, Jimmy? Could be purely my nerved-up imagination. But all week, no Jimmy. Couldn't you at least have got as far as a phone booth? Oh hell, I'm writing like a sniveling brat.

"Lately I've been having too many morbid thoughts. I know I behaved badly Friday evening—you didn't want anything to get started, and I had to act like a whining bitch in heat.

You should know there's more to me than that—I guess you do, I guess you do. Well, since that evening I've now and then thought of us—I even dreamed something of the kind—as if we were no wiser than a pair of kids slipping out behind the barn to study the difference between a boy and a girl—with peevish grown-ups likely to come around the corner of the building any minute. I've lost some of the dream—I think we did get caught and stood there frozen waiting for the wrath. Only the boy in the dream wasn't quite you. Be jealous, damn you.

"Are we so terribly far apart? I'm beginning to understand there's plenty about me you don't even like. It's not strange. Didn't I tell you at the start, or try to, that I'm not easy to get along with? I often have a bad enough time trying to get along with myself. But Jimmy, Dearest, *all* people are far apart in a lot of important ways. No exceptions. And all people have elements in common too, things they can share, use to bridge the gulf between self and self, if they only knew it. Don't you think we have enough in common so that if we both tried hard and honestly and lovingly, we could live happily together?

"I know, I know—I wrote that as if I were assuming that Ann would set you free. Oh, I like you and don't like you, for not wanting to talk about her with me. Like you for it because I know it's loyalty, you're trying to be fair to her, spare her pain, you still love her in many ways—and somehow I know about all of them, and respect every one of them whether you believe that or not. And dislike it, it hurts, because—well, because I happen to be the one under the gun, Jimmy, and I keep thinking if I knew more about her I might see my own way better. I love you in ways she never imagined, couldn't imagine. She's not a passionate woman, Jimmy—as I don't suppose you need to be told. She's sweet, possessive, domestic, good to you so far as she knows how to be, loves you in her fashion so long as you conform to what she wants you to be. Undoubtedly it troubles her that you haven't happened to have children yet. Loves you in her fashion—oh, Jimmy, to my thinking, and I'm not a fool, loving an image of what you'd like another person to be, that's not love at all, just self-love and arrogance.

"Am I doing it too? Am I in love with what I wish you were? I mustn't *always* shy away from that thought—I'll have to look at it straight some time, can't now somehow, not now, not now. I don't think it's true. Anyway I will assure you, pretty Ann never woke up at night whimpering your name and tasting blood on her lip.

"There's no solution that won't hurt somebody. I'm selfish too—like you, like Ann if she knew and understood, I don't want to be hurt any more than I have been. I don't hate Ann, I don't want to hate her. I don't want anything except to get away somewhere with you—are we savages to be held in line by magic words mumbled in the mouth of a priest?— because I love you best and need you.

"Silence is the cruelest of a coward's weapons. It's not like you to use it against me. Please write, or call me. Please come to me.

"Callista."

The fourth letter is typed, dated July 5th, 1959, and signed only with a typed capital J. You remember yesterday Mr. Lamson testified that James Doherty himself, as well as Miss Blake, acknowledged his authorship of this letter. It reads:

"Dear Callista:

"I meant to write to you sooner, but have been very busy, so am afraid the time has slipped by, besides I do not know just how to say what I ought to, except that we must relinquish the prospect we have discussed and that you mention in your letter, as it would not work out for the best but am afraid would have bad consequences to all concerned. I consider myself very much to blame having given you a wrong idea of the situation, although that certainly was not my intention. I think all we can do is try to forget about it, because that is what we must do, unless the situation changes some time. I am sorry to have to say it as you may feel disappointed and that I have let you down, as a matter of fact I feel that myself, am afraid I may have treated you rather badly letting you take things for granted when I ought not to have done so, although that was not my intention, and am very sorry if it is so. I feel you are not to blame in any way but I am, I know, and the only thing we can do is sort of forget the whole thing and hope you can forgive me for letting you down.

> "Sincerely,
> "J."

"P.S. I feel we ought not to get in touch again about this for a while as there is nothing we can do. Please read between the lines and don't be angry."

Since the defendant appears to find this letter amusing, I can only say that her sense of humor has not much in common with mine.

MR. WARNER: Is the defendant on trial for changes in facial expression? I did not know that an unhappy smile was an indictable offense.

JUDGE MANN: The comments of both counsel are out of order. Continue, please.

MR. HUNTER: As you have already heard, members of the jury, the last letter we have here was not mailed, but found in Miss Blake's possession. During her interrogation by Mr. Lamson, she stated certain reasons for not mailing it—part of the testimony which you have heard, to which you will give whatever weight you believe it deserves. This last letter is dated August 8th, 1959, more than a month after Miss Blake received that letter from James Doherty. I would remind you too that August 8th was the day after the picnic which has been mentioned several times in the testimony. The letter reads:

> "Dear Jimmy:

> "Understand, before you start reading this, that you need not answer it unless you wish. I will wait a while, and then take silence for your answer if that is how it must be. I had almost accepted silence already, or thought I had, most of the time this last month. But I saw you yesterday—might have stayed away, meant to, could not—with all the fog of company manners between us, and discovered what I should have known: I am not cured of you. I wish I were, and I shall be after a while. I've wished I could hate or despise you—can't do that, but I'll be able to forget you sometime, and if there's no happiness at least there will be peace, of one sort or another.

> "I have gone by two periods, Jimmy. In those good days of June—yes, they were good—we evidently managed to start a certain arrogant little Blake-Doherty thing which now lives in me as if he belonged there. And he does. What does

- 167 -

this knowledge do to you? Sorry? Scared? Maybe a little bit happy, or proud? Or just angry with me? I'm shocked to realize I don't know you well enough to guess the answer.

"One thing I will not do—and your religion would approve my decision, I believe (at the same time that it provides some cruel obstacles in the way of carrying it out). I will not, Jimmy—I will *not* creep off on the wrong side of our idiot laws and have an abortion. I want this child. Crazy of me it may be, but I already love it, while it's just a blob of almost-nothing that'll soon be making me sick and physically scared. I want it.

"And I want the child to have a father. From the start. I've seen too much of petticoat government—it reeks. I don't trust my own self to bring up a child alone. In spite of all the best knowledge I have, sooner or later I'd have some damned uprush of maternity to the brain and start making a lot of the mistakes all mothers make—including some my own mother made with me, no doubt—and nobody to check me, nobody to fill the father's place that must not be empty if a child is to grow up straight and good. I won't have my baby crippled that way.

"He's yours too, Jimmy. It's your seed in me, the life-package from all your grandfathers and grandmothers. He's from Ireland, dear, he's from Italy where my father's mother was born, he's from one of the embraces when your sweet strong body could not free itself until I was willing to let you go. I frightened you sometimes, didn't I? I will again, or at least I dream of it.

"All right, let's be sober. For religious reasons, Ann will never even consider a divorce. There is such a thing as separation, that would allow you to provide for her but live with me. The legal formula is not too important to me—I wish we might have it, but it would not hurt me to live without it, and we could educate the child so that his understanding would be too big to care for such cretinous words as 'illegitimate.' With your training you could find work anywhere in the States—or abroad for that matter, Canada, England, Australia. So could I. I understand the kind of art work that makes money, as well as photography. I also know shorthand and typing. We'd make out wherever we went, and be the same as married. It only needs your will for it, Jimmy, and an amount of courage that isn't abnormal. Others faced with the same difficulty have done it.

"Granted, Ann would be hurt badly, for a while. She'd consider us both lost in sin. (Do you?) Her pride would be hurt, and her love for you, which may be strong—I don't know that, yes or no. Jimmy, you and Ann don't have children. You and I do have a child. Granted also that Ann is good and sweet and conventionally right. Does that give her the right—

Members of the jury, three words are crossed out here, but not illegible. It is my understanding that these letters will be available for the inspection of the jury; the purpose of reading them is to save time and to make sure of the correct interpretation, as Mr. Warner pointed out. Now I think I should read these crossed-out words, but will not do so if the defense has any objection. Do you wish to look at the page again, Mr. Warner?

MR. WARNER: Not necessary, but wait a moment, please. [*Conferring with defendant.*] The crossed-out words may be read, so long as the jury is given the whole picture. The words are still legible, it's true, but not clearly, and it was evidently not Miss Blake's intention that they should be legible, if she had ever mailed the letter.

MR. HUNTER: Thank you, Counselor. The words crossed out are "to destroy us"—"Does that give her the right to destroy us"—but with those words crossed out, the letter reads thus:

"Does that give her the right to keep you and me apart and prevent my child from having a father?

"Living seems to be full of situations where you can't do a good thing without an accompanying evil. I suppose it's questions of this kind that make people give up trying to solve their own ethical problems and ask some supernatural authority to do it for them. And yet I would think that the only answer in any such dilemma is to decide which is greater, the evil or the good. If they seem to balance, doubtless inaction is better than trying to perform your good act. But if one is clearly greater than the other, isn't the answer plain? I know this goes contrary to your religious views, but Jimmy, this once, think whether I may not be right and yourself mistaken.

"I am trying to think straight, about the years ahead, the child, about living with you, the difficulties we'd face. I'm trying not to remember that you did look at me yesterday once or twice as a lover might, and with the sunlight falling across your cheekbones, before I quit playing with the Wayne kids and wandered off. Maybe some time I'll tell you where I went and what I did.

"I can't think of Ann as anything but an innocent bystander. She needs you in the common ways, but I—"

Members of the jury, the letter ends there. The State rests.

JUDGE MANN: The Court will hear any motions.

MR. WARNER: Your Honor, I move that the case of the People against Callista Blake be dismissed on the following grounds: one, that the prosecution has not demonstrated that the death of Ann Doherty resulted from a criminal action; two, that the prosecution has not, by witnesses, connected the defendant Callista Blake with the death of Ann Doherty beyond a reasonable doubt.

JUDGE MANN: The motion is denied, Mr. Warner. Are there other motions?

MR. WARNER: No, your Honor, not at this time.

JUDGE MANN: The Court stands adjourned until 1 P.M.

7

Upon this, by us has she been required to voluntarily declare herself to be, and to have always been, a demon of the nature of a Succubus, which is a female devil whose business it is to corrupt Christians by the blandishments and flagitious delights of love. To this the speaker has replied that the affirmation would be an abominable falsehood, seeing that she had always felt herself to be a most natural woman.

Then her irons being struck off by the torturer, the aforesaid has removed her dress, and has maliciously and with evil design bewildered and attacked our understanding with the sight of her body, the which, for a fact, exercises upon a man supernatural coercion.

BALZAC, *The Succubus*

I

In the robing room after the noon recess, Judge Mann was assailed by a feeling of being out of place, ludicrously so, dismayingly. The village atheist blundering into a crowd of churchgoers to retrieve his hat; or an explorer required to take part in a tribal ritual without a briefing on the rules. Innocent oversight, by the way, on the part of local chieftains and witchdoctors, for why wouldn't they assume that everybody knew the rules from infancy as they did? *What am I doing here?*

He could ask the question of Joe Bass and receive an intelligent answer. No good. No use making Joe uneasy about the Judge's state of mind.

Even the door to the courtroom looked unfamiliar. Why had he never before noticed that the swirling grain of the oak resembled the smoke lines of a bonfire? He stood with his hand on the knob, reflecting also that technique is not enough: he should spend several months, say a year, in a special kind of discipline, before it would be right to start taking piano pupils—supposing he had any such intention. He turned the knob, hearing the muted uproar of a hundred conversations in the dull room beyond; opened the door a crack, and the noise became a sonorous flow; opened it then all the way, and the roar was shut off by the action, since every talker had been watching that door, impatient for the continuation of ritual. *For example, I would have to learn much more about children—*

"All rise!"

He walked to the Judge's bench a stranger. Why the devil must they stand up? Settling their damn lunches?

Seated, noticing how quickly today the rustle and throat-clearing subsided, his eyes were annoyed by shabbiness. Old stains, scratches on the woodwork, in every corner a pinch of dust; on every face—Callista Blake's, Hunter's, even Mr. Delehanty's—the marks of that peculiarly human strain that people experience in the presence of the heavy institutions they themselves have made. Maybe his eyes were exaggerating the dust, to support the bias of his mind, which insisted on pointing up the dirt, cracks, awkwardly mended spots and general bad housekeeping of the law itself. *Well, there are certain things to do before I go.* "Are you ready for your opening, Mr. Warner?"

"Yes, your Honor." The Old Man could hardly say that no one is ever ready to send his love into the bonfire. "Members of the jury, I don't think you want to hear any elaborate opening speech from me. A great part of the defense of Callista Blake has already been brought out by testimony for the prosecution. I am not referring only to the transcript of the interrogation of Miss Blake by District Attorney Lamson, in the course of which she told practically everything that she can tell if I put her on the witness stand. I am thinking, for example, of the testimony of a very honest and impartial State policeman, concerning footprints and other evidence by that pond in Shanesville. I'll revert to his testimony in my closing words. I'm thinking of the testimony of Mrs. Jason." Anyway, Mann thought, Cecil Warner's voice was in good shape; he was slow, and calm, and steady on his feet. "And I am thinking, of course, of those letters written by Callista Blake which the District Attorney by some process of reasoning utterly beyond me—I suppose it's reasoning—appears to regard as evidence of guilt.

"We're confronted here, ladies and gentlemen, by a case in which the most vital elements are intangible, subjective. Now, the law doesn't like intangibles. That's natural. If we're dealing with clear, everyday facts of observation we know where we are, we're used to thinking in those terms, we can manage as well as if we were manipulating a solid object in the hand. Take a common sort of case for an example: a man falls in getting off a bus, is injured, and sues the traction company. All right: you've got eyewitnesses, medical testimony, and a few fairly simple questions to decide: did he fall? was he injured, and if so how badly? was the bus company at fault, and if so what's a just compensation for the injuries? A jury will have minor difficulties in a case like that: there's the possibility that the man's a clever fraud, and since most people are not good observers, the eyewitnesses may contradict each other a little, but on the whole juries don't have too hard a time in reaching a fair verdict in such cases.

"Here it's not so. In this case the tangible facts are hardly in dispute, the vital problem is the interpretation of those facts. There was aconitine in Callista Blake's apartment; the defense has not denied it. I know, and Callista Blake knows, why it was there; the State will try to tell you it was there because of a deep-laid premeditated plot to kill Ann Doherty. Ann Doherty did drink the poison there, undoubtedly; we know it happened accidentally, the State will say she was intended to drink it. The State has demonstrated an affair between Callista Blake and James Doherty; we have not denied it nor thought of denying it. And the State, by inference, supplies Callista Blake with the motive of common jealousy and argues that this led to premeditated murder. Now Callista herself knows that isn't so; I know it, and so do a few others really well acquainted with her: they're aware that no degree of sexual jealousy would ever drive her to perform such an act. But how in the world is she to prove it to twelve honest jurors who never saw her before the trial? It's just not in the field of tangible proof. I could put her on the stand, and if she talked to you all day long, what could she say on that subject that isn't already said in the traditional words she's already spoken when she was indicted?— 'I am not guilty.' Finally, the defense does not deny that Callista Blake drove out to Shanesville soon after Ann Doherty left. The State will have it that she went out there in a sort of pursuit of Ann Doherty, to make sure Ann died. We know she did it because she had just discovered that Ann might have got some of that stuff; we know she went out there in an attempt to reach Ann before it was too late and save her life; and it was too late, and Ann Doherty was dead. So there you have state and prosecution asserting precise contraries. We cannot, by tangible evidence, prove the intentions, motives, ideas of Callista Blake; neither can the State. In this connection I'll merely remind you for the present that the State's own witness Sergeant Shields very clearly and carefully said there was no way of telling how Ann's body got into the pond; he made it clear there isn't a scrap of that precious tangible evidence to show that Callista Blake did anything except stand there and look down, as she told Mr. Lamson she did.

"Because of the nature of the case, the primary questions of reasonable doubt and criminal intent or absence of it, I am intending to call only two witnesses for the defense. As a prosecutor, and taking it for granted that he has somehow honestly convinced himself of Callista Blake's guilt, it was unavoidable that my able adversary should have piled up all that mass of circumstantial evidence, even though hardly any of it was in dispute. As a prosecutor, he had to do it; trying to your patience as well as mine, but that's how the law works. Yet when the dust of argument has settled and you've gone into that jury room, I think you'll see—or more likely you do already— how the whole thing comes down to the question whether or not you believe Callista's word. The two witnesses I mean to call are the two who can come nearer than any others to telling you, showing you, convincing you, what kind of girl, what kind of human being Callista Blake really is. And I have no more to say by way of argument until after they have been heard. Miss Edith Nolan, please!"

She came forward not briskly but with poise, her thin face showing the gravity of concentration. She wore the same green tweed suit, in some need of pressing, that she had worn all through the trial. The dark shade, nearly the green of hemlock, set off her red hair pleasantly, the Judge thought, but did not belong too well with light blue eyes; and to wear the same costume four days running was maybe a little odd. He noticed also, and hoped the jury would not, her moment's hesitation as Mr. Delehanty recited the oath and held out the Bible for her. Probably she would prefer to affirm but had decided against such action to avoid offending the jury, accepting what to her might be a distasteful absurdity for the sake of her friend. Edith Nolan would not be, like Mrs. Jason, a truth-teller at any cost, though the Judge supposed that whatever she said would be in the service of truth as she saw it.

And what would Callista Blake do if and when it was time for her to take the oath? If Callista had learned anything yet about the grown-up necessities of compromise, it did not appear in the evidence nor in her own actions thus far. The girl who made the responses in the Lamson interrogation seemed too young, too sharply earnest to understand flexibility or the art of yielding minor issues for the sake of great ones. He thought: *Let her learn it quickly!* And instructed himself irritably to quit borrowing trouble ahead of time.

Miss Nolan also took care to make no open demonstration of the friendship which the Judge knew existed between herself and Cecil Warner. One swift eloquent glance he saw, a silent declaration: "*I'm with you and will do whatever I can.*" Then she was in the witness chair, private tensions skillfully hidden, giving routine information: age thirty-one, unmarried, portrait and free-lance photographer, A.B. Radcliffe plus a year of art school, studio and residence at 96 Hallam Street, Winchester.

"Is that address near to 21 Covent Street, Miss Nolan?"

"Yes, four of those long uptown blocks."

"How long have you known the defendant Callista Blake?"

"It's almost a year and a half now. She's been my assistant at the studio since July of last year. She answered an advertisement of mine, I employed her, and we very soon became close friends."

"Did she take her apartment at Covent Street soon after she began to work for you?"

"I think it was the same week. I helped her look for it."

"The close friendship you speak of—tell us more of that, will you? For instance, you're familiar with the details of Callista's life—past history, opinions, tastes, temperament, things of that sort?"

"Yes, Mr. Warner. A year and a half isn't a long time, but I think I know Callista as well as I could know my own younger sister if I had one, or better. Interests in common, a natural sympathy I suppose it might be called. We agree on many things, and when we differ we know how to talk, get our ideas across to each other."

"Your shared interest in artistic work has been a large part of that bond of friendship, hasn't it?"

"Yes, it has."

"Do you at present do any artistic work yourself, besides photography?"

"Not just at present. I have in the past. Illustrations for a children's book a couple of years ago. Nothing grand, but I hear the kids liked them. A few things like that."

"In any case you do have professional training and professional standing. I'm going to ask you for what the law calls an expert opinion. Miss Nolan, if you were not personally acquainted with Callista Blake, and if you were called on to judge her work, say in an exhibition of good serious modern painters, how would you rate it?"

Judge Mann saw T. J. Hunter consider an objection and settle for a somewhat elaborate bored look. The red-haired woman smiled, for the first time. Mann's pencil on the doodle-pad rather angrily crossed out its attempt to draw her face, not in cartoon but in a portrait sketch. It had escaped him altogether. *I haven't got it.* He laid the pencil down.

"It's hard to imagine myself not acquainted with Callista. But I think I can do it, Mr. Warner, for that one question. If I knew nothing about her, if I were seeing her painting or drawing for the first time under those conditions, I think it would be likely to outshine anything else in the show."

"If it were like this, for instance?" Intent on Edith Nolan's face, Mann had not been aware of Warner's drawing from his pocket a folded cover paper. Now it was in the red-haired woman's hands, and she was taking from it a page, evidently from a small scratch-pad, gazing at it and steadying it with her other hand because her fingers had started to shake. He thought in distress: *Damn it, we do have to have some rules—*

"Oh! When did she do this, Mr. Warner?"

"This morning, in court. Scratch paper. Before the reading of the letters, when Mr. Hunter and I were in side-bar conference and nothing else was happening."

"She was remembering little Doris Wayne."

"May it please the Court, is Mr. Warner introducing some of the defendant's art work as an exhibit for the defense, or is this just a love feast?"

"Mr. Hunter, I think your sarcasm may be distasteful to the jury as well as to the Court." *But it isn't, and Terence, for Christ's sake hold your water! That was too strong.* "May I see the sketch, Miss Nolan?"

Warner handed it up. Turned away from the jury, his round sagging face showed nothing of triumph, looked only tired and frightened. Another face confronted the Judge, with the arrogance and pathos and curious vulnerable mirth of childhood. Doris would be about ten, said Callista's affectionate unsentimental lines, and she was amused about something: perky, uncertain, lovable, maybe a bit dangerous. He thought: *Now I know. And though I know it, she still could die. Judge Cleever*—"I don't suppose it would qualify as an exhibit, Mr. Warner, since it isn't directly relevant to any of the legal issues. However, if you wish the jury to see it, the Court has no objection."

Hunter said quietly: "But I object. I haven't seen it, but I consider the introduction of it an unwarranted attempt to influence the jury's sympathies with irrelevant matters, and by an improper method."

"I will overrule your objection, Mr. Hunter. The defense is privileged to question Miss Nolan as a character witness. Miss Blake's artistic ability is an aspect of her character that it would be absurd to ignore. No objection was made by you when Mr. Warner asked Miss Nolan for an expert opinion in the field of art, in which she's evidently qualified to speak. The introduction of this sketch is merely a natural means of supplementing and demonstrating what Miss Nolan has to say."

Reluctantly, for it was loss of contact with something valued and not yet understood, he watched the drawing pass into the lumpy hands of Peter Anson, foreman, hands that held it briefly under bothered eyes and passed it on. Casually, and perhaps to cover the intentness with which he was watching the jury, Cecil Warner said: "Being older, more experienced, art school and all that, you've taught Callista to some extent, haven't you?"

The drawing escaped from the blank glance of Emma Beales into the hands of LaSalle, which held it for some time, and gently. Edith Nolan said slowly: "About technique, handling materials, things like that, yes, Mr. Warner, but ..." The drawing rested in Mrs. Kleinman's lap while she changed to reading glasses; probably the good lady couldn't get used to bifocals. "Her ability is very much greater than anything I have, so it would be truer to say, Mr. Warner, that she has taught me." Mr. Fielding looked at the face of Doris Wayne with lifted brows that might mean indifference or annoyance, and passed the drawing to Helen Butler. "You see, aside from her own talent, Callista has that faculty of searching out whatever's best in anyone, and—" *Why must Helen Butler look at me? I am not Callista's accuser!*—"and making it better if she can."

Don't get too rich for their blood, Miss Nolan! Hide a little the fact that you love her, or they'll begin to discount what you say. And yet, the Judge reflected, she could hardly be expected to dissemble; there would be a false note if she did. And how softly the woman was speaking!—as if they were here not to consider Callista Blake's life or death but only to talk about her as friends might talk affectionately of another in absence. He looked again at the jury. Miss Butler had relinquished the drawing to a hand from the back row and was frowning into the distance, her mild intelligent face more disturbed than he had seen it at any time during the trial. A Sunday painter, wasn't she?—he tried to remember her answers during voir dire examination, but they had gone vague: a rather mousy personality, good and pleasant but not strong.

The foreman Peter Anson fidgeted irritably, and settled into a glumness. Something wrong there. Judge Mann felt a kind of pain, in its beginning hardly distinguishable from a twisted muscle or the first warning of nausea. Anson's blunt face had become readable; at any rate Judge Mann's interpretation of its look came to him with such force that it was difficult for him to doubt his own insight: the blobby features were saying that to Mr. Peter Anson long-hairs and especially long-hair intellectual women were one big pain in the ass. You could understand it. Anson was a man who liked things simple and comfortable; he wanted larger issues settled by authority and formula, and you could say the wish derived from an honest humility, inarticulate awareness of his own mental limitations; unfortunately it meant that anything not covered by authority and formula must be brushed aside, or ignored—or hated. Confronted by a manifestly human Callista Blake or Edith Nolan—well, Anson was a good little joe and would try to be fair about it; BUT ... Only later did the Judge admit that his sense of unease, so much resembling obscure physical pain, could be the beginning of despair.

The drawing came back to Warner from the hands of Peter Anson but without another glance from him; for a moment his stubby hands were eloquent, saying: "*This paper has nothing to do with me.*"

"It's true, isn't it, Miss Nolan, that although you're naturally fond of Callista and loyal to her, the fondness and loyalty are based on understanding? I mean, you know your friend's faults and weaknesses too. You have, maybe, something of an older sister's detachment?"

"Yes, I think it's fair to say that. Mr. Warner, if that drawing isn't to be used further, as an exhibit or anything—may I have it?"

"Well ..." The moment was a long one, Cecil Warner turning to look at Callista Blake with something more than inquiry, Edith and Callista gazing at each other directly, unsmiling, yet the Judge wished the moment might be prolonged for the sake of his own understanding. A kind of brilliance and a hush; the courtroom no more present than the ocean is present at some moment of wind and shining sand and sunlight: only the three of them; the three of them, and himself somehow more than a simple observer. Callista smiled: climax of a moment that could have lasted no longer. Warner was saying quickly: "Of course, my dear—" and giving the drawing to Edith, who put it away in her handbag and shut the clasp with care. "Now would you, as an observant friend, say that Callista is moodier than most people? Subject to depressions?"

Hunter bayed: "I suggest Miss Nolan's qualifications as a psychiatrist have not exactly been established."

"My question refers to a simple observation anyone might make."

"Is that a formal objection, Mr. Hunter?"

"No, your Honor. But I hope the testimony isn't going to stray into fields where only a psychiatrist would be competent to speak."

"Let your mind be at rest on that point, Mr. District Attorney. Is Callista Blake subject to periods of depression, Miss Nolan?"

"Yes, decidedly." Judge Mann considered the possibility of exaggeration, not falsehood exactly but close to it. Surely Callista Blake was not what his brother Jack would call a depressive type, if that word was still favored in the jargon. "However, Mr. Warner, I think Callista's depressions are generally related to some external cause. Related to things that happen to her." *Yes, Redhead, that helps—some.*

"Were you at all acquainted with Mrs. James Doherty?"

"By sight, hardly more. I believe I met her three times in all, when I was visiting Callista's family in Shanesville."

"Have you met Mr. James Doherty any more often than that?"

"I don't think so. Same occasions, and then one or two times since Mrs. Doherty's death, in connection with this case."

"Callista never told you much about the Dohertys, either of them?"

"No, not much, until last July. Then she took me into her confidence about the episode with Doherty, which had ended then, or so she hoped."

"She said that? That she hoped the affair was ended?"

"Just that, as I recall. She showed me that letter from Doherty, the thing that was read in court, and then later—well, next morning in fact, she said: 'I hope it's over. I hope I'm done with the fever and the blindness.'"

It could be despair, that dullness in him like a bodily ache. The Judge found he was again studying faces on the jury. Emmet Hoag bored, half asleep by the look of him. Ancient Emerson Lake neither bored nor hostile, his gaze rigid, vaguely vulturine, apparently hypnotized by the swell of Edith Nolan's breast, under the tweed suit hardly more than hints of fullness and softness, but evidently enough to set an old man dreaming in his rank and lonely antiquity; would he be hearing what she said at all? Young LaSalle seemed indecisively friendly, Mr. Fielding remote behind an unreadable pallid front. The Beales woman studied Edith Nolan's green handbag, possibly wondering if it was a style that would suit herself. Mrs. Grant appeared grumpy; likely her bony frame was uncomfortable in the graceless seat of the jury box. The only faces of the entire jury that showed any positive liking for Edith Nolan were those of Helen Butler and Rachel Kleinman. He saw Dora Lagovski apparently submerged in moist daydream; recalled that when Callista's drawing had reached her he had seen the damp lips form (in merciful silence) the word "cute." Emerson Lake's jaw was now moving slightly, approximately in time with the mild rise and fall of Edith Nolan's breathing—damn the old buzzard. But what about himself, aged forty-seven and for the last few minutes intensely aware of Edith Nolan as a desirable woman? Weren't his own wits wandering?

So far as the Judge could see, Edith Nolan was doing nothing to flaunt her personal attractiveness. Probably to many eyes she would have none. Her make-up was not prominent, the tweed suit practically dowdy, her manner consistently simple and direct. If his wandering middle-aged eye wanted a tickling, why not choose an obvious pin-up type like the juror Dolores Acevedo? He forced himself to glance in that direction once again. The black-haired beauty was showing no more emotion at present than Mr. Fielding. Very lovely indeed; made more so by her position next to the sallow weediness of the schoolteacher Stella Wainwright. Lovely like a conventional painting, Acevedo—and no more disturbing. Her face blurred; the instant's involuntary motion of his eyes transformed it to another, also under black hair: but these were close-set curls, the face altogether different, not beautiful at all by common standards but rather homely, big-nosed, small-chinned, the eyes sea-blue and, not for the first time, frightening. "*It wasn't natural how men went crazy for her—not even pretty—any man, garage man, anything in pants....*"

That peevish outbreak from Maud Welsh had puzzled the Judge at the time. Now he could sense the quality in Callista that Maud Welsh had meant. Earlier perhaps he had been too intensely preoccupied with other aspects of the case and with his own situation as Judge, the lawyer and judge dominant, the male animal quiescent or at least temporarily locked up in the cellar. Yes, she had it, the quality sensed but not understood because understanding is a verbalizing process and there aren't any words for the electric something-or-other that will make men turn in desire toward one particular woman in a crowd, ignoring others who may be in a dozen ways prettier, more agreeable, more available. Callista had it. Edith Nolan, in her own totally different way, had it, at least for himself, perhaps not for most others. No: Maud Welsh wouldn't have been likely to make that remark about Miss Nolan. *Yes, they are wandering.*

"Do you recall, Miss Nolan, what day it was that this conversation took place, about Doherty's letter?"

"Yes, it was the evening of Monday, July 6th, the same day Callista had received that letter."

"I'll ask you to tell the circumstances more fully in your own way."

"She telephoned me, that evening, soon after going home from my studio. Asked me to come over to Covent Street. Her voice sounded as it might if she'd been in physical pain. I went at once, and found her—well, dazed, sick, in shock you could call it. She'd been in one of her blue moods all week, I didn't know why. She held out that letter to me. I read the thing. I remember I told her she'd feel better if she could cry, or smash dishes, anything to break the tension that was making her sick. She did cry, the only time I've known her to do so. And told me about it. Everything, I think. Except at that time she didn't know she was pregnant—a few days past the period, not enough to signify. When she was able to talk she was much better, got things in proportion, summed it up quite realistically herself without my saying much. She'd loved him a while, the kind of infatuation any lonely and imaginative girl might experience; then when she most needed him he'd broken it off, and that was that."

"Objection! Irrelevant opinions."

"Objection overruled." Judge Mann reflected dourly on the legal unwisdom of what he was about to add, and added it: "It appears to the Court that the witness is concerned with matters of fact as she saw them, speaking to the best of her knowledge and belief." *Old buzzard, pint-size Emerson Lake in a black silk nightie, you wanted that startled blue-eyed glance, the warmth of it and the friendliness, and you knew you'd get it: consider whether that was why you spoke.*

"Exception."

"Did Callista say anything to suggest she was thinking of suicide?"

"Two things, Mr. Warner, which I didn't understand at the time as I should have. When she was crying and hysterical, she said: 'I want my father, my father, I can't find out how to live without him.' Well, I knew he'd died away back when she was seven years old. Then later she said, twice I think: 'I wish I was dead.' That—oh, I took it to be simply an unthinking expression of grief and exhaustion. It seems to be a thing people say without considering quite what it means. I took it that way: alarming but not to be understood literally. But I think now, she meant it literally."

"You stayed with her a while, I suppose?"

"Yes, took her back to my place and made her go to bed there, gave her a sleeping pill. I played some hi-fi records, things she liked, until she fell asleep. In the morning she seemed to be in good command of herself, sense of humor restored anyway. That's when she said she hoped she was cured, and for a while I stopped worrying about other things she'd said."

"But only for a while?"

"Only for a while. During the following month, the rest of July, it was clear that things weren't right for her. Not herself. Deep abstractions for instance, when she wouldn't answer because she really didn't hear. Normally with me she's completely courteous, wouldn't dream of ignoring a question if she heard it. In July she was slipping down into the bluest of blue moods, and I couldn't reach her. I wondered about pregnancy because of what she'd told me, and asked her about it, I guess a week after she'd first told me the situation. She said: 'Oh, I'm all right.' Mistakenly, I took that to mean she'd had the delayed period. Either she answered evasively, which isn't like her, or she didn't understand my question. The last, I think. I think she was in such a faraway mood it was hard for her to get hold of what people said."

"Did she say any more, that month, about suicide?"

"Indirectly, yes. One evening we got into a sort of general talk, just kicking ideas around. She said some individuals are deficient in the will to live; living is desiring, she said, and such people don't desire strongly enough for a complete effort to stay alive. Well—something in it if you're speaking of certain pathological cases—catatonics I think the doctors call them— patients who just lie around, won't eat or even move, a kind of death in life. But that's so far from anything in Callista's make-up, I couldn't believe she was talking indirectly about herself. She said not all zombis are in the psychopathic hospitals. Later—this did alarm me—she remarked that she'd have no problems worth mentioning if she could discover any purpose in existence. A depressive remark, certainly. She wouldn't have said it if she hadn't felt she was losing her hold on things, losing her interest in living—and if I understand it correctly, Mr. Warner, that loss of interest is the danger sign. People can talk a lot about killing themselves, and nothing happens. But if the interest in living goes—"

"Objection! This is exactly the sort of thing I was afraid of, your Honor. I don't care what she calls it, Miss Nolan is now lecturing us like a professional psychiatrist, and I object."

"Overruled." *I believe I snapped; the rumble on the left is the noise of calf-bound law books revolving in the grave.* "The Court has not received the impression that the witness is claiming any professional standing in psychiatry. The remark you object to, Mr. Hunter, was a general one, to be sure; but she was speaking of matters that are either common knowledge or ought to be. I must rule that the defense is within its rights to let her follow this line, to help clarify her testimony on matters of fact." *And where in the pluperfect hell do I dig up a precedent on that one?*

"Exception."

"Yes. You may complete what you were saying, Miss Nolan."

"If the interest in living is gone—I mean the simple wish to stay alive and see what will happen next—then I think there's real danger of a suicide. And as the Judge said, Mr. Warner, I guess that's pretty much common knowledge. Callista herself was certainly aware of it, from her reading, her general education. Well, that remark about discovering any purpose in existence—I caught Callista up on that, I remember. I reminded her that we make and choose our own purposes—" (*Watch it, Red!*)—"so far as we know them." She understood the danger, probably, the risk of touching on any questions that, for most of the jury, were settled on Sunday morning and decently ignored the rest of the week. "She—thought about that, I'm sure, and for a while I think she came part way out of her depression. Not all the way."

"Summing up then, Miss Nolan: knowing her as you do, and seeing her, I suppose, every week-day during last July—you're convinced that most of that time she was behaving like one in the grip of a serious depression with the possibility of suicide?"

"I don't have any doubt of it, Mr. Warner—now. I ought not to have been in doubt at the time. If anyone is guilty in this case it's myself, because I ought to have stayed with her just about every minute until she won her way out of that mood. Then there would have been no chance for the horrible accident that makes it possible to charge her with—"

"Objection!"

"Objection sustained." She looked up with understanding and no reproach. The man in private applauded her doubtless intentional violation of rules, while the Judge must condemn. "The witness's answer will have to be stricken." *It comes to me, I did not add that the jury is to disregard it. That all right, Red?*

"Miss Nolan, I understand you weren't present at a certain picnic in Shanesville last August 7th. Did you know about it at the time?"

"Yes. I closed the studio that afternoon—the weather was impossibly hot. Cal said her mother was having one of her picnics, and thought she might go. Cal didn't ordinarily care for that sort of thing, but I—oh, I guess I just told her to run along and have a good time."

"Did Callista speak later of seeing the Dohertys at that picnic?"

"Yes, Monday. All she said was that they were there, and she hadn't talked with either of them. I asked if she was—cured, and she said: 'Oh, Edith, I can't talk about it yet, I can't.' I had to let it go at that. All that week she was very blue. She was working hard—too hard; volunteered to straighten out some of my records. Afraid to relax, maybe."

"When did you last see Callista before her arrest?"

"Friday, August 14th, when she left the studio after work."

"What did her mood seem to be at that time?"

"Tired, unhappy, withdrawn—but maybe a little more composed. I knew that, left to herself and barring unforeseeable accidents, she'd find good and reasonable answers to her troubles, but—Mr. Warner, it's strangely difficult to help anyone you love."

"Did you talk to her on the phone that week end any time?"

"Yes, late Sunday afternoon, the 16th. My father was in town that day, a flying visit, unexpected. Callista had never met him. I wanted her to. I called her late in the afternoon, past 5:30 I think—to ask if she'd like to come over in the evening. She said she might, but there was something she had engaged to do first. She sounded very much better. Not happy, but—calm anyhow. She didn't say what the engagement was, and didn't make it sound like anything too important. It could have been a reference to Mrs. Doherty's coming to see her—I mean, nothing Callista said was inconsistent with that. She could hardly have talked to me as calmly, almost cheerfully, as she did, if she'd still been overwrought or—or had known she was heading toward something disastrous."

"When she didn't come to meet your father, did you call her?"

"Tried to, a little after nine—that would have been when she was out in Shanesville, according to what she told the District Attorney. I wasn't worried when she didn't show up, just supposed that something had delayed her until too late, and that she'd bring me up to date when I saw her Monday."

"What was her usual time for coming to work in the morning?"

"Any time before ten was all right with me. That Monday, August 17th, she telephoned me at about ten and said she was sick. Her voice was completely changed: flat, dead. I asked of course what was wrong. She said in the same tone, without hesitation: 'I've been pregnant since June and last night I had a miscarriage.' I told her I'd come over as soon as I could get rid of a client who was waiting in the studio. She said then in a very distressed way: 'No no, Edith, please don't!' She insisted she was all right, and then for a moment or two she was almost incoherent, saying she—oh, refused to drag me into her troubles, things like that. I said nonsense, I was her friend and that's what friends are for. Finally I asked if there was anyone with her, and she said no, but there would be presently. I thought she meant her mother or maybe her stepfather or both—she didn't say so, it was just one of those mistaken impressions you get under stress."

"You didn't go over?"

"No, sir. I thought that if Mrs. Chalmers was there I'd likely just be crashing in and doing more harm than good. I called again, later. Busy signals. When I finally got through, about one-thirty, the phone was answered by some policeman who asked me a few dozen questions and was finally willing to tell me that Miss Blake had been detained for questioning on a certain matter, as he called it, and was at the courthouse, at Mr. Lamson's office."

"Who was that policeman, if you recall?"

"Gage or some such name."

One for the Chief of Detectives. The Judge will not smile. There is no reason to smile.

"Did you then go to the District Attorney's office, Miss Nolan?"

"Yes."

"Were you given any information about your friend?"

"No, sir, just a brush-off from some clerk. That's when I started trying to call you, Mr. Warner."

"Yes. I have only one or two more questions, Miss Nolan. Did Callista ever express to you any hostility toward Ann Doherty?"

"Never. I recall that she spoke of her several times, but never with hostility or resentment or anything suggesting jealousy. No exaggerated friendliness either. I got the impression they were—acquaintances."

"Well, for that matter, did you ever hear Callista speak maliciously about anyone?"

"Never."

II

"Your witness, Mr. Hunter."

Edith Nolan thought with an edge of panic: *Is that all, Cecil?* The Old Man's face was saying a kind of good-bye to her, turning away, not apparently displeased or disappointed—satisfied rather, so far as one could hope to read a face that must also be presenting a front to the gaze of the jury. But there was so much more that ought to have been said! The intimate truths of personality, relation, individual quality, that become no longer small once your vision is clear enough to separate the general from the specific, to see the primary core of self and the universe its matrix at one and the same time, neither too much distorted. It seemed to Edith that she had hardly begun to talk to those twelve, who were certainly not all dull, not all hostile.

Was there, for example, no way at all to explain that Callista had a comic brown mole near her navel, that when she was absorbed in reading her left forefinger twisted a black curl above her ear, always the same curl, the same small motion—and that these facts, alone and of themselves, were reasons as great, valid, finally convincing, as any of the other reasons why she must not be slain?

Still it was not, ultimately, a question of explaining anything, of offering facts to twelve other minds with the assumption that they could view them as you did. They could not. If it isn't in nature for two pairs of eyes ever to observe a simple physical object in quite the same manner, how grotesque to expect twelve minds to agree, or even approximate agreement, in the consideration of an abstract idea! What was needed, she thought, was that twelve minds should learn (here and now and very quickly) a type of humility in the face of the unknown that even the strongest and best schooled intelligences found it hard to achieve with study and leisure and every advantage of the past's accumulated resources. Unknown indeed—these people knew nothing of Callista Blake. They never could, in the nature of things, know much, never acquire more than a brief distorted glimpse of her, and that under conditions so outrageously far from the daily norm that her actual self appeared to them as no more than the flicker of a shadow. The kindly and badly troubled little man up there on the bench knew far more about her than they did, simply because he was trained to observation and the disciplines of independent thought; and he knew only a trifle. *How little I know myself, or ever will know!*

She controlled her face to the semblance of tranquillity. The long-jawed man had arrived with his athletic grace, a foot raised comfortably on the platform that elevated the witness chair, his charcoal-gray suit just right for the occasion, neat and grave like a uniform. At close range, Edith noticed his expression was not particularly cold or severe. His eyes were thoughtful, his features betrayed no ugly tension. What is cruelty anyway, and how do you read it in another? It seemed to be present like an occasional tic (but might not really be) in the vacuous face of that oaf Hoag in the front row of the jury box. But in T. J. Hunter? At the moment he looked like a solemn salesman about to give her a well-spoken pitch, say on insurance or a middle-priced car.

"You would do virtually anything, would you not, for your friend Callista Blake?"

"The best thing I can do for her is tell the truth about her and about these events, so far as I know it, and that I've done."

"Your answer is not quite responsive, Miss Nolan."

"I think it is, but I'll be more specific if you wish. I would not commit crimes for Callista Blake or any other friend, if only because in the long run you do your friend no service that way—compounding wrong things instead of lessening them. And I would not lie for her on any important matter, because it happens the truth is best for her as well as for me."

"That's quite a pragmatic attitude, isn't it?"

My, the high intellectual plane! "Naturalistic might be a better word, Mr. District Attorney, but pragmatic if you like. If an ethical principle isn't at least theoretically practical in human affairs, I'd rather leave it in the books."

"I see your point." *If only you did!* "You wouldn't kill in defense of Callista Blake?"

"Why, I might. If it's a clear case of protecting a friend's life, the law generally calls it justifiable homicide, doesn't it?"

"But for you it would have to be a clear case, is that right? I mean, you're referring to something on the level of shooting a burglar to protect the household, something like that?"

"I suppose so. I've never encountered any situation like that, so I really can't predict how I'd behave."

"Let me make sure I understand your position, Miss Nolan. You do not believe in absolute ethical principles?"

"Before I can answer that I must have your personal definition of the word 'absolute'."

"You must be familiar with the term, are you not?"

"Yes, but there would be at least five or six definitions of it in any unabridged dictionary, and I can't know which one you have in mind unless you tell me."

"Well, I had in mind the meaning which I think is generally used in philosophical discussions: self-contained, self-dependent, ultimate, in other words free from the limitations of human error, human perception."

"Thank you." *He is a shade tougher than I thought.* "In that case the answer would have to be that ethical principles are human achievements, human ways of thinking and acting, and I don't see how a human activity can ever be free from the limitations of human error and human perception."

"Very plausible. I see you've done quite a bit of thinking along these lines. That is what you mean by what you called a—a naturalistic attitude, I think that was your term?"

"In part, yes."

"Oh, there's more?"

"As a well-read man, Mr. Hunter, you must know that the conception of naturalistic ethics is at least as old as Confucius, that libraries have been filled with it, and that we could talk here on the subject until the end of next year with a great deal left unsaid."

"Well, I'm afraid there might be a fatigue factor."

"There might indeed." *Was I quick enough to steal some of that applause of witless laughter?* "It would take quite a while just to find a little agreement on definitions and first premises."

"Maybe." He looked downright friendly, she thought, until you noticed the rigid watchfulness. His smile was comfortable; he probably felt that the rumble of amusement was, on the whole, one for his side. It probably was. She risked a glance toward the jury. Most of them looked puzzled, but none really irritated except little Mr. Anson; Flint-face Fielding seemed coldly interested, but whether in a favorable or hostile way there was no telling. In

Helen Butler Edith saw a tiny flicker, surely friendliness, as their eyes met for an instant. It might mean recognition and memory, but if Miss Butler had any thought of disqualifying herself because of a trivial meeting months ago when they had not even exchanged names, she would surely have done it already. *Best not look at her again.* "I think, Miss Nolan, I'd better go back to my original question. I gave you my definition of 'absolute,' you remember, and you said—which sounded reasonable to me—that human activity can't very well be free from human error. Now, may I take that as a positive no to my earlier question: you do not believe in absolute ethical principles?"

"Not quite, Mr. Hunter. Some ethical principles take on the apparent quality of absolutes, or of universal law, simply because virtually all the members of a society endorse them. In other words we act as if those principles were absolutes, whether we can justify it logically or not. So let me put it this way: I believe in following certain ethical principles as strictly as though they had the nature of universal law, so long as my own conscience, my own intelligence, can agree to it."

"I see. But that means, doesn't it, that your conscience is actually, to you, the supreme judge?"

"In a sense it has to be."

"For example," said Judge Mann suddenly, and Edith turned to him feeling as though he had reached out a hand to aid her in crossing slippery rocks above a torrent—"for example, if an individual accepts the orders or doctrines of an external authority, would you agree, Miss Nolan, that his acceptance is itself an act of his own conscience, or will, or intelligence?"

"Yes, your Honor, that expresses what I had in mind."

The Judge said: "In fact the individual can have no dealings, no contact with ideas or doctrines or even with simple observation of the physical world, unless there is first a positive action of his own intelligence. Is this still in line with your thought, Miss Nolan?"

"Yes, your Honor."

"And—I'll be done in a moment, Mr. Hunter—and finally, would you agree, Miss Nolan, that this decidedly elementary fact is often overlooked in our everyday thinking, perhaps because it's so obvious that we aren't willing to give it a second glance or work out its implications?"

"I believe so. We accept the fact the way animals accept the air they breathe, and with no more thought."

"Yes," said Judge Mann, his gaze leaving her, maybe reluctantly, as he scribbled something on his note-pad, "life was breathing air a good many million years before a fairly advanced science noticed that air was a mixture of different gases, had weight and mass, other properties. Well, go on, Mr. Hunter."

Edith thought: *Maybe that'll larn him.* And over there beside her friend, the Old Man's dark eyes were watching, saying as plainly as eyes could say it that he was pleased with her, and that he was profoundly frightened.

"I've enjoyed this little excursion into philosophy, Miss Nolan, and I'm glad his Honor lent us a hand with it—'way over my depth, I'm afraid—but now I suppose we'd better get back to the facts. Well, one thing first: am I right in supposing that in your view, this—this act of acceptance, I think you called it, has to happen first before one is even allowed to believe in a Supreme Being?"

She could not help glancing toward the Judge, who was watching the prosecutor, coldly intent and unjudicially angry. The corner of her eye gave her the solemn approving nod of the juror Emma Beales, the sudden relaxation—*everything's all right, boys*—in the foreman Peter Anson. She understood that Judge Mann was waiting for her. "Mr. Hunter, I also enjoyed that excursion into philosophy, but unless the Court rules it's relevant, I will not discuss my views on religion with you."

"They are not relevant to the case," said Judge Mann, "and the witness is not required to answer."

Hunter nodded politely. "I've certainly no wish to press the point. But may I ask—and by the way, I won't urge you to respond to this question either if you'd rather not—may I ask, Miss Nolan, whether you're willing to state the reasons for your refusal to answer?"

"Quite willing. Religion is a topic that too easily stirs up a lot of emotion if there's any serious discussion or conflict of opinion. I assume the members of the jury belong to more than one religious faith. Some of them might share my views, others might be offended by them—I can't tell. But since religion, so far as I can see, has absolutely nothing to do with the guilt or innocence of my friend, I think it would make no sense anyhow for me to get into the subject."

The Old Man over there nodded slightly, maybe a kind of cheering, a way of saying his gal Red could take care of herself. *But can I?*

"That's reasonable," said T. J. Hunter almost affectionately. "You're right it's a touchy topic, right also that it has no direct bearing on the question of guilt or innocence; and I'm as anxious as you are to avoid stirring up needless emotions or side issues. The only thing I do wish I could get at along this line—my only reason for speaking of it at all—well, Miss Nolan, if you have no unqualified belief in absolute ethical principles, and if a question about belief in God is merely distasteful to you, don't you think that might have some slight bearing on your credibility as a witness in a murder trial?"

The Old Man was standing up, his voice slow in coming, slow-moving when it came as if each word must force its way past an obstacle in his throat: "Mr. Hunter, that is vicious and contemptible."

And before stage anger took control of the handsome mask with the shovel chin, Edith glimpsed the fact that T. J. Hunter was at last genuinely pleased about something. "I must ask you to watch your choice of language, Counselor."

"No more of this," said Judge Mann. "The attention of both counsel, please. Your question, Mr. Hunter, was entirely out of order, because it implied that a person with independent views on religion has a lower regard for the truth than others—an implication with no slightest basis in fact or logic. From her answers, her manner, her educational background, there is every reason to suppose that Miss Nolan has quite as high a regard for the truth as anyone else who has testified in this case. You will withdraw your question. Mr. Warner, your remark to the prosecutor was ill-chosen and unparliamentary. It calls for an apology to him, I think."

Hunter spoke gently: "I withdraw my question."

"Mr. Hunter," said the Old Man wearily, "I was influenced by personal feeling as I should not have been, and my words were ill-chosen. My apology, sir, if you can find it acceptable."

Very gently, Hunter said: "Why, of course, Cecil." And more gently still: "I will ask no further questions of this witness."

She stood up, dizzy. Some passage of words between Cecil and the Judge. Redirect examination—there would be none. She heard the Judge say after an impatient throat-clearing that she was excused, and through a sudden maddening colorless blur she saw or imagined that Cecil was achieving a sort of smile for her. She stepped down carefully, concentrated on preventing her fingers from reaching after a handkerchief or rising toward her face. If she could keep her head turned away from the jury, they might not see. Her seat was over there somewhere, beyond the bald skull of the fattest reporter at the press tables. Cecil was still smiling, more or less.

But I lost. I lost.

Callista, what have I done to you?

III

Callista thought: *I am stronger than she is, and never knew it before. Why is she crying, after she was so wonderful?*

It was no trick of vision; no mistaking the intrusive brilliant glitter on her cheeks as Edith stepped down and walked rather clumsily—but head high— toward her seat. She would not retire in any sniffling droop: rather, Callista knew, she would be furious at the weakness, and maybe not reach for a handkerchief even when she was clear of the arena but keep her head high and angrily observant, let the sparkle dry on her face and stay there, the hell with it. *But I am much stronger. I can hold up too, even better. I won't let hunter-Hunter trick me into saying anything he can use. I'll play the act to the limit. For Cecil. For Edith. For myself. And isn't it time now?*

Yes, it was time. Cecil was whispering to her. Watching Edith still, ready with a smile if Edith would only look her way, Callista lost his words and had to ask him to repeat. "I'm putting you on now. Feeling all right, Cal? Steady?"

"I'm fine, Bud. Steady. Let 'em all come." It occurred to her that she really did feel in excellent condition. This was the end of the long affliction of waiting, mute listening, anticipation: now at least she could attempt to do something. Cecil rose and moved away; he was up there near the witness stand, calling her name, smiling a little—*Himself, not like my father. It is time. First to Mr.-Delehanty-which-is-the-Clerk.*

At close range Mr. Delehanty's eyes appeared curiously vacant. She found a moment's fantastic pleasure in proposing to herself that the poor guy might actually have died long ago, leaving a fruity voice, a magnificent suit of clothes, and some structure (partly plastic?) designed to hold the two together world without end. The arm mechanism must be especially clever, to carry on that Bible routine. She held her hands at her sides, and before the melodious rumble (a concealed recording?) could start, she spoke quickly as she had rehearsed herself last night while Matron Kowalski was playing the usual games with that light bulb in the corridor: "I affirm that I will tell the truth, the whole truth so far as I know it, and nothing but the truth."

At the corner of her eye she glimpsed Cecil's stricken look, and thought: *Oh yes yes, I should have warned him.* Her thought continued with an irritation which love somehow magnified instead of diminishing: *What's the matter anyhow? Must we be so timid? They're not going to condemn me for such a thing as that. Are they?*

Mr. Delehanty made an indeterminate fogbound noise.

Judge Mann said evenly: "The oath is binding in that form—should there be a question in anyone's mind. The witness is exercising a constitutional privilege which ought to be familiar to everyone." She felt he would have liked to speak to her directly, humanly. Instead he turned to the still faintly resonating Delehanty and remarked in a casual undertone too low for the jury's hearing but not for hers: "You might be interested to know, Mr. Delehanty, that I chose to affirm when I took the oath as a justice." *You were not actually speaking to that-which-is-the-Clerk—I heard and I'm grateful.* "You may take the stand now, Miss Blake."

They were trying to help her. Cecil, Edith, now Judge Mann who, as Cecil said, had tried all along to give her every break—tried too much for his own good, maybe, and hers too. She understood that he not only desired to help her: he *saw* her.

Her mind grew dizzy, shifted, retreated, sought to steady itself, reason and unreason quarreling within. Were they, the three of them, treating her as they might treat a difficult child? She fought down the illogical resentment, despising it, conquering it—almost. She was seated, the ungainly witness chair still warm from Edith's body. How different the courtroom looked from up here! A whole new orientation. Just look, for instance, at that big slob in the back row smuggling a candy bar up to the pink slot in his shiny face. Had that operation been going on since Monday morning? *Look, Daddy! Is he s'posed to eat in here, Daddy, is he s'posed to, huh, Daddy?*

The jury too. (*Where's Jimmy?*) The jury was closer, much closer. She could smell them. One of the females gave off a powerful tuberose reek, variable as drafts in the large room stirred it about. (*Where's Jimmy, if it matters?*) Callista decided the smell was generated by the Lagovski, probably in heat. Any minute now—well, Emerson Lake was the biggest, but pretty old; maybe one of the more vigorous younger males—

"Callista—" *Please stand near me always!*—"you're a resident of Winchester, aren't you?"

"Yes, sir. 21 Covent Street."

"You've kept that apartment?"

"Oh yes. Edith Nolan is taking care of it for me."

"Ought to be back there in a few days." *How do you do it, Cecil, that casualness? You're hurting inside worse than I am. I feel fine.* "You were attentive to all of Miss Nolan's testimony, weren't you?"

"Yes, I was, Mr. Warner."

"Before we go on to other things, is there anything in that testimony that you want to comment on, or add to, maybe?"

You told me, give them modesty. "Every one of them knows, Cal, that you're in their *power. Think what that does to twelve human egos, and show them the respect they believe*

- 192 -

they deserve. In fact don't just show it: try to make yourself feel it." I will give them modesty, *Cecil.* "I think she overrated me as an artist, Mr. Warner. It's her honest view, I know, but I'm not that good." *Who knows for sure? Maybe I am.*

"Well, as you know, I set a very high value on your work myself." His quick relaxed smile was including the jury somehow. *Wish I could do that.* Or some of the jury: his glance had been directed, she thought, toward the crinkle-faced middle-aged lady. *Name?—Butler, Miss Helen Butler.* Callista ventured to meet the woman's eyes, did so, and was frightened to realize that for the instant's duration she was not certain what her own facial muscles were doing. *What did I actually do?—make a face?* Surely there had been a gleam like friendliness in Helen Butler; just as surely, the woman was now looking down at her hands, and away across the room, troubled but otherwise communicating nothing at all. "However, Callista, I was thinking chiefly of other things Miss Nolan said—for instance her belief that you might have been experiencing a serious depression, perhaps suicidal, last July and part of August. Was she right, Callista? Were you at that time, or any part of that time, actually contemplating doing away with yourself?"

"Yes, I—yes, I was."

"It was a definite intention, my dear?"

"For a while, yes. It wasn't so until I happened to see those plants in my mother's garden. Maybe not too definite even then. I only thought: this would be one way. Then I was thinking, why not take a few, have them on hand if things got worse? Then I was actually taking them, breaking off the tops and shoving them away in the tall grass, keeping the roots."

"But I presume you must have been working up to that state of mind for quite a while?"

"Yes, I had been. It was like a progressive illness—well, I suppose that's what it really is. Each day a little emptier than the one before, a little harder to care about anything."

"You made that infusion of the roots in brandy?"

"Yes, the next day."

"Do you recall the circumstances—what part of the day it was, say?"

"It was evening, after I'd stopped trying to write that letter—the one I didn't finish, didn't mail."

"You gave up entirely on that letter, didn't you?—I mean, you decided it couldn't do any good?"

"Oh, that's true. I was imagining communication when—when in the nature of things there just couldn't be any. Jimmy—Jim Doherty and I never really—never *saw* each other, never heard—"

"Callista, I'm not sure the jury—it's a difficult thing to express."

"I know, Mr. Warner, and I'm doing it badly. Well—sometimes a person can get rid of the self-preoccupation long enough to really *know* someone else, without illusion or pretense. It's like that with Edith Nolan and me. We—communicate. But with Jimmy—with Jim Doherty and me it was all illusion. On both sides. And I gave up on that letter because I realized rather suddenly that I was—talking to someone who wasn't there." (*And he isn't here in the courtroom—he is—it doesn't matter.*) "You asked something else—oh, about the monkshood. Yes, I made the infusion that night, and then pushed it away to the back of the shelf. I don't know how to tell this either, Mr. Warner. There's a fascination about an ugly and foolish thing like that. I don't understand it: it takes hold of you in spite of yourself. I remember I almost poured out a drink from it, that night, simply from a sort of curiosity, and then I thought—this is going to sound idiotic—"

"Never mind, just tell it as it comes to you."

"Well, I thought: Look, Callista, if you can be interested and curious about a miserable thing like this, maybe you could be interested in better things. After a while if not now. So don't drink it. And I didn't of course—I just pushed it to the back of the shelf and—oh, I read that evening, I think. Some book or other. It didn't hold me, I wasn't quite alive, but it was something to do. That Saturday evening after the picnic was probably the time I came nearest to actually drinking the stuff."

"I see. A week later, Callista—I mean Sunday, August 16th—did you telephone to Ann Doherty?"

"Yes, early in the afternoon."

"You wanted to reach her and not Jim, is that right?"

"Yes. If Jimmy had answered the phone, I don't know—I suppose everything would be different, wouldn't it? I wasn't prepared to talk to him then. Maybe I'd've hung up without speaking. Anyway Ann did answer, and I—asked her over."

"Did you say why you wanted to see her?"

"No, I—hadn't quite braced myself up to telling her the situation. I kept it to small talk, on the phone. She sounded very friendly—well, she always did. She happened to mention that Jimmy had gone to New York for overnight, and that's when I asked if she'd come over—said I wanted to talk to her about something. I don't suppose I made it sound important—as I say, I hadn't fully made up my mind about telling her anything."

"Were you in a different mood that day, Callista?"

"Very different. Some other things—nothing to do with Jimmy, or with Ann—had been sort of cleaned up for me, the night before." As she spoke, Callista was meeting her mother's gaze across the courtroom for the first time that day. Her words had no visible effect on the fixed pose of sad quiet, the dignity of the rejected Mother deeply wronged. Callista deduced that the Face of The Mother was saying: "*You see how it is: I her Mother am not even allowed to testify.*" "I'm not sure, Mr. Warner, if it's what you call relevant."

"Well, Callista, your mood, your state of mind at that time, is certainly relevant in the ordinary sense. Legally, the question of relevance gets difficult when we're dealing with subjective matters. If I correctly understand the rulings during previous testimony, the Court is taking a generous and realistic attitude on this question. The nature of the case demands it, since, as I said in my opening words, we are not contesting most of the circumstantial evidence. Subject to correction by the Court, Callista, I'll leave it to you whether you think that a mention of what happened the night before would help the jury understand your situation. If you feel it would, go ahead and tell it, and we can check you if it seems to be going too far afield."

"I think it might help to explain things. But I'll leave out the details—they don't matter." *By the way, Mrs. Chalmers, I'm your daughter—remember? They tell me I'm on trial for murder.* "It had to do with my relation to my mother, Mr. Warner. There had been some—tensions between us for quite a while, and that Saturday evening—it was the 15th, wasn't it?—yes—we sort of cleared it up. In a way." *Mrs. Chalmers, Mrs. Herbert Chalmers, I am about to smile at you, toward you anyway. Will it make any difference?* "You remember, sir—Miss Welsh testified about my going out to Shanesville that Saturday evening, and how bad-mannered I was—and I don't doubt I was too, I can be pretty stupid— call it a one-track mind. Though it's a fact I just didn't know Ann Doherty was there on the porch, until Miss Welsh testified to it. She must have been back in the shadows, I suppose, and I was thinking so hard about what I wanted to talk over with my mother that I didn't hear her speak." Callista felt her lips curve. It was surely a smile; she meant it for a smile. "I guess I was in a fog." Yes, fog—as inexorably as deepening fog, the realization came over Callista that Mrs. Victoria Johnson Blake Chalmers was quite simply not listening. Present in the courtroom, knowing at least as well as most of the other spectators the general story of what was going on down here in the arena; but not listening. Mrs. Chalmers was maintaining a Face; a very necessary thing to do. She would have been perfectly willing to smile back,

Callista guessed, if she could have divided her attention, listened just enough to understand that it might be appropriate, right now, for the Face to smile. "So I went indoors to—see my mother, and we—talked." Fog—words pushed into fog move sluggishly, as if through pain.

"Miss Welsh also testified to overhearing a few things. Was that testimony accurate, Callista?"

"Oh, reasonably, so far as Miss Welsh knew, I'm sure. Mother was crying a little at one time, and I guess I did quote something or other from Shakespeare. I was sort of making a fool of myself." *Ten minutes from now, Mother, will it dawn on you what I said? You see, I haven't a notion what I'll be saying ten minutes from now. By the way, Mama, I don't see Cousin Maud. Is she home with the Plum Jam?* "What Miss Welsh didn't hear, couldn't very well know, Mr. Warner, was that at the end we did get things sort of cleared up." *All right, stranger—no smile, just sad maternal forgiveness. One of Callie's little emotional upsets, you know—children are SO difficult!* "And—here's why I thought it might not be out of place to mention it—that evening, that's when the suicidal depression left me. I wanted to live again. After I'd—said good-night to Mother." *Mama darling, why don't you lean over the rail, ask that fat guy at the press table, the bald one who looks intelligent—I think he'll tell you this is a murder trial. They're trying the funny-looking broad with the gimp leg.*

"It left you suddenly, Callista, the depression? Like the end of a sickness?"

"Yes." *Cecil, I love you.* "Yes, it was very much like that, Mr. Warner. Like coming out of a fever, or pain all at once ending. There was—too much upswing also, I guess you might call it. I was back with some of my illusions. I mean the illusions about Jimmy. I'd once more talked myself into imagining there might be—you know, a separation, what I'd been trying to write Jimmy about in that letter I never mailed. Most of the day, and even while I was talking with Ann on the phone, I was able to fool myself with that. Self-deception, it's like walking a tightrope, I guess: so long as you don't look down at the *fact* of the ground a long way below, you can truly believe there's no danger, you're just walking. I think that all that day, until Ann came, I was—living inside of that illusion. Wanting something so much I couldn't see how ridiculous it was to expect it." *Look, Mother: I know I hurt you plenty of times. I was always nasty and hellishly difficult until I escaped from Shanesville and from you—but I never hurt you THAT much.*

"I think now, Callista, you might go ahead and tell, in your own way, everything that happened that Sunday evening and night. I realize you'll be mostly repeating what you told Mr. Lamson last August, but I believe the jury wants to hear it direct from you, so—so just go ahead, my dear—take your time, try to remember everything important."

Don't be scared, Cecil. Yes, I know: this is it. "Ann came to my apartment about quarter to eight, Mr. Warner. I can't bring back the early part of the conversation too well, except I know it was nothing important. Just usual comments on the weather, I guess—it was a very hot evening, sticky hot. Her suit—the powder-blue—it was summer weight of course, but I remember it looked sort of warm, I think I asked something silly about how could she stand wearing even the jacket in such weather, and—Mr. Warner, do I understand it right, that I shouldn't repeat any of the things she said? It seems reasonable that I shouldn't—after all, Ann's not here to set me right if I misquoted her."

"That's how it is, Callista. I'm sure you understand it. Just tell your own side of it—what you did, what you observed, what happened."

"Yes, I'll try. There was that small talk for ten minutes or so, and then I was going ahead, very clumsily I guess, telling her about—Jimmy and me. Oh, wait, one thing—I remember that at the start, when she'd just arrived, I was going to offer her a drink, and I didn't because I had a sort of half-memory that she didn't take alcohol. A mistaken memory—likely had her tastes confused with someone else's—but I know that was in my mind, that's why I didn't offer her one." *Cecil, I just invented this: is it any damn good?*

Apparently he was not displeased. "You didn't offer her a drink then or any time, is that right?"

"That's right. You see, I—Ann Doherty and I were never really very well acquainted. I knew the Dohertys as neighbors of course, from the time they moved in there, but my mother and stepfather saw much more of them than I ever did. I can't say I really knew Jimmy, either, I—" *(Cecil, please give me a lift with this one)*—"well, I said something like that before, didn't I?"

"The episode with him was—really no more than that, an episode?"

"Midsummer madness. I must have been ready to go overboard for someone. It was chance we happened to meet, that May-day." *Handkerchief back in the sleeve, girl—let the palms stay wet, wouldn't look good to be wiping them.* "And things got out of control. So far as the affair is concerned, Mr. Warner, if there's any question of blame or responsibility, I'll take it. Nothing could have started if I hadn't allowed it. And Jimmy—well, I can't speak for him, but I know he didn't realize until much later how terribly important I'd let it become to me, for a while. He just slipped, but I went all the way over, head over heels, for a while, and nobody to blame but myself." *(Give me that look, won't you?—the Cecil Warner special. Tell me I'm doing all right.)* "Then later when he did understand how I was making such a thing of it—well, poor Jimmy, he's not an unkind person and never would be, he was in a spot, I think. He couldn't bear to hurt Ann or me either, and couldn't do anything at all without hurting one of us. I don't know what he could possibly have done except what he did—break off the relation and let time take care of it." (*Did the jury see him go? I didn't. Here at the start of the day, that I know.*) "Do I need to say any more about this, Mr. Warner?"

"I don't think so. You're free to of course, if anything else occurs to you later. Do you want to get back to the Sunday evening now?"

"Yes." *Mother's gone too, behind the Face—but that happened a long time ago. And Cousin Maud with the Plum Jam, I hope. What's the matter, you nice people—isn't the Monkshood Girl putting on a good show? Herb—shall I project the voice at you, Herb?* "Where was I?"

"You'd spoken of starting to tell Ann Doherty about it."

"Yes. I tried to do it reasonably, but I think all I did was blurt one hint after another until she—understood. She did, I know—that is, she understood what had been happening. As I think I told Mr. Lamson, I didn't get as far as telling her I was pregnant. I got the other facts said, somehow or other, and she—said something that showed she understood, and then I was suddenly sick to my stomach."

"She didn't appear angry?"

"No, Mr. Warner. I believe—I believe what I said could have been taken to mean that the thing was completely ended. Of course I've no way of knowing if that's what she thought. She wasn't angry. And then my sickness, coming like that, confused everything else. I ran for the bathroom. I know Ann was sorry for me, trying to help. I was—call it hysterical. I yelled at her, couldn't stand the idea of her touching me while I was sick, only wanted her to go away. But she wouldn't, so I ran from her again, into my bedroom, and I locked the door." (*Help me now!*) "Yes, I know I locked the door."

"That part is a perfectly clear memory, Callista? The physical act of turning the key or throwing the latch or whatever it was?"

"Yes. Old-fashioned key—why, I probably never had used it before, no occasion to. But I did then. I threw myself down on the bed. My throat was still raw and sour from vomiting, I remember that."

"Now you told Mr. Lamson that there's a stretch of a few minutes, in the bedroom, that won't quite come back. I take it for granted that since then you've been trying to fill in that gap in memory. Suppose I put it this way, Callista: is it possible now for you to add anything to what you told Mr. Lamson that day in his office?"

Not quite a direct lie required—thanks, friend. Not that it matters, direct or indirect. The letter killeth—inner Puritan, drop dead, drop dead! "No, Mr. Warner—as you say,

I've tried ever since to clear up that part in my mind, but—I can't add anything now." *I don't dare look toward a certain flinty intelligent face—the name is Francis Fielding—and yet I'll do it.*

He was very quiet, Mr. Fielding, alert, interested; no change or wavering in his smart bird-like eyes as she met their probing and tried briefly, unavailingly, to win a glimpse of the self behind them. *Once I watched a heron in my famous field glasses, motionless at the edge of a stream. Motionless, hunting motionless.* That had been only the summer before last, a trip alone in the Volks to the hill country. More of the day came back, a good day and the summer hush. Eighteen. The heron had remained a somber painted image until the frog returned to the bank; then he got his meal: too large a frog to swallow whole, so he knocked it to pieces against a rock and resumed his stillness. But Cecil was speaking.

"I'll make a suggestion, Callista—a sort of hypothetical question, though I won't try to phrase it in precisely that form. Before you broke away and went into your bedroom you'd been, as you say, hysterical, sick, nauseated: too early for ordinary morning sickness I suppose, but the pregnancy must have had at least some influence on your condition. And you had undergone, were still undergoing, an intense emotional strain: the anticipation, the build-up to your interview with Mrs. Doherty, then sudden realization that it was wasted effort. Now I suggest that all those things coming together at once might have produced a plain old-fashioned fainting spell, a blackout from exhaustion. And I'll ask: is everything you remember about those moments consistent with that? It makes sense to you, that this could be what happened?"

Again the aid and comfort to the idiot Puritan: don't know why it should help to avoid the phrasing of a direct lie—superstition—somehow it does though and he knows it—my love is wiser than other men—"Yes, it could have been like that, Mr. Warner." A half-seen glimpse of something kind in black-haired Dolores Acevedo might mean feminine sympathy, fellow-feeling—or something else, or nothing at all. The experts say, Callista remembered, that a person with an obsessive notion never actually performs the fantastic act he imagines performing— like for instance leaning forward in this chair and saying: "Dolly, I bet you know how it feels to go nuts for a good lay."

"After going into the bedroom, what is the next thing that you remember positively?"

"The next thing—the next thing I am really certain about is hearing Ann walk across the living-room—her high heels—to the front door. I heard the door close, heard her car start up and drive away. It somehow—released me—I can't think of a better word. I unlocked the bedroom, came out, got myself a drink of water. I went into the kitchenette to get that instead of to the bathroom. Then—not right away but very soon—I saw the brandy bottle had been pulled forward on the shelf, and there was a glass with a few drops in the bottom, and I knew what must have happened. It brought me out of my fog anyway. I knew I had to get to her at once if I could, and I wasn't able to think beyond that. What I ought to have done—I know it now—was call the police and tell them the emergency. They might have got to her in time and done something for her. But I was shocked silly, I couldn't think of anything except going after her myself, and that's what I did—tried to do."

"Well, you didn't lose any time, I'm sure."

"No, just grabbed my handbag off the living-room table and ran down to the garage. It's back of the apartment—overhead door always sticks, I remember I had to struggle with it as usual but it didn't hold me up long." *Nice old Em Lake, you had such a time yearning after my friend's mammaries—how will these do? Not big, but I bet anything you've seen worse. Drool, old boy, drool all you like if it makes a difference. Will I twitch my jacket back a little? Better, huh? Besides, away up there, sixty-five or whatever it is, doesn't it seem too bad to die at nineteen?*

"Can you judge about what time elapsed, from hearing Ann's car start to getting your own out on the road?"

"It could have been as much as ten minutes. Until I saw that brandy bottle I was just dazed and stupid, not hurrying about anything. I don't know how long I was, coming out of the bedroom, getting that drink of water. I didn't look at the clock or anything, no reason to."

"To be sure. Well—you drove on out to Shanesville?"

"Yes, fast as I could. Wasn't delayed on the road. I pulled into the Dohertys' driveway, alongside the Pontiac—it was just as Sergeant Shields described it. The house was dark. My headlights picked up her handbag lying in the path, so I knew at once she must have gone that way."

"Did you take the flashlight from your car?"

"No, didn't think of it till I'd started down the path. The moon was hazed over, but still pretty strong light." *The Monkshood Girl will now look at the Foreman of the Jury.* "I supposed she must have gone to my mother's house, but when I came to that spur path I—thought—" Peter Anson would not look at her; she was certain he had been doing so, and intently, the instant before her own eyes shifted.

"Take your time, Callista—by the way, would you like a sip of water?"

"Yes, please. Thank you." *Thank you for more than that.* The water was cool and perfect; she held and turned the crystal of the glass until it gave her the excellent diminished star of the ceiling chandelier. Had it been burning all day? She couldn't remember. Probably; a gray series of hours, this Thursday, with a whimpering of December wind. *I'm sorry, Cecil, I know I'm stumbling, not doing very well—keep thinking about twenty-to-life—it wouldn't let me come to you.* "When I came to the spur path it was—oh, just a sort of sick feeling that I ought to look at the pond and make sure she hadn't—it was only a few steps, the light fairly good through the trees. I saw something in the water. It was white, some part of her white blouse."

"You went down that steep path to your left, Callista? Stood on the path first and then over on the left side of the pond?"

"Yes. I could see—enough to know. Then the pains began. I knew she was dead, and I knew what was happening to me. I guess I said, didn't I, that I'd wanted the baby, I wanted to bear it? Did I say that?"

"Yes, my dear, you told Mr. Lamson that—I believe it's not been mentioned here until now. You really did want it, didn't you?"

"Yes."

"You needn't say any more about that now unless you wish."

"All right. I ... well, I don't quite remember getting back to my car. I did it though, and when I reached the junction I remembered that thick second-growth woods across the road from my mother's house. So I parked by the pines, got over there—" *Don't do it, Mrs. Kleinman: Mr. Fielding wouldn't like it, anyway crying is just the glands going into an uproar. I'm not crying—see? Of course, if it means you don't want to burn me—*

"About that also, Callista, you needn't say any more than you want to. The fact of the miscarriage is enough, and I haven't heard the prosecution contesting it. Did you happen to have your wrist watch on, by the way?"

"No, the sticky hot weather, it was chafing my wrist—I'd taken it off at my apartment. Well, when it was over I got back to my car, made the turn in my mother's driveway—" *Sorry, Herb, manner of speaking: she's a very important lady, you know how 'tis—*"and I guess that was the way Miss Welsh described it."

"Do you recall seeing Dr. Chalmers on the porch, turning on the light?"

"I think so. I was clumsy with the gears, backing and turning. Then I held up all right till I got home."

"And then?"

"I found I'd left the apartment door open. I remember closing it and leaning back against it. Then I was on my knees—I don't mean I fainted, I don't think I did. I think—does this sound possible?—I think I just fell asleep.

Remember being on my knees, dropping forward on my hands, thinking how soft the rug would be if I could hitch over to it, and I must have done so, because when I came out of—it seemed like a sleep—I was there on the rug with my handbag for a pillow. After I got up I couldn't stop shaking for a long while. I wanted a shower, but couldn't make my fingers take hold of my clothes. The shoes were the worst. Did finally, had the shower too I think, and dozed off again. I didn't see the sun come up—it was in my eyes when I woke. By ten o'clock I'd pulled myself together somehow, got dressed. I called Edith. I knew I'd have to call the police."

"You hadn't done anything with the brandy bottle after you first saw it had been moved?"

"No, I hadn't, and I did nothing with it that morning—just left everything as it was. I supposed that was the right thing to do. But I didn't get up my courage to call the police until after my stepfather had telephoned me, and told me about finding Ann's body. I think it was about eleven o'clock that he called."

"And when you did call the police, what you got was Sergeant Rankin."

"Yes." *When we get this one over with we're done, aren't we, Cecil? Except for—except for—*"He turned up about twelve o'clock."

"You recall his testimony on the stand?"

"Yes. It was accurate except for what it left out, and his denials to you in cross-examination."

"Before we go into that, do you want to tell your side of that thing about the aquarium, Callista?"

"I might as well. It was a foolish impulse. I loved the things, and I had a picture of them going hungry and dying off with the apartment closed. If I'd stopped to think, I'd have known of course that Edith would take care of them for me." *I can't look across the room at you right now, Edith; I don't dare.* "After all she gave them to me herself. It was an impulse of—despair, I think. You see, until Sergeant Rankin made it plain to me, I actually hadn't understood how things were going to look for me. I wasn't thinking clearly at all until then. What he said—and did—showed me how it would be, that I'd be accused of murder and there'd be nothing to disprove it except my word— no tangible evidence in my favor, no one else with any first-hand knowledge of what happened. Naturally as a police officer, Rankin saw that aspect of it right away. Well, the aquarium—I wanted the little tropicals to die quick and easy, that was all."

"I see. You said Rankin's testimony was accurate except for what it left out, and those denials. Will you fill in that blank? Just tell what Rankin did, to the best of your recollection."

"When we were going back to the living-room after I had shown him the brandy bottle, he grabbed hold of me from behind. I was still feeling sick and confused, and startled by what he'd said a minute before—something to the effect that no one would believe my story. I wasn't expecting any physical approach like that. I guess I was aware that he'd started to get excited, but I supposed that being a policeman, he'd at least control himself. I said: 'Take your hands off me!'—something like that—or stronger, I guess—'Take your ugly hands off me, you fool!' He didn't let go. He said he could 'give me a lot of breaks,' as he put it, if I would—'put out.' I tried to break free of him, but couldn't. A sort of stupid wrestling match across the living-room. I couldn't get my wrist free. He forced me down on the couch. I tried to tell him then that I was ill, but it's possible he really didn't hear that. He was in a state of violent excitement—had opened his trousers and was trying to swing my legs up on the couch without letting go my wrist. I told him the Police Department would smash him for it and he'd wind up in jail no matter what happened to me. He managed to say: 'The hell with that—who's going to take your word against mine?' I said that anyhow I could testify he was circumcised, and since he wasn't Jewish that ought to give my word a little weight. It got through to him, and scared him. He gave me an open-handed slap across the face—just a nervous explosion, I guess, hardly knew what he was doing—and let go my wrist, stepped away from me across the room, got himself under control. When he turned back to me he was well behaved. He apologized, said there was something about me that made him lose his head. I think he spoke of having a wife and children, and then something more about it's being my word against his. I don't believe I was able to say anything except that I'd make him no promises about telling or not telling of it. He made his call to headquarters, and the aquarium thing was after that, I guess—yes, it was. What he testified about just sitting there till the others came—that was true. I don't think he looked at me once after that remark I made—something about a spring morning warmed up in the oven."

"Yes, that seems to have made an impression on him." *And yet after all, Cecil, wouldn't we have done better to show Rankin as just one more creature caught in a drift of confusion, half ape, half civilized, like the rest of us?—or maybe we did succeed in doing that—I wouldn't know. LaSalle and Miss Wainwright look quite angry on my behalf. The Face of the Hoag expresses a certain disappointment: 'Wha'd he give up so easy for, and him a cop?' The Face of Fielding says quite truthfully that it hasn't a damn thing to do with the death of Ann Doherty.* "Well, Callista, I suppose Gage and the others arrived quite soon, as he testified. Do you want to add anything about that?"

"No, I don't think of anything important. It was all about as Rankin told it, and then I was taken to Mr. Lamson's office."

"And questioned there—do you happen to remember how long?"

"I think, from about two o'clock until seven in the evening, when I signed that transcript."

"Callista, I will ask you: was there ever any genuine hostility between you and Ann Doherty?"

"When two women want the same man, there's bound to be, Mr. Warner. As a person—if it were possible for me to think of her apart from Jimmy—I had nothing against her. It's true to say I hardly knew her. We had nothing in common. She was a sweet, harmless girl who never did the slightest thing to rouse any hostility in me."

"And I'll ask you, Callista: did you ever, at any time at all, entertain any sort of intention of doing away with her, or in fact of doing her any kind of harm?"

"No. No, Mr. Warner. The worst I ever wished against her was that she would—let Jimmy go."

"Callista, after signing that transcript in Mr. Lamson's office, did you receive medical attention?"

"Oh—yes, I did. I sort of blacked out, after signing it. Came to in some kind of infirmary room—in this building, I guess it is. The police doctor was—all right."

"Do you recall seeing me that evening?"

"Yes, you were there at the infirmary, soon after I came to myself."

"You remember my explanation of why I couldn't be there sooner?"

"Yes, you told me you'd been out of town, and Edith couldn't get word to you until after six o'clock."

"Did you see your mother or your stepfather that day?"

"No. They came, I understand, but weren't allowed to see me."

"So it adds up this way—correct me if I'm wrong: you had a miscarriage about nine o'clock Sunday evening, were in a state of partial or total collapse the greater part of the night. Then official questioning, briefly interrupted by attempted rape, from noon Monday until seven in the evening. Then medical attention. Do you think of anything you want to add at this time, Callista?"

"No, I—" *There must be something. I am not ready*—"No, I don't think so, Mr. Warner."

"You may cross-examine, Mr. District Attorney."

The Hunter is coming forward—

8

Whosoever now, Ananda, or after my departure, shall be to himself his own light, his own refuge, and seek no other refuge, will henceforth be my true disciple and walk in the right path.

Reputed saying of GAUTAMA BUDDHA

I

"The chips are down now, aren't they, Callista?"

She'll understand that the best answer for that one is no answer. But I might—Cecil Warner remained on his feet by the defense table until he could reassure himself that Callista did understand. She was watching the prosecutor with outward calm, her hands folded—white hands, actually strong, now seeming small and frail.

"Mr. District Attorney, I have one or two old-fashioned quirks. It was natural for Mr. Warner to use my first name because he is a friend as well as my attorney. From you I would prefer a reasonable formality, do you mind?"

Yes—good—perhaps. Too highbrow for the jury, but it may upset his pace a little. Warner sat down, forcing upon himself once more the resolution that he would not intervene except as strategy required it. She was, within obvious limits, on her own, and must fight in her own way. He must protect her to the full extent of his position and powers, but the jury must not feel that she was being overprotected. His own words must have the force of economy, and not be wasted merely to relieve his own anguish.

T. J. Hunter was brooding over it. The hour was 4:15, the sky beyond the high windows altogether dark. The day would end with whatever Callista was able to say now, and perhaps in some short redirect examination after Hunter had finished. Closing arguments tomorrow, and probably Terence's summing up: T.J. was not likely to call rebuttal witnesses, and his method did not call for long-winded oratory at the end. The case was likely to go to the jury tomorrow afternoon or evening. *I am not ready.*

"Very well, Miss Blake. I'm a plain man myself with only a commonplace education, and I'm afraid I'm a little bit given to plain speech. Did you kill Ann Doherty?"

"No."

"Why—she died of aconite poisoning, didn't she? And drowning? We've all heard that testimony."

"Yes."

"Are you saying someone else gave her the poison?"

"She found the poisoned brandy in my apartment without my knowledge, she drank it without my knowledge. When she drowned in that pond, I was not there. I found her too late."

"That is still your story, Miss Blake?"

"Objection!"

"Sustained." Except for silence, his graceful body stooped slightly forward as though setting itself for a predatory leap, Hunter gave no sign of noticing the interruption. "Do you wish to take an exception, Mr. Hunter?"

"No, your Honor. Miss Blake, in your direct testimony I recall that you chose to qualify one of the remarks made by your friend Edith Nolan, a remark concerning your artistic ability. I believe you said she overrated you. Does that mean that in your estimation, your own estimation, you are really not much of an artist?"

"No, that isn't what I said."

"Then you do consider yourself an artist?"

"Yes, but with less ability than Miss Nolan gives me credit for."

"I see. In how many lines, Miss Blake?"

"Drawing and painting. Nothing else worth mentioning."

"Not in fiction?"

"Objection! The question is wholly improper."

"Sustained."

"Exception. I was using the word in the purely literary sense—literature, fiction-writing, is surely one of the arts."

"Mr. Hunter, since the question of Miss Blake's literary ability has never been introduced at any time in this trial until you mentioned it just now, the Court does not find your explanation altogether acceptable. You may have your exception of course. As you continue, you will avoid sarcasm and innuendo. Miss Blake is entitled to the same respect as any other witness."

"I regret it very much, your Honor, if anything I said had the sound of sarcasm. It was not so intended. Miss Blake, as an artist, in your own estimation, do you share the attitude which I understand is fairly common in some quarters, that an artist is—well, a sort of privileged character? Not to be judged by the standards we apply to ordinary mortals?"

"I do not, and I never knew any artist who held that attitude."

"Have you met a great many of them?"

"No. A few."

"But never met one who felt that he was, let's say, a special sort of being? Someone apart?"

"Special perhaps, or apart, but not specially privileged."

"Not even the beatniks?"

"I don't know anything about the beatniks."

A swift small worm of pain ran down Cecil Warner's left arm, puzzling him. He said with care for the sound of his voice: "Is all this leading anywhere? Does it have any possible relevancy?"

"If the Court please," said T. J. Hunter melodiously, "there has been a great deal said about Miss Blake's state of mind at various times. I have not objected to it. This is in many ways an uncommon case. I am inclined to agree with a remark made by my very honored adversary a little while ago in his opening, when he pointed out how much depends on whether we can or cannot believe Miss Blake's word. He is naturally convinced that she is telling the truth. I am not. She is now on the stand, having affirmed that she will speak truthfully. It is my necessary task to test her credibility in any proper manner that is open to me, and my present line of inquiry is directed to that end."

"The point is well taken," said Judge Mann. Warner heard or imagined a note of weariness or doubt. "Are you making a formal objection, Mr. Warner?"

"No, your Honor. I only wish the prosecutor would get to the point, if there is one."

A mistake; he'll catch me up on it too. "There is one," said Hunter mildly. "Perhaps I can make it clearer to counsel later on. Miss Blake, you must have believed—did you not?—that something—maybe not your position as an artist if you say it wasn't that—but something excused you, made it appear all right to you to enter blithely on an adulterous relation with James Doherty."

"I did not enter on it blithely, nor make excuses for myself. I was aware that such a relation is contrary to the principles we give lip-service to in this part of the world."

She can't—she mustn't—

"And also contrary to law?"

"Mr. Hunter, I'm afraid I never stopped to find out whether this is one of the states where adultery is listed as a crime."

With deepening terror Warner understood that she was already becoming raw and recklessly angry, though Hunter had scarcely begun. *I must be heard.*

"I take that to mean that you hold yourself above the law?"

"I object, your Honor. I submit that in his opening Mr. Hunter laid considerable polite stress on the fact that the indictment charges murder and nothing else. If now he has elected himself some kind of guardian of public morals, if Callista Blake is to be tried after all for a violation of sex conventions—"

"Sir, that's uncalled-for and unjust. My question was phrased in general terms. I think nothing could bear more directly on the credibility of the witness than her respect for law, or lack of it."

"You were asking," said Judge Mann, "in general terms, whether or not the witness considers herself above the law? That was the meaning of your question and the extent of it?"

"It was, your Honor."

"I must overrule your objection, Mr. Warner."

"Exception."

"Yes, certainly. Answer the question, Miss Blake."

"I do not consider myself above the law." *At least she's quieter; her hands not shaking.* "Like everyone, I've probably broken a number of minor laws without even knowing it. As for the matter the prosecutor specifically mentioned, adultery, I don't know, as I said, how the state of New Essex technically regards that action. If it's a crime, then I'm a criminal—on that charge." *No more, Callista! LOOK AT ME!* "I'm quite aware you can't have a human society without laws. I try to respect them so far as I'm able—I—"

"Miss Blake," said Judge Mann, "there is no need to go beyond the question. For your own sake I must instruct you not to do so. Limit your answers to what Mr. Hunter asks, so far as you can."

He may have saved her—I don't know—I don't know.

"You respect the laws so far as you are able—now what does that mean, Miss Blake? At what point, please, does it become impossible for you to respect the laws?"

"No one could answer that exactly. As a lawyer, you certainly know that many laws are obsolete or foolish. Dead-letter laws—Sunday blue laws—that sort of thing. I would never willingly break any law that the majority considers important."

"I see. You have decided then that the majority doesn't consider the law against adultery important?"

"I don't know—I've already said I don't even know what laws New Essex has about that. If people are ever prosecuted for it—I suppose they are—I never heard of it."

"Your answer isn't quite responsive. Do you mean you believe that in breaking the seventh commandment you were merely doing what everyone does more or less?"

"I didn't say that. I—"

Warner let his voice go: "I will inquire again whether the District Attorney believes he is trying a case of adultery."

"I will reply again that I wish to discover Miss Blake's attitude toward law itself, as it bears on the reliability of her statements."

Judge Mann spoke with acid: "Gentlemen ... Mr. Hunter, your point may be still defensible, but I think you're going too far afield. I suggest you bring your inquiry back to factual evidence and the material of direct testimony."

"Very well, your Honor. Miss Blake, do you have a clear recollection of those letters of yours which were read in court this morning?"

"Very clear."

Warner saw him take them up from among the exhibits; fought back his surge of resentment that those hands, clean, excellently shaped, well manicured, should be handling them at all. "I recall, Miss Blake, that before these letters were read, quite a point was made about seeing to it that the jury heard a correct interpretation. This seems like a good opportunity to clear up one or two points and give the jury your own views on what they mean— that is, I take it you have no objection?"

"You needn't make such a production of stage politeness." *Callista, don't!* "I'm prepared to answer any legitimate questions as well as I can."

Hunter's eyebrows rose and fell. He read to himself, slipped the first page under and read on. "Well—'my love (you know it) is nothing like what could happen for you with anyone but me. And there's my cure for jealousy—if I could apply it, if I could make my head rule a little more, my crazy heart a little less.' That appears, Miss Blake, to be among other things an admission that you did experience what's usually called jealousy. 'Something that could not happen with Ann. Or anywhere in her world.' That's jealousy, isn't it?"

"I did experience it. I haven't denied it."

"No? Now I thought that in direct testimony you said something to the effect that you had nothing against her. I think that—in direct testimony under oath—you called her a 'sweet and harmless girl'—something like that."

"I think I said—apart from Jimmy—meaning—apart from the fact that she was his wife—oh, it's perfectly clear what I meant."

"That is, you had nothing against her except that she was in the way?"

"I never said that—never put it that way, even to myself."

"I'm sorry, Miss Blake, I think you did." He turned pages slowly. "Not in those exact words perhaps. 'Granted also that Ann is good and sweet and conventionally right. Does that give her the right—' and then the crossed-out words that I think you remember, and then—'to keep you and me apart and prevent my child from having a father?' Miss Blake, how much nearer could you come to saying that she was in the way without actually using the words?"

"The marriage—the fact of their marriage was in the way. I never thought of her as a—a person to be removed—oh, I'm not saying it clearly—I never wanted to—do away with her. My letter says—my letter simply asks him to do something about a separation. And that's the letter I never even mailed."

"All right—it sounds a little involved—the letter doesn't sound to me as if you were writing about the 'fact of their marriage,' but let that go for the present. This is from the first one, a letter you did mail: 'I fit no pattern. No one can own me, no one can make me over. I was born a heretic and so live. No one can catch me except if I will.' This time I am frankly puzzled, Miss Blake. It is by chance a quotation from something?"

"No."

"You had been writing affectionately—and poetically, I must say—and then all of a sudden you throw this at him: 'No one can own me—born a heretic and so live.' I'm simply puzzled, Miss Blake. Why in the world were you moved to say to James Doherty: 'No one can catch me except if I will'— why?"

Warner saw the violent tension and forced relaxation of her folded hands. She said: "It must be—it must be it never occurred to me the letter would be examined by a district attorney."

"What?—you mean it's a form of doubletalk? Hidden significance, something that might be damaging if it came to the eyes of that lowest form of life, a district attorney?"

"No—no—no hidden significance." She was turning her head from side to side as if in search of physical escape. "I don't know how you dissect a love-letter. Do it yourself—do it yourself—"

"'No one can catch me except if I will.' And then you were caught, weren't you?"

"Objection!"

"Sustained—sustained. You know better than that, Mr. Hunter. And step back from the stand a little. I will not have the witness abused."

"My regrets, your Honor. I had no such intention." *Throws it like a bone to a dog—Terry's no dog—but—*"Miss Blake, I will read to you from the second letter. You had been asking about Doherty's religious views, and then you wrote: 'I wasn't asking about *Ann's* views, blast you—I know she'd condemn the whole thing without a moment's pause for thought.' Miss Blake, by what reasoning it is possible to reconcile that remark with your alleged intention of asking Mrs. Doherty to agree to a separation? How could you write that about her, and then in the very same letter talk about her meekly agreeing to a separation?"

"I suppose—I suppose the remark about her condemning us—I suppose I wrote that in a moment of exasperation, and was calmer later on. I don't know—must a love-letter be consistent like a dictionary?"

"All right, I see what you mean, but on that point the inconsistency is really glaring, isn't it? You knew—elsewhere in the letters you even grudgingly admit—that Mrs. Doherty loved her husband. You knew, and you specifically said, that she would regard your adulterous relation with him as sinful—of course, how could you doubt it, what wife in her right mind wouldn't regard it so? Yet in almost the same breath you're talking about a separation, as if you expected Ann Doherty to throw away her marriage, violate her deepest religious convictions, humbly agree to letting her husband go live in sin with his ... with you. Consistent?"

"I suppose it's inconsistent, if you make no allowance for the other things I said."

"Oh—there is something else in the letter that makes it consistent?"

"I don't know—I don't know."

"Miss Blake, on the basis of these letters, and your testimony, I will ask you: weren't you, in all this talk of a separation, simply proposing an impossibility, knowing it was one, to—well, what? See what Jimmy would do? To feel him out maybe, find out if he'd go along with you on some much more direct method of—eliminating the woman who was in the way?"

"That's idiotic."

"Well, if I'm an idiot you should have no trouble defending yourself."

"Witness and counsel will both confine themselves to the issues. No more of that sort of thing."

"My apologies, your Honor. All right, Miss Blake, we'll let that stand. But in my—simple way, I keep trying to understand. Now for example in the rest of this second letter, where you attack Doherty's religious faith—"

"I never attacked it! In that letter I was *asking* about his beliefs, and stating some of my own ideas, nothing more."

"Oh? I must have misunderstood. Let's see—you wrote here, speaking of his religion: 'Isn't it mostly a matter of being brought up in a certain way that automatically shuts out other views without seriously examining them? I'm trying to suggest that unlike Ann, you're really not embedded in religion like a fly in amber.' That's not an attack?"

"No, it is not."

"I see—the fault's with my understanding. And further on you wrote: 'just where is the mercy, the rationale, the loving-kindness in an ethical-religious system that makes me a whore bound for hell because I love you and welcome intercourse with you and want to live with you?' But you're telling me seriously now that this isn't to be called an attack on the man's most vital and deeply cherished religious convictions?"

Callista said: "Mr. Hunter, I think your A is a little bit flat."

One giggle sounded, in the back row, probably the same adenoidal snigger that had punctuated the trial from the start. There was no other laughter. Only a hush. The same kind of hush, Warner thought, that might have held the crowd in shock and incredulity, hundreds of years ago, if some candidate for an Inquisition bonfire had ventured to poke a little fun at the officiating priest. And T.J. was in fact performing certain priestly functions. *So what am I then? Advocatus diaboli?* He saw Terence Mann's hand clench spasmodically and fall in a droop.

Hunter said somberly, when the moment was right: "I have no objection to your odd sense of humor, Miss Blake, if you are enjoying it. But I would like a responsive answer."

"Mr. Hunter, I did not think of James Doherty as a child. At any rate I tried not to. Apparently I rated his intelligence more highly than you do. I did not think that his religious beliefs had to be coddled and protected, or avoided the way you might avoid too much comment on a child's make-believe. Therefore in that letter to him I asked him about his beliefs, as one might ask any adult, and I wrote a little about my own ideas. It can't be called an attack unless you feel that the mere mention of an unreligious idea is an attack on religion. I'm aware that a lot of people do feel that way. They take all dissent as if it were an unkind criticism of themselves. Maybe Doherty did too, but I didn't think so at the time."

Could she have won that round, or partly won it? It seemed to Cecil Warner that her voice had recovered some steadiness and coolness. Fielding looked somewhat impressed, as well as Helen Butler, LaSalle, and maybe Miss Wainwright. But the others were annoyed, or puzzled, or not listening. And about Fielding it was never possible to be sure.

"He's 'Doherty' to you now? Not 'Jimmy' any more, just 'Doherty'?"

She turned her face to the Judge with a look of blindness. "Must I answer that?"

"You need not," said Judge Mann. "I think you might withdraw the question, Mr. Hunter."

But even at that moment—the Judge manifestly friendly, Hunter showing up badly as his antagonism became too obviously personal and overdramatized—even at that more or less favorable moment Warner felt a change in Callista, a retreat or a weakening, as though before his eyes she had slipped further away from him, almost out of sight and hearing. He might, he supposed, be exaggerating her look of increased exhaustion, a fault in his own powers of observation. The pain slid down his arm again, compelling some part of his mind to mumble: *Heart?—and irrelevant?* Callista was not necessarily in flight, not necessarily losing her desire to live. A better part of his mind recalled a better voice, speaking with a nearly incomprehensible sweetness: "*Living is journeying, and love's a region we can enter for a while.*"

"I withdraw my question. Miss Blake, as the author of these letters, I take it you are the one person best qualified to explain this sentence: 'You are already a prisoner, and I wish I might set you free.'"

"Oh—oh—explain it by what follows, can't you? I think when I wrote that I wasn't referring to Ann."

"Well, not exactly, Miss Blake. The words I see on this page are: 'No, I don't hate Ann, I was not thinking only of Ann when I wrote that.' *Only*, Miss Blake—that seems to say pretty plainly that you're at least including Ann Doherty in what you wrote about your Jimmy being a prisoner. Doesn't it?"

"All right—if you wish."

"It's no question of what I wish, Miss Blake."

"I think it is—I think you—no, never mind, I don't mean that. Go ahead and ask your question—what do you want to know?"

"I am asking for your interpretation of that sentence: 'You are already a prisoner, and I wish I might set you free'—insofar as it does refer to Ann Doherty."

Her voice had gone dull and flat, hard to hear from Warner's place: "No interpretation except the obvious one. His marriage trapped him, confined him." Warner's ears had begun a faint ringing; he undid the top button of his shirt—a little better. "I suppose marriage does that for anyone, man or woman, and usually the restrictions are voluntarily accepted, welcomed, or so people like to think. I suppose that's all I meant."

"But the rest of the sentence, Miss Blake—'I wish I might set you free'—what did you mean by that?"

"Why, the—the separation—what I've said repeatedly—I think I wrote about that in the very next paragraph, didn't I?"

"Yes, you did," said Hunter in a dull and abstracted voice that curiously echoed her own. "So you did. 'You are already a prisoner, and I wish I might set you free.'" He came out of his abstraction briskly. "Well—no more about that? Nothing you wish to add?"

"Nothing."

"I see. 'Are we savages to be held in line by magic words mumbled in the mouth of a priest?'—do you want to comment on that sentence from your letter, Miss Blake? Explain, perhaps, why it's not to be taken as an attack on James Doherty's religion?"

"Genuine faith can't be attacked, Mr. Hunter, because it hasn't anything to do with reason. Religious people sometimes admit that themselves, if they've done any thinking about it. I remember hoping rather foolishly that he would be able to see my side of the question. As for what I wrote there, it's a—a comment on superstition. If you heard it in ordinary conversation it wouldn't trouble you much. It's important now only because you've decided to try me for irreligion as well as murder."

"No, Miss Blake, I am still concerned with your attitude toward law, as it bears on your credibility and on the issues of this trial. Now I hear that the marriage sacrament to you is a superstition proper to savages—that's what you meant, isn't it?"

"Marriage is a legal status. A marriage certificate is a legal document. When you talk about the sacrament of marriage you're expressing a religious view that has no legal meaning."

"Oh, well—"

"Ask any lawyer."

"Why, as an amateur lawyer, Miss Blake, you happen to be perfectly right. But that isn't quite the point, is it? It seems to me that in tossing off a comment like that to James Doherty on the subject of his marriage to Ann Doherty you were placing yourself pretty far above the law as well as above religion. Heard now, under these circumstances, doesn't it sound pretty arrogant even to you?"

"Not nearly as arrogant as the first premises of a true believer or a prosecuting attorney—"

The break in her voice had been unmistakable. Warner knew that if he stood up then and spoke, he would only be compounding disaster by drawing more attention to it. *When did I lose her? When did she go away? A little while ago she still desired to live.* He tried to recast the outline of his closing speech—more emphasis here, less there. And perhaps in redirect some of the damage could be repaired. *The defense never rests.*

"I suppose I must leave it at that," Hunter said. "But maybe I ought to remind you, Miss Blake, that I could have no interest in making any personal attack against you, as you seem to feel I'm doing. I am simply a servant of the State, with a duty to perform."

"No," she said emptily, "that's not quite true. Impartiality isn't any part of the system. You hate and fear me because—"

"Miss Blake," said Judge Mann sharply, "for your own sake there must be no such expressions of personal feeling. It's perfectly true that impartiality is hard to achieve, because we're all human. But in a law court we do try to achieve it. This procedure, this sometimes clumsy mechanism of a trial—it's an attempt at fairness, objectivity, the best we can do under the present conditions of society. Now I must warn you, and very urgently: simply answer the prosecutor's questions as plainly as you can, unless the Court rules you need not answer, and don't try to go beyond those questions. That rule—in fact the whole procedure—is for your own protection."

Directly to the Judge, and quietly, but also as though she had not really taken in his words at all, Callista said: "I never wanted her to die."

Warner saw Judge Mann turn to him, distress momentarily plain to read, as though the Judge and not the defense were most in need of help. "Mr. Warner, if you wish a recess—"

"No!" said Callista, and that was a cry. "I want this to be finished. I'm perfectly able to answer the questions, but I can't go away and come back to it, I can't do that. No recess now, please!"

"Your Honor, I think—so long as my client feels able to continue and wishes to—but—reserving the privilege of asking for a recess later if—"

"Yes, certainly, Mr. Warner. Whenever you want to request it."

Hunter said, gently and mildly, no longer half-crouched like a man readying himself to rape, but standing some distance from the witness stand, almost careless in his quiet—"You never wanted her to die, Callista?"

"No, I—yes, when—nobody ever answered Pilate."

"Yes some of the time, no some of the time—that would be natural, perfectly human, wouldn't it, Callista?"

"I suppose...."

"Does it mean, Callista, that you've remembered what happened in that lapse of memory—the thing you couldn't tell Mr. Lamson?"

"Yes."

Warner understood he had risen. But there were no words. She must know that he would come to her if he could; but she would not look at him now—only at Hunter, and without hostility, but with somber recognition, as if suddenly after much bewilderment she understood why he was there and what purposes he might serve.

"What happened, Callista?"

"I heard her take the bottle from the shelf, and the sound of a glass. I heard her come to my door, and knock, and say that she'd poured a drink for me. I lay still. I deceived myself a little, I think—I tried to imagine it was not the poison, then I tried to tell myself she would not drink it. But for a few seconds or minutes the strongest part of me was the part that held me there, willing that she should drink it. When she was gone, and I knew what had happened, that self, that part of me, was no longer in command. Then I became—whatever else I am, and have been since then. Now I'll answer no more questions, even from those I love."

II

The courtroom had gone into a silence where voices were remembered with uncertainty, like the dead. The judge's chair was empty. Three reporters talked in small murmurs at the press table, waiting it out, and a few spectators remained. Edith watched Mr. Delehanty appear from the small side door at her left, take up with quiet importance a manila folder from his idle desk, mutter inaudibly to one of the bailiffs, glance first at an old-fashioned gold watch from his pocket and then toward the door on the right through which the jury had disappeared three hours ago; then he tiptoed in dignity away. It was nine o'clock in the evening of Friday, December 11th. Closing speeches, the judge's summing up and charge to the jury—done, and anticlimactic all of them, for it seemed to Edith that it was Callista herself who had closed the trial, yesterday. "*I'll answer no more questions—*" standing up then, even before she was dismissed, but waiting with the politeness of a tired guest until Hunter murmured something that Edith did not hear; and she stepped down, took hold of Cecil Warner's hand, and walked with him drowsily to the defense table, and sat leaning her head back against his arm, eyes closed, until the Judge announced adjournment for the day. No part of the courtroom ritual now remained—except one. The long finger of the electric wall clock jerked, and was still a while.

After today's ordeal of listening—anticlimactic, yes, the Judge's voice roughened at the end of his summing-up, at moments not plainly audible, running down like a mechanism with a used-up spring—after the jury had retired, Edith had seen Victoria Chalmers press her hand to her broad pale forehead, rise, accept with sad patience the Associate Professor's fumbling courtesy with her coat, and move away. She would be having one of her headaches. No nod for Edith—Herb Chalmers gave her one—and no backward look at the arena; but as Victoria turned her head the light washed coldly across her face, and Edith saw plainly that even Victoria was a little changed. A sag of the mouth, a droop of shoulders and sturdy frame, a slowness and uncertainty in the hands adjusting her coat that suggested old age, although she was still in the early forties. She seemed doubtful of her steps, an unsteady hand undecided whether to grasp her handbag or tuck it under her arm. At the exit she did look backward once, with vagueness, as though there might be something she wished to say; or even someone she wished to find. Then like an old lady she rested her arm on Herb's clumsy hand, and was gone.

Edith found it was now natural, inevitable, to pity Victoria Chalmers— whatever pity might be worth. Earlier, until the jury went out through that doorway, there had somehow not been time. There was time now for every sort of thought, regret and fear and wonder, time for a swarm of thoughts crowding for attention, pity the least of them—time for anything the mind could do except for the discoveries of happiness and peace. Pity, maybe, was no more than a private vice, with varied by-products, some good, some bad.

Herb Chalmers had come back an hour later, alone. He made as though to sit down by himself, but seeing her look his way, he shambled to her, side-stepping along a row of vacant seats, and let himself down by her in a long-legged sprawl. "I suppose nothing's happened yet?"

"Nothing. Is Mrs. Chalmers all right?"

"I don't know," he said, his weariness lending the force of truth to the absent reply. He yawned convulsively, apologizing for it in a mumble. "She's pretty used up of course. Felt she couldn't stay, and I thought that was sensible. I took her home, and maybe she can sleep. It's not as if we could do anything now. For a while. You see, I feel sure that they—" he rubbed large hands over his face and shook his head—"no, God knows I don't feel sure of anything any more. Anything at all."

Herb also had aged. More deeply sunken lines, more gray in the thinning hair. He had evidently cut himself shaving that morning; the scab at the edge of his gaunt jawbone was overlaid by the day's growth of silvery bristle, making a sort of Skid Row shadow across his wan, weak, intelligent face.

"They can't find first degree," Edith said. "It's not possible." Yet she might be only trying to convince herself; she heard no strength in her own voice. "The Judge's summing-up—oh, he had to define all the possible verdicts, but the way he did it, the stress he laid on reasonable doubt—and then even the very fact that she said what she did, at the end—they can't do that."

He mumbled what might have been agreement, then turned to her suddenly, large-eyed, wounded, ineffectual. "They could though, Miss Nolan. Juries ... we have to face the fact, anything's possible from acquittal to—first degree. Law tries to go by logic, but never quite succeeds." More than one way, she thought inconsequently, of facing facts: walk up to a fact and spit in its eye,

Callista's way; or, like Herb Chalmers, just stand there. And you could make out a pretty good case for Herb's way, sometimes. *My way—my way...* "Why didn't he call me, Miss Nolan?"

"Well, he—I think he felt that character witnesses—and that's all I amounted to—couldn't help much. Any more of that would have pointed up the lack of any other kind of evidence. I suppose juries discount the word of friends and relatives; it's natural."

He wasn't listening much. "I would have done anything. I failed her somehow, somewhere along the line. From the start, I guess." He sighed and fidgeted. "But maybe she'd have resented anyone situated in her father's place. I remember when I first met her, a kid of eleven, I said: 'Look, Callie, I'm not your father and couldn't try to be anything like him. I'm just me, a person, and I'd like us to be friends.' Eleven—it never got across, you know? Infantile glowering, and then a kind of frozen politeness that I never could break through." He sat quiet, perhaps aware of her as a listener, gazing aimlessly at the broad knuckles of his bony hands. He said with curious humility and no resentment: "She's always had a good deal of contempt for me, I think. Children grow up so fast, and we grow old so fast. You know, Miss Nolan, a while ago I started something, a piece of writing—nothing very much, but it might prove interesting. A study of the Cavalier and Courtier Lyrists. I want to relate them to certain trends in modern poetry. You know, it's never been done. Oh, I suppose it'll turn out to be just another trifle of academic stuff. But the curious thing—look, I'm afraid I'm boring you or getting on your nerves at a bad time—"

"No, you're not, not in the least." Her impulse toward callous and hopeless laughter ceased of itself, no need to fight it down. Abruptly, there was nothing funny at all about stringy Herb Chalmers having an affair with the saucy music and tenderness of the Lyrists. He was a scholar; he knew his subject; he might even have something to say.

"Well, the curious thing—" he blushed briefly like a schoolboy, and blew his nose, and sighed—"curious thing, when I was getting together some of my notes for it the other day, I kept thinking—imagining Callista reading it. Escape psychology, I suppose."

"Why call it that? 'Escape' is just another one of those two-for-a-nickel derogatory noises that people use in place of thinking. Why not escape from ugliness toward something better? Escaping doesn't mean you've forgotten the ugliness is there."

"Something in that. Is Warner with her, do you know?"

"I think so. He wouldn't leave her unless she asked to be alone."

"He surprised me this morning, that closing speech. Two and a half hours. I never thought he'd take all morning, and repeat himself so much. It was—effective, maybe, but it scared me too. I couldn't help thinking it was effective only for people who already *know* Callista. I tried to think myself into the position of a juryman, a mind totally alien to Callista's. Everything he said was good, but he said too much. Trying to ram it through a stone wall.... I suppose you saw how once or twice he lost the thread of what he was saying and just stood there. Looking lost."

"Yes. He's not just a defense lawyer in this thing. He loves her."

"I've felt that, yes. And so did the jury, I'm afraid—more than he should have let them feel it. It even gave Hunter his cue, I think. After all that thunder and pleading, he could afford to be quiet and cold, and make the mere contrast seem like a virtue. Taking it off now and then to abstract principles the way Warner did—that was good, for us. I can't believe more than two or three of the jury went along with it. 'The defense never rests'—yes, but what can that plumber foreman make out of it? Ah, I don't know...." The intelligent professor faded, leaving a collapsed and tired old man. He shrugged, looked at his watch, gathered his legs under him. "I'm going out for a smoke. Want to?"

"No, I'd better stay, Dr. Chalmers. She'll be coming back when the jury returns, if it does return tonight. She's always looked for me when she first comes in. I've got to be here."

"Yes, I—of course." He blundered away a few steps and turned back to her. "Miss Nolan, I thought you were quite wonderful on the stand—said a number of things I would have liked to say."

Edith winced inwardly, wishing he would go. "In the jury's view I wasn't good. Another maverick."

"Oh, I don't know." He rubbed his sagging face. "Shouldn't underestimate their intelligence, I suppose. It's—democracy in action, you might say—something like that."

"Democracy be God-damned," Edith said. "It's a human life."

"Well, I—see what you mean of course." He stood tall and drooping near her, so that she must bend her neck awkwardly to see his face as he went on, driven by some compulsion to talk when perhaps he had no real wish to do so: "Strange thing—had a dream a while ago, possibly an echo of my reading—Huck Finn likely. Lost in a fog, on a raft, watching the river stream past me—sometimes the water'd slop up between chinks in the logs. All under a milky fog, no landmarks, but I could see the river all the time, the dark flow of it, now and then trash and broken things sliding past. It went on, you know, years, a hundred years, who could say? And I thought I was motionless, nothing more than a pair of eyes, brain somewhere back of them. Well, but—here was the nightmare, you see—I suddenly understood that I was drifting too, had been all the time. Doesn't sound like anything in the telling, but it was horrible—I can't tell you. Drifting all the time when I thought only the river was in motion. The sleeping brain's comment on myself, you see?—myself as summing up all human stupidity. Or blindness— much kinder word, isn't it? 'So may you, when the music's done, awake and see the rising sun'—that's from Thomas Carew, I think, died 1639 or around there. My head is an attic, you know, full of little facts with dust on them. They were so concerned, those poets, with treating love itself as a work of art, you'd think to read them superficially they had nothing else on their minds. But there was a depth, Miss Nolan, something you don't discover right away. All that polish, glitter, gracefulness, word-play, that was something they produced *after* accepting the squalor and danger and confusion of seventeenth-century living. They knew what they were doing. Reading the avant-garde stuff of nowadays, usually the contrast is merely grotesque, still I keep finding parallels. Here and there. It keeps an old man interested. Well, I'm babbling like second childhood. Telling dreams, at my age! Look, can I get you anything? I think I'll take a walk around the block, can't sit still. Coke? Sandwich?"

"I guess not, thanks all the same. Jumpy stomach."

"Mm, I know." Her neck ached. *Please go!* He was leaning down, a remote, remotely friendly ghost, a friend of Thomas Carew, also a human being in distress. "A thing like this—you know, Miss Nolan, I believe the very worst of it is that we *forget*. Because we have to, maybe. We're beaten down somehow, used up, licked in the end by the daily littleness—head colds, weakening eyesight, the brush-your-teeth-and-put-out-the-milk-bottles sort of thing, and there's no defense." At any other time, Edith thought, she would have enjoyed listening to this particular Herb Chalmers. "My God, littleness steals everything, including the last breath. And before then, you see, no matter what we resolve, what we hope for—we forget."

"I sha'n't forget."

"I'm fifty, Miss Nolan. You're still very young. Thirty years from now, d'you think you'll know just as clearly what's been happening here, what will happen when those people come back through that door? Ah, I don't know, I'm talking like a fool—who's going to see thirty years ahead? Jim Doherty's already forgetting. In a bar."

"What? Did you see him?"

"Last night he was anyway, and it looked as if he was laying the foundation for a long one. After I took Vic home last night I came back to town, to the college—had to make some kind of pass at the week's work that's piled up on me—they've been very nice, leave of absence and so on, but I notice things pile up anyway, letters, term papers, what not. On the way home I stopped at Judson's—that's uptown, bar where I used to go sometimes with Jim and—Ann, before all this. He was there, tight as a tick, must have been working on it all afternoon. Not here today, I notice. Last night I tried to get him to go home with me, but he'd made friends with some character who looked respectable, capable of putting him to bed right side up."

Edith said absently: "Someone will always be around to put him to bed."

"Know what you mean. Democracy in action." *I can't smile, Herb.* "Well—go for a walk, I guess. Can't sit still. 'Bye." He stumbled off, a weary progress with a slow grab at every chair-back along the awkward route...

Cecil Warner came through the doorway at the left, alone, his broad face sallow, all ruddiness washed away. He passed the press table with a shake of the head and no other answer to some tactless and poorly timed question. He came up the aisle, and sank with slow motion into the seat beside Edith, relaxing his bulk all at once with the suddenness of an old man's muscles letting go. "Tell me," she said.

"A message. She wanted me to come to you with a message. 'Tell my friend Edith I'll sleep well tonight, and ask her whether she'd like me to try Doris Wayne in oil or watercolor.'" He would not quite look at her. "She was smiling, Edith. It seemed to be a little flash of happiness, like a breeze on a still day."

"It's good if she can think ahead. I've been trying to, but I can't. Herb Chalmers was here, wandered off—good Lord, half an hour ago! I've just been sitting like a vegetable." She saw his eyes were held by the clock, against his will. "Cecil, does it necessarily mean anything at all, when they stay out this long?"

He looked at her then, studying her face as if from a distance, deeply aware of her and certainly no less aware of the girl in the detention cell. He said: "It's not good."

"It's what would happen if there was a disagreement, isn't it?"

"Yes. A disagreement would not be good. A new trial very likely wouldn't come before Terence Mann. And I wouldn't be competent, physically competent, to go through it again. I'm getting pains down the left arm, other things—" he waved his hand quickly and irritably to dismiss the concern in her face. "Couldn't risk conking out in the middle of a trial. That would make a mistrial, then another wait, a third trial with some other attorney, quite likely some other judge—Hangman Cleever for instance. No good, no good. Oh, I shouldn't have taken it on this time. Or I should have got someone younger to work in court with me. That's only one mistake I made. I've made hundreds. Vanity, vanity, thinking myself better able to defend her than anyone else, and blundering all the time—"

"No."

"Don't waste your breath comforting me now. I can see it, Edith, I can see it. My last mistake was talking too long this morning. I couldn't let go, even when I knew I wasn't getting through to them. Some kind of idiot compulsion to hold off the moment when T.J. would start—as if that could make any difference. A cub fresh out of law school wouldn't make such an error—I've been at it forty years."

"Cecil, stop whipping yourself. You did everything possible."

"Everything I could, yes. But everything I could do wasn't enough, and a lot of it was done wrong. A stronger man could have done more, done it better. Why, there's the big evil of the adversary system, Edith, right under our noses. Should the life or freedom of a human being depend on the perfectly irrelevant strength or weakness of opposing counsel? What in hell do my skill and brains, or T.J.'s, have to do with Callista's innocence or any of the other facts? What could be more medieval? But we accept it, have accepted it for hundreds of years, meekly, stupidly, as if no other method were possible or worth a thought. I've spent my life inside the propositions of a vicious fallacy, and discovered it at sixty-eight."

"One man couldn't do away with the fallacy. It's too heavily established, and maybe there isn't enough wisdom in the world yet to develop a better way. You had to work inside of what you found, and it's not wasted effort. Within the system, you've saved a good many lives from public vengeance—and never mind whether they've been good lives like Callista's, or the lives of crooks and psychopaths, that's not the point. Each time you've set your face against public vengeance, you've brought some minds that much nearer to learning that the whole notion of vengeance and punishment is wrong. You've done your share. You've been on the side of mercy. How many can say that?"

"Well, my dear, you're good for me. Maybe I should have been a doctor. I remember thinking of it for a while, when I was in college—but I felt that the wish wasn't enough, that I didn't have the other qualities it needs."

"I think a defense lawyer—your kind of defense lawyer, Cecil—is in something like a doctor's position, but without any adequate sciences to support him. A doctor can draw on chemistry, physiology, pharmacology, a dozen other disciplines, and rely pretty solidly on what he gets from them. A lawyer trying to be useful according to rational ethics—what is there to help him? An infant science of human behavior, full of errors and contradictions and blank spots, hardly more advanced than physiology was in the eighteenth century; and haunted by the crackpots and manipulators too, so that it's sometimes hell's own job to separate the science from the special pleading. So I think, Cecil, that anyone who defends a life against the crowd's desire for a victim, who shows up the flaws in the system by bucking it—he's pioneering, he's taking a part in bringing law nearer to reality. I'll set Clarence Darrow in the same company with Semmelweiss and Pasteur, any time, no strain. And you."

He covered his face quickly with his hands; said after a while: "I wish I were a younger man, to hear that."

Edith looked away at the clock. Her mind was caught in a brief paralysis of waiting for the next twitch of the minute hand. "I drew something the other night, Cecil, a memory sketch of that jury. It's curiously good." She heard his breathing slow and become quiet. "My own style, but the kind of thing I was never able to do before. I want you to see it. Come over soon anyway—I need my friends too, you know. We try, Cecil, oddballs like you and Callista and me, others here and there. Herb Chalmers told me he's having a thing with the Cavalier and Courtier Lyrists. I started laughing inside—just started because it seemed so damn far away from everything—and then stopped laughing. It's Herb's way of trying, using his brains in his own style on what's nearest to his reach."

"Callista and I put the human race on trial the other night. We came to no conclusion, no verdict."

"Well, I think there's an obvious verdict in that case, and maybe only one possible at the present stage."

"So? You tell me."

"Not proven."

"I should have thought of that. Cal would like it. I'll remember to tell her." Beyond the melancholy and desolation of his face she saw Herb Chalmers returning along the row of empty seats. Warner nodded to him morosely. "Herb. All by yourself?"

"I took Vic home." Herb Chalmers showed the dubious tension of a news-bringer. "Cecil, what way does the jury-room face?"

"What way?" The Old Man's eyebrows bunched aggressively in perplexity. "The Court Street side. Why, Herb?"

"They're yawping a *Courier* extra on the street. Judd died in the hospital a couple of hours ago." He pulled a smeary paper from his overcoat and handed it to Warner, who stared at the splash of black ink and let the thing slither to the floor. "A brass-lunged newsboy, Cecil: 'Blake Case Witness Dies ree aw abowit!'"

"Some fool," Warner said—"some fool in the jury-room is bound to open a window, to let the smoke out."

"He was shouting pretty plain. I could make out the words a block away. Any legal significance, you think?"

"I doubt it, Herb." Warner looked up hopelessly. "Anyway she gains nothing from a mistrial. Likely it wouldn't even go before the same judge, a second time. Everything that could happen," he said. "Malice, chance, blind circumstance, human frailty. Even the malice nobody's fault really—not even T.J.'s. He's something worked by strings."

"They can't find first degree," Edith said, and hated the querulous shake in her voice, its jaded insistence on what she could not know.

"Twenty to life," said Warner.

"She's young," Edith said. "She's very young."

Herb asked: "Wouldn't actually be twenty, would it? Don't they—"

"She's young," said Warner, his voice all bitterness, "and it wouldn't actually be twenty years."

The door on the right opened for a court officer, who spoke to someone over his shoulder. Warner stood up, breathing carefully. Edith caught his arm; he looked down almost angrily. "Cecil, tell her I'd like her to try it in watercolor."

"Oh. Yes. I'll go with her now." He was hurrying down the aisle.

Herb said: "What—he meant to say he'd go to her, I suppose."

"He knew what he was saying. Sit here. Stay with me, please."

She watched the courtroom coming alive. Knowledge of the jury's returning had spread as if by a spark of telepathy. A group of the last-ditch curious straggled back from the corridors, and newsmen who must have been waiting at some point of vantage outside, and Mr. Delehanty—gravely ready at his desk before the Twelve filed in.

Judge Terence Mann came in and took his place without delay, moving for once not easily but with a suggestion of middle age. He did not reach as usual for his note-pad and pencil; he dropped his thin rugged hands on the desk and stared at the space between them until his eyes must turn, like all the others, to the door on the left.

She was with Cecil Warner. She looked at once for Edith, and seeing her stepfather also she smiled once, quickly and warmly—a new thing to remember. She held closely to Warner's arm until they reached the defense section; then she stood alone, not troubling to seat herself. No doubt someone, the Judge or Mr. Delehanty, should have told her to sit down; but she remained standing until the jury, at Judge Mann's word, self-consciously rose.

Mr. Francis Fielding looked tired and for the first time regretful.

"Members of the jury, have you reached a verdict in the case now before you?"

Peter Anson said: "We have."

Callista looked on the jury as Edith had never seen her look on others before. It was a look of patience resembling friendliness, a look that one might naturally give to strangers who were confronted by a painful difficulty and not quite able to understand its nature.

"What is your verdict?"

"We find the defendant, Callista Blake, guilty of murder in the first degree, without recommendation of mercy."

III

From a letter written by Terence Mann, formerly Justice of the Court of General Sessions of Winchester County, New Essex, July 17, 1960, to Dr. John Sever Mann, of Boston:

> ... For that matter, I can hardly understand that more than a week has passed since Callista died. My sense of time seems to be still slightly distorted. For many days and months, too much to endure and understand, hope for and relinquish; then quiet, aftermath. Finished. The new things that begin, some of them surely good, are not yet clear in my mind, nor in Edith's—we're tired, Jack.

Last night I finished and mailed that letter I told you about, to the president of the New Essex Bar Association, setting out in writing my reasons for resigning from the bench. Mr. Paulus, president of the B.A., is a very pleasant character, a successful gentleman but also mellow and moderately philosophical, capable of filling that position with no sense of strain, and yet able to see quite a distance into a stone wall. In him, I'd say that intellectual compromise rises to the level of a fine art, a hedonistic achievement which I respect, though I can't imitate it—my own hedonism requires its ethical frame of reference to be in plain sight, accessible, subject to change if reason demands. You might understand Paulus better than I do, since in your work compromise (though a very different kind) has to be the order of the day. You try to help your patients live in the jungle, which must mean plenty of yielding here to gain a little there. Well, what I started to say—Paulus is a good joe. It was Paulus who kindly suggested, away back at the time of my resignation, that I should write such a letter, and he gave me advance permission to send copies to newspapers if I cared to— which I've done. Perhaps some of them will allow my cerebral verbiage to rub for a moment against Miss Americas and Russian face-making.

I wasn't able to start that letter at the time of my resignation. I kept putting it off. For a while—April and most of May— Edith and I were in a suspended mental state, waiting out the appellate decision. I couldn't say it to Edith—(especially since we knew by that time that she was pregnant, your first nephew apparently aiming for next February)—I couldn't say it to her, but after the appeal was denied I never had any hope of the Governor. I know him, a cultured nothing, mentally gelded by the modern political rule, never stick your neck out. Even his fishing trip last week was perfectly predictable.

I began my letter to Paulus after the appeal was denied, and it may be worth something, for the record, but not very much. The memory of newspaper readers is remarkably short, I think. Last week there was the inevitable frenzy over the execution here in Winchester, and I guess elsewhere— I haven't looked at the out-of-town papers. Mostly pointless—all of it, so far as saving Callista's life was concerned—the few reasonable voices drowned out by the crackpots petting their emotions in public. This week—oh, in the houses and bars and restaurants this week I doubt if there's very much talk about Callista Blake. And if a few newspapers publish my letter, or as much of it as will fit comfortably in half a column, most readers will be honestly puzzled: Terence Mann, who the devil's he?

It's natural, you needn't tell me, Jack. We aren't geared to endure sustained high tension very long—though didn't I hear you say once that some patients have surprised you in that respect? The week of the trial was enough to kill Cecil Warner—understandable of course, he must have been ill before it began. I wish you could have met him. I saw him only once after his collapse the night of the verdict. He got home—I think I never told you this—by himself, walked home I believe. His housekeeper called me in the morning because he was asking to see me. His doctor wouldn't let me stay very long—he grew too distressed by the effort to tell me something when words wouldn't come. It was mostly about Callista's letters, something he wanted me to understand, as if I were capable of sitting in judgment—but I was not then, Jack, and never have been. Edith was there too—the first time I'd met her outside the courtroom. Warner said, so far as I can bring back the words: "I couldn't believe the letters wouldn't get through to them. I thought they *had* to hear the truth in them, the reason and the sweetness—but I was only sending a child into a snake pit." He said: "The guilt's mine, Judge—I've killed her, by trusting human nature." That's when his doctor told me I had to go, but he let Edith stay, easy to see why. She has that ability—I think you've felt it yourself—of sharing her own steadiness. It's a personal magic—I'll never know how she does it. I have, myself, achieved enough tranquillity, mental security, to see me through, especially since our marriage and my resignation from the bench. But I seldom seem able to give others the benefit of it; they are most likely to be irritated because I don't share their excitements of the moment. You have a good deal of her kind of magic yourself.

Well, there at Warner's house she came out to me later, told me how he'd talked more quietly a while, forgetting much of the present, and taking pleasure in the sound of ocean, which no one else would hear in this inland town, but he could hear it out of childhood. He died that night.

My letter to Paulus was, as I said, too cerebral, and that's why it has left me discontented, aware of much that still ought to be said.

In that letter I marshalled all the familiar arguments against capital punishment, for the sake of logic and completeness. Paulus has heard them all, and so have most citizens above the moron level. Capital punishment does not deter, nor have any effect on the crime rate one way or another— repeatedly demonstrated by statistical study long before the time of Warden Lawes; vengeance does not restore life, but only adds another evil, namely murder by the state; there can never be complete assurance that the innocent will not be punished and the guilty go free; punishment itself serves no purpose except to excite the self-deceptive emotions of the punisher; and so on, Jack. While I listed and discussed these and lesser arguments in my letter, I grew increasingly discouraged, mostly by realization that it has all been said before, more persuasively than I know how to say it, that the arguments on the other side seem (at least to my best understanding) monstrously shabby, unrealistic, archaic, some of them plain sadism with its nakedness barely hidden by doubletalk, and yet the laws remain on the books.

You're a headshrinker, Jack—why do so many minds cling to unreason with such a sullen fury? I am thinking of people like Judge Cleever, or people who can read the entire transcript of the Sacco-Vanzetti trial and still declare briskly and earnestly that the innocent are never punished. How do they do it? What's the faculty of the mind that makes it possible for an intelligent being to look directly on a glaring fact and somehow will it out of sight? For my part I *cannot*, from sheer physical inability, believe a lie when the demonstration is before me.

And so finally, when I had done all I could with the clear, sensible, familiar arguments that have beaten on Paulus' head for forty-odd years without ever moving him to act on them, I found that I was closing my discourse with nothing more nor less than a plea for humility.

This was perhaps a little different, a little new—or would have been if I had not felt obliged to write my letter in academic and parliamentary language. I think no one ever said to Mr. Paulus: "You, sir, although an exceptionally decent and clever sample of *Homo quasi-sapiens*, are much too stupid and ignorant to decide whether another human being shall live or die; and so am I, and so are all your colleagues, and all policemen, all Governors, and all juries." I did say, in terms not obscure, that my reason for resigning the judgeship was that I felt my own self incompetent to decide a question of that magnitude. Since he knows I am not a fool, not badly educated as such things go, not grossly inferior to others in my profession, and not given to false modesty, maybe the implications were clear enough to exert some force.

Then having gone so far, it was necessary for the sake of honesty as well as politeness to say what I could for the law on the credit side. You can't (as Callista Blake said) have a human society without laws. The civil law, and with many reservations the criminal law, stumbles and bumbles through a vast amount of necessary work, and not too badly. Concepts broaden, eventually. The law in these years begins to listen more intelligently to your (very young and new) profession, Jack; I predict that quite soon the dear old McNaughton Rule will find its proper place—in historical textbooks. And so long as there are laws, why, the function of a judge is probably required at certain times, and if the judge has intelligence it is a potential means of serving order and human approximations of justice. On the personal level, I admitted to Mr. Paulus that if I had remained in office I could have done much useful work for many years, doing at the same time no more harm than most judges do, and less than some.

But I did not retreat into the formula of declaring that my decision was purely a matter of private conscience. Mr. Paulus may so describe and pigeonhole it, but I did not say that. What is so private about a conscience if it directs the life and actions of a man? I could not soften the implication that any judge who opposes capital punishment and yet remains in office in a state which keeps that on the books is obliged to justify such compromise before the bar of his own reason. He can do that: he can say that his compromise enables him in the long run to do more good than harm. That is honest; that I can respect. But I say, let him remember that it is still a compromise with evil. And I say also that it cannot be my way.

I think that in the end all honest reasoning does arrive at the necessity of humility. In effect you say to all your patients: "I don't know much about you, you don't know much about yourself; let's try to find out more, and make what use of it we can, and remember then that we still don't know very much." Or as my own dearest teacher used to say to me: "Bring out the inner voices." No one ever knew all he was capable of learning, or all he needed to learn. The individual self is the heart of everything we understand, the world's endless complexity being the product of all individual selves living and dead. About the self of another we know one thing for certain and only one: it exists. Therefore, not as a supernatural dictum but as the command of a human being to himself: Thou shalt not kill. Therefore, more light! Therefore, humility.

I am one of the fortunate of course. I think, Jack, that by next September I can decently start teaching music—with humility, at least something of the strength and humility that I felt in my teacher Michael Brooks but was too much of a child to understand. I shall write books and articles—I told Callista that; or rather I agreed, for it was the first thing she thought of when she learned of my resignation from the bench, and all I had to say was yes. I have a redheaded wife who doesn't allow dull moments, though we have many peaceful ones, and we shall have children who will undoubtedly teach me a good deal about humility, if only through the slow and touchy business of learning it themselves. But Edith and I will not turn smug and insulated with our good fortune, I think—we know and remember too much for that.

I was able to see Callista several times in the death house. I remember I wrote you a little about some of those visits, probably not too well. The first time was right after my resignation. I felt I had to see her and talk to her, if only for my own sake. It was no crawling search for "forgiveness"— she would have thought that absurd and contemptible; she knew (I think) as well as I know, that during the trial I was partly a mechanism on the bench, partly a bewildered and rather inexperienced man who liked her and did not want her to die. But I was undeniably in search of understanding. She was someone who had gone into regions I had never known—not all of them dark and fearful either, for surely her brilliance, insight, humor, daydreams, were quite as meaningful as her suffering. She was also someone who was articulate, observant, wise, and could therefore tell me something of those regions, if she was willing. In meeting Callista you somehow by-passed "forgiveness" and other vanities. I think it was because, when she was not too unhappy, she was often able to speak from mind and heart at the same time. She had no acidulous interest in puncturing sham for the sake of puncturing it. It was simply that, once friendship and communication were established, she was so straightforward and clear-minded that one's own shams and self-deceptions showed themselves up as abominations, and one could only wish to be rid of them, and to exist for a while on her level. She would never have thought of asking a friend to be honest; she merely took it for granted that he would be, took it for granted with an innocence and uncalculated kindness that even Edith says she can't understand.

Never suppose that Callista wanted to die. She wanted life, and all it might have brought her. She followed closely and hopefully everything that we were trying to do, the appeal, the later efforts. She was happy and intensely *interested* when she learned that Edith and I had become close friends and then lovers; it was Callista who urged us to marry without too much waiting. She wanted to know everything about this Emmetville house we've bought—yes, I listen for The Express, though it's always a Diesel now and doesn't sound quite right to you and me—and she seemed to get a wholly relaxed, natural fun out of telling us how to fix the guest room where she would sometimes be staying. When I told her of Edith's pregnancy (not even sure that I ought to) she was happy—I swear there was not one moment in the little time I had with her that day when I could see any shadow on her face, any hint that she was comparing Edith's lot with her own. Later of course, after I was gone—but no one will ever know about that.

And in spite of all this, her manifest interest in living, I think she sensed all the time that the appeal would probably fail, and the appeal for executive clemency. Once or twice—only once or twice—she was bitter and miserable. I will not make a saint of her, and so lose what she really was. She was greater in many ways than most of us; she was also a nineteen-year-old girl, unfortunate, frequently sharp-tongued and hasty; loving beyond measure to her friends but incapable of suffering a fool with patience. Once, only once, I saw her truly angry. Well, she had said to Warden Sharpe himself that she wanted no visits from the chaplain, and then after respecting her wish for quite a long time he had come in anyhow, poor earnest man, and prayed at her—just unable, in his good intentions, to understand that there really are those who prefer to employ their minds in other ways, especially when the time is short. But I found out on talking with her, after her anger had given way to amusement, that what had chiefly exasperated her was her inability to recall chapter and verse numbers for the quotation from Exodus she wanted to cite to him: "Thou shalt not suffer a witch to live." (It's XXII, 18, if you're curious.) She said: "I did want to give him just the numbers so he'd have the fun of looking it up himself."

Later, unsmiling, she asked me: "Will it accomplish something, do you think, if I'm able to demonstrate with what peace a freethinker can die?"

She was like that. She could say that, and saying it, compel me to answer straightforwardly instead of with a mere desperate insistence that I didn't think she would die. I said: "Yes." Then of course I was driven to say the other thing too, because, like Edith and Cecil, I loved her and I could not look at the thought of her death. But the yes was what she wanted and what she remembered.

She would not permit me to be present at the execution. She said I must stay with Edith at that hour, and that was right, and I did so. We lived through the time—I don't care to remember any of it except that Edith took hold of my hand and held it above the life growing in her body, until the minute hand had gone past that mark.

Warden Sharpe has told me there was "no confusion." Callista walked alone—of course. Sharpe says she smiled suddenly at the chaplain, patted his arm, said: "It's all right. Come with us if you want to." When they strapped her in the chair she said only: "You people here are not responsible for any of this. I'd like you to know I understand that." Then the hood was over her face, and an employee of the sovereign state moved the switch to perform on her body the ultimate indecency.

She was one of the lonely and strange. Though we destroy them, they give us a light that can become our own.

THE TRIAL OF
CALLISTA BLAKE

EDGAR PANGBORN

In 1959, in the state of New Essex, a witch was on trial. Or so she seemed to many of the jurors who would ultimately decide her fate, and to the people who thronged the crowded courtroom, many of them friends of the murdered woman. On trial for poisoning her former lover's wife, she would—if found guilty—be executed.

Callista Blake is nineteen years old at the time of her trial. She has a very slight physical deformity, and the much greater mental ones of apparent aloofness, fierce independence of mind, a laconic and sometimes sarcastic wit, marked but unconventional artistic talent, avowed atheism, and a complete inability to compromise. Added to all this, although she is not beautiful by any of the usual criteria, men find her overwhelmingly attractive. No wonder the good people of Winchester and Shanesville dislike her, fear her, and, subconsciously, at least, think she is a witch. No wonder they do not believe Callista's story that she had mixed the deadly potion of Monkshood and brandy for herself at a moment of suicidal depression, and had been prevented by a miscarriage from saving Nancy Doherty, who had drunk the stuff accidentally. The circumstantial evidence against Callista could not be more damning, yet there are one or two people unshakeably convinced of her innocence.

This is the story of their struggle in the courtroom to save her. On her side are one witness—Edith Nolan, her friend and former employer—her defending counsel—Cecil Warner, a sick, aging man who loves her—and Terence Mann, who in his role as judge is obliged to attempt impartiality but, trying his first case carrying the death penalty, is appalled that the fate of a human being can be at the mercy of anything so haphazard as the adversary system and the whim of a jury. We see Callista's ordeal and the events that brought her to it from the viewpoints of all these people, as well as that of Callista herself. We see T. J. Hunter, the formidable District Attorney (they call him hunter Hunter), Jim Doherty, only too willing to accept his confessor's view that he was an innocent ensnared by a temptress of whom he is now happily free, Callista's well-meaning stepfather, hopelessly dominated by her overbearing, histrionic mother, the perfect Gertrude to Callista's Hamlet, and many others who indirectly hold Callista's life in their hands. We gradually learn the history of Callista's passionate affair with Jim, told with a compassion and insight which contrast poignantly with the chilling ritual of the courtroom.

Edgar Pangborn knows and understands the people he writes about. And with irresistible force he shows that no one is good enough or wise enough to hold the power of life and death.

Mr. Pangborn, who lives at Vorheesville, New York, attended Harvard and the New England Conservatory of Music. He is the author of three previous novels: *West of the Sun*, (1952), *A Mirror for Observers* (1953), and *Wilderness of Spring* (1958). He has also contributed short stories to various magazines.

Jacket design by Paul Bacon

ST MARTIN'S PRESS

Milton Keynes UK
Ingram Content Group UK Ltd.
UKHW040831071024
449371UK00007B/712

9 789362 096739